JEWISH GIFTEDNESS

AND

WORLD REDEMPTION

The Calling of Israel

If the statistics are right, the Jews constitute but one per cent of the human race. It suggests a nebulous dim puff of star-dust lost in the blaze of the Milky Way. Properly the Jew ought hardly to be heard of; but he is heard of, has always been heard of. He is as prominent on the planet as any other people, and his commercial importance is extravagantly out of proportion to the smallness of his bulk. His contributions to the world's list of great names in

literature, science, art, music, finance, medicine, and abstruse learning are also away out of proportion to the weakness of his numbers.

He has made a marvellous fight in this world, in all the ages; and has done it with his hands tied behind him. He could be vain of himself, and be excused for it. The Egyptian, the Babylonian, and the Persian rose, filled the planet with sound and splendor, then faded to dream-stuff and passed away; the Greek and the Roman followed, and made a vast noise, and they are gone; other peoples have sprung up and held their torch high for a time, but it burned out, and they sit in twilight now, or have vanished.

The Jew saw them all, beat them all, and is now what he always was, exhibiting no decadence, no infirmities of age, no weakening of his parts, no slowing of his energies, no dulling of his alert and aggressive mind. All things are mortal but the Jew; all other forces pass, but he remains. What is the secret of his immortality?

Mark Twain
Concerning the Jews, Harper's Magazine,
September, 1899.

JEWISH GIFTEDNESS

AND

WORLD REDEMPTION

The Calling of Israel

Jim Melnick

Lederer Books
A division of
Messianic Jewish Publishers
Clarksville, MD 21029

Printed in the United States of America
Cover design by Lisa Rubin,
Messianic Jewish Publishers
Graphic Design by Yvonne Vermillion,
Magic Graphix, Westfork, Arkansas

2017   1

ISBN: 978-1-936716-88-3

Library of Congress Control Number: 2017935424

Published by:
Lederer Books
A Division of Messianic Jewish Publishers & Resources
6120 Day Long Lane
Clarksville, MD 21029

Distributed by:
Messianic Jewish Publishers & Resources
Order line: (800) 410-7367
lederer@messianicjewish.net
www.MessianicJewish.net

Dedicated in memory of my beloved mother,

GLADYS MARIE PEPPEL MELNICK
(1924-2014)

*who gave me a love of music, a love for the
Scriptures and a desire to strive for excellence*

GENESIS 12:3

By you all the families of the earth will be blessed.

"The LORD your God has chosen you to be a people for Himself, a special treasure above all the peoples on the face of the earth."

DEUTERONOMY 7: 6-8

"This people I have formed for Myself. They shall declare My praise."

ISAIAH 43:21

"I will betroth you to Me forever..."

HOSEA 2:19

"There yet remains a special, unique, and irrevocable calling upon Israel as a corporate people."

JOEL RICHARDSON,
When a Jew Rules the World, p. 63.

"[The Jew] has made a marvelous fight in this world, in all the ages; and he has done it with his hands tied behind him...The Egyptian, the Babylonian, and the Persian rose, filled the planet with sound and splendor, then faded to dream-stuff and passed away; the Greek and the Roman followed, and made a vast noise, and they are gone...The Jew saw them all and is now what he always was, exhibiting... no slowing of his energies, no dulling of his alert and aggressive mind. All things are mortal but the Jew; all other forces pass, but he remains. What is the secret of his immortality?"

MARK TWAIN,
Harper's New Monthly Magazine, Vol. XCIX, 1899.

"Israel today concentrates the genius of the Jews...Israel's rarely celebrated feats of commercial, scientific, and technological creativity climax the Jews' twentieth-century saga of triumph over tragedy."

GEORGE GILDER,
The Israel Test, p. 4

Foreword

I n the secular world, there is a group of Gentiles usually described as philo-Semites. Yet, not every philo-Semite is motivated by Scripture. I thank God for every non-Jew who loves my people, but appreciate even more those who are like Jim Melnick, the author of this wonderful book, who is a self-confessed philo-Semite for deeply spiritual and biblical reasons.

I am glad that my friend Jim Melnick turned his many years of theological studies and deep reflection as a spiritually-minded Gentile Christian philo-Semite into a most thoughtful, engaging and well-researched book.

Jewish Giftedness and World Redemption: The Calling of Israel is going to make a big difference in helping Jewish people in particular to understand the mystery of being chosen, and, more importantly, that true Christians generally believe that the Jewish people have been chosen by God for a holy and lofty purpose.

Jim Melnick presents a multitude of facts which demonstrate the specialness of the Jewish people, echoing and amplifying the verse in Deuteronomy 7:6 where the Lord tells Moses that the Jewish people are a particular or peculiar treasure to the God of Abraham, Isaac and Jacob – *a people for His own possession out of all the peoples who are on the face of the earth.*

Throughout the book, Jim provides many reasons and illustrations as to why he believes this to be a conclusion corroborated by both ancient and modern history.

I must admit that this made me feel somewhat uncomfortable. I had heard the litany of Jewish achievements before – that Jewish people have won so many Nobel Prizes, produced some of the world's greatest intellectuals, musicians, writers, philanthropists and scientists that the world has ever known. Yet, for some reason, I still felt that it might be better if God's choice of the Jewish people be defined spiritually or left more ambiguous rather than be illustrated with real-time historical examples.

Yet Jim did not let this concern go unanswered, as he knew some Jewish people might feel uneasy about a Gentile calling attention to the achievements of the Jewish community. Jim helped ease any concern through his gracious and factual presentation.

This book is well researched and makes some very powerful historical and sociological arguments for its thesis – which is that the achievements of the Jewish people are founded upon God's supernatural calling of the Jewish people to be a light to the nations. I highly recommend *Jewish Giftedness and World Redemption* and believe it will and should be taken seriously by both Jews and Gentiles, especially during this critical time as we see the rise of a new global anti-Semitism that threatens the well-being of Israel and the worldwide Jewish community.

DR. MITCH GLASER

President, Chosen People Ministries
New York, New York
December 2016

Preface

"And you shall be a kingdom of priests for me, a nation set apart."

EXODUS 19:6

A Priestly Nation and a 'Light to the World'

The Jewish people are a nation of priests. Yes, that's right – *a nation of priests* to the world. That may sound strange – indeed, it *is* strange, but it is nevertheless true. Why this is so and what this means for the world are the central messages of this book. One author writes that "[t]he call of Israel is to function for humanity in the essential priestly role before God for the sake of the redemption of the world."[1] Another has written that "…it is God's prerogative to choose one nation through which to bring redemption to the entire world."[2]

Being a nation of priests also means being a 'light to the world.' In a book of essays titled, *I Am Jewish*, written in response to the widely publicized murder of Jewish journalist Daniel Pearl at the hands of Islamic terrorists, David Suissa, editor of *Olam* magazine, wrote of "…our eternal mission" – meaning a *Jewish mission* – "of lighting up the world."[3]

What does this really mean?

I shall try to answer that question. It's not an easy thing to do. It must sound like nonsense to those Jews who don't even believe in God. Yet I believe that the very real factors of Jewish giftedness, drivenness and generosity that we see so evident in our world today - plus the very real desire on the part of so many Jews to 'repair the world' (*tikkun olam*) - are somehow related to this fundamental role. If I haven't lost you already with such statements, please read on to see why I believe that this is so.

Jewish giftedness, genius, creativity, pre-eminence, success, achievement, and accomplishment – at times I use these terms rather loosely and inter-changeably in this book, far more than if I were specifically trying to define each one in a technical journal, for example. In so doing, I am attempting to describe similar aspects of the same phenomenon, not trying to confuse the reader. So, if I use the word 'genius,' for example, where I may have used 'pre-eminence' before, or if I skip to using another term in between, I hope the reader will indulge me for the sake of argument.

A Love-letter to the Jewish People; Growing Anti-Semitism

This book is a love-letter, of sorts, to the Jewish people. Yes, for better or worse, I am a philo-Semite, whatever that really means... I *do* love the Jewish people. Not that I don't love other peoples as well – *of course* I do! My heart aches for all people who do not know the salvation of God. But this book is about the Jewish people and is written, principally, with them in mind. However, although what revolves around the Jews and what I reveal in this book, will, I believe, eventually touch everyone in the world.

The world today is caught up – *again* - in a new wave of global anti-Semitism. *Judenhass,* a phrase in German meaning "hatred of the Jews," is once again rearing its ugly head. Its polar opposite is the Hebrew phrase, *ahavat Yisrael* – "love of or love for the Jewish people."

Under the guise of anti-Zionism, anti-Semitism is being peddled on many university campuses today with impunity. Jews remain the special targets of Islamic terrorists around the world, such as the 2015 attack on the Paris kosher supermarket following the Charlie Hebdo magazine office massacre. Decades ago, Polish Jewish scholar Isaac Deutscher astutely observed the following about European anti-Semitism: it "invariably reflects or foreshadows," he wrote, "a diseased condition in European civilization. Its rise and fall is perhaps the most sensitive index of Europe's moral and political sanity."[4] We certainly see that today: the madness is beginning all over again.

The Jewish people have faced many hardships and much opposition over their 4,000-year or so history. In his 2015 book, *Anti-Semitism,*

Jewish author Frederic Raphael asks the age-old question, Why anti-Semitism, over and over again?[5] Why indeed?

What is the root cause of anti-Semitism? There are many, and we shall examine some of them in this book. But strangely enough, one reason for anti-Semitism – though this must sound quite bizarre to many – is, I believe, the failure of the Jewish people to take up their priestly role to the rest of the world. I will explain why in the following pages.

Messianic Jewish believer Murray Tilles has written, "God chose the Jewish people to be His first ambassadors to the world...they were His 'first loved' people...Modern Judaism has failed in its biblical mission to reach the world with the message of God."[6] The Jewish people's 'election', their 'chosenness' was for this specific purpose. As Israeli pastor Eitan Shishkoff has written, this special people has "a servant role among the nations." But this role of bringing redemption to the world, a role that has not yet been fulfilled, "carries a weighty and sacred responsibility."[7]

We see some 'first fruits' of this future priestly role reflected today in the modern Messianic Jewish movement, and, while far from being insignificant (God is doing some amazing things through the movement), it is still relatively limited in impact in global terms. But more than that, it is only a foretaste of what is to come.

There are some fourteen million Jews in the world today out of a global population of some 7 billion people, making the Jewish percentage of the world's population an extremely tiny 0.2%. Despite this very small percentage and despite the horrific devastation of the Holocaust, Jews still lead the world today in all sorts of fields; however, they are certainly not a nation of priests to the world. Globally, the Jewish people worldwide constitute a 'nation' (if you will) of the greatest number proportionately of leading academics, Nobel Prize winners, famous entertainers and cultural producers and philanthropists in the world, but they have never truly taken up their global priestly role. As such, the rest of the world has suffered that loss and looked on with envy, hatred, ignorance, and suspicion. *Why do the Jews excel?* many ask. Why are they even still around despite all the efforts to destroy them? Why do they end up in places of influence again and again, even after they are put down again and again? Virulent anti-Semite Henry Ford asked this question incessantly. So did the authors and adherents of the arch-statement of anti-Semitism, the fraudulent "Protocols of the Elders of Zion," proclaiming, 'It must be a conspiracy!' These voices of hate and intolerance have persisted throughout the centuries asking the same unanswered question. Meanwhile, the answer has been staring us in the face all along.

No, Jewish survival and success are not a conspiracy – unless you want to call them part of 'God's conspiracy'. On the contrary, they represent a central part of His plan for the redemption of the world.

The people of Israel today have a "Masada complex"

The mountain stronghold of Masada overlooks the Dead Sea in Israel. It was the scene of one of the most famous events in Jewish history. Most readers know the story – how a small band of Jews held out against the Roman authorities following the destruction of the Second Temple and survived on that mountain for as long as they could...

I have climbed Masada many times (I've lost count how many) – most recently via what I call the 'Roman way.' Unlike the famous 'Snake Path' up the mountain, this was the way that the Roman Tenth Legion eventually completed its final offensive in crushing the last Jewish stronghold against the power of Rome. Many Jewish prisoners of war are said to have been forced to build that ramp for the Romans that eventually brought down their fellow Jews.

It is a sobering and a solitary hike – going around and then up the mountain via that Roman ramp, thinking of those who stood alone on the top of Masada, facing inevitable death, watching and waiting for the Roman soldiers who climbed this path to eventually break through. They chose suicide instead.

Masada today has more and more become a symbol of modern Israel. This can be termed "the Masada complex." With enemies everywhere bent on her destruction, Israel itself seems to be morphing into a 'national Masada'. The post-Holocaust cry of 'Never again' rings in the ears of the current generation. It seems more probable that the

Middle East will face a major conflagration before it ever sees a time of peace and tranquility. But Israel will not go down quietly.

'The Masada complex' – and all its attendant psychological implications – permeates Israel and much of Jewish life today. But the Jewish people are worn-out from fighting endless enemies and endless anti-Semitism.

This was not the way it was supposed to be. In ancient times Hebrew prophets wrote of future wars against Israel, Jerusalem and the Jewish people, but they also wrote of the nations of the world coming to Israel to learn from the Jewish people, a time when there would be unprecedented peace and the world would be transformed - a time when "the lion shall lie down with the lamb." Which is it, or is it both?

Will the Jewish people ever be a nation of priests to the world at large? The answer is *yes!*

How that will begin to take place will be presented within the pages of this book.

Jim Melnick
November 2016

"Is there any one that desires God's special blessing? Then let him labor in the cause of Israel, and he shall not fail to find it."

J.C. RYLE,
"Scattered Israel to Be Gathered." (May 1858),
reprinted in *Coming Events and Present Duties* (p. 91)

The Jewish people "in a wonderful manner continue numerous & distinct from all other nations: which cannot be said of any other captivated nation... & therefore is the work of providence."

SIR ISAAC NEWTON
S. Snobolen, p. 99, citing Bodmer MS

"And they shall be My people, and I will be their God... Yes, I will rejoice over them to do them good."

JEREMIAH 32: 38, 42

Contents

PART II:THE JEWISH PEOPLE AND WORLD REDEMPTION

Introduction

It all began when I was about eleven or twelve – sometime before Bar Mitzvah age, although I was never bar-mitzvahed, since I am not Jewish.[1] My beloved mother Gladys imparted to me a deep love of music and, along with my father, a quest for excellence. I grew up playing the violin over her shoulder at church as she played the organ week after week. She once said, "Music is my life." Over the years, as I grew in ability, I began to feel how music could be expressed beyond just the plain notes. My mother taught me how to let go and to let the melodies soar – thrilling my heart and soul. She imparted to me a deep love of music and encouraged my musical gift in every way that she could.

And so it was that, even at that young age, I fell in love with something extraordinarily beautiful – the Brahms Violin Concerto and other great violin music. For those old enough to remember not Wi-Fi but Hi-Fi and long-playing records, I would listen over and over again to a recording of Isaac Stern playing the Brahms concerto - so moving, so exquisite, it seemed to represent the essence of excellence. Stern played with such passion - passion that almost seemed to come from another world, or at least another place than our day-to-day world.

Then one day it struck me – nearly all the greatest violinists in the world: Stern, David Oistrakh, Jascha Heifetz, Yehudi Menuhin, and other names that I would learn later, such as Bronislaw Huberman - were all Jewish. That realization impacted me at a very deep level, one that I can't really describe, but it would later affect my life in many unforeseen ways. It began to embed in me a deep love for the Jewish people. In a remarkable way, it helped lay the groundwork for this book.

I had stumbled upon something very special, if rarely explained as a phenomenon – a Jewish commitment to excellence, combined with the reality of Jewish giftedness. Where did it come from and what does it mean? This phenomenon has intrigued others, but, except for a handful of Jewish scholars who have written mostly for academic or Jewish audiences, it has largely been Gentile writers who have been the most vocal and expansive on describing this phenomenon – from Mark Twain in 1899 to Thorstein Veblen in the early twentieth century to authors such as Steven Pease and George Gilder today. Jewish observers have understandably been restrained in exploring this topic. Gentiles who have been struck or deeply moved by the phenomenon have sought to fill the gap. I follow in that tradition, but I go one step further: I don't just describe it; I try to explain *the reason why*.

A Challenge to Atheists

Jewish giftedness is real. Its existence is undeniable. This giftedness is a source of curiosity for some Gentiles, and, unfortunately for many others, a source of envy, hatred and suspicion. But before getting into that, allow me to issue a challenge to any atheists – either Jewish or non-Jewish[2] - who may be reading this book – **consider the evidence and the arguments I present and ask yourself, is there is any explanation beyond what I present and analyze here that *better* explains the phenomena of Jewish giftedness and pre-eminence and the reasons behind them?**

What does the scholarly literature say, when it ventures to say anything at all about this? I examine the literature thoroughly, as well as considering the implications of recent research and related commentaries on the subject. Some have come up with what they believe are the best arguments to try to explain the phenomenon of Jewish giftedness. Many of these explanations are fascinating and carry elements of truth in them, but, I believe, they all fall short of providing an over-arching *reason why*.

Be honest with yourself - I don't think you will find any 'reasonable' explanation for Jewish giftedness outside of the one that I provide – which you will discover if you read on! But if you think you have a better explanation, please drop me a line at: info@frji.org. I would love to engage readers on this point – especially if they believe they have something novel and useful to add to the discussion.

Before going further, I should specify how I define "Jewish" in this book. I follow the definition laid down by the *Dictionary of Jewish Biography* (1991), which states: "we go by the traditional Jewish religious principle that a person born a Jew is always regarded as a Jew 'no matter how much he sins'." Extending this further, this definition applies "even in the case of converts to other faiths or those who publicly dissociate themselves from Judaism or the Jewish people..."[3]

So that is our working definition in terms of birth and ethnic background. In terms of identity, the definition gets more tricky. As Messianic leader and scholar Daniel Juster has noted, "when asked who is a Jew," even David Ben Gurion himself "was so loose in his definition that he simply stated that it was anyone who desired to identify himself as a Jew. This seems to overlook the seriousness of taking on a Jewish identity with real conviction."[4]

Rabbi Sherwin T. Wine has been even looser in his definition. Being a part of Jewry, he writes, "is open to anybody who wishes to join... joining the Jewish people means loving the Jewish people, Jewish culture, and Jewish achievement – and the willingness to identify with the history and social fate of the Jewish people."[5] By that definition, I, too, would be 'in the club'. But it is not quite so simple – being Jewish consists of more than just identifying with the Jewish people. It *is* related in part to birth and to growing up Jewish, regardless of Rabbi Wine's breezy entrance requirement or Ben Gurion's loose view on Jewish identity. Within that context, then, we shall examine the phenomenon of 'Jewish giftedness' and 'Jewish genius'.

Leftist billionaire financial wizard and funder of radical causes George Soros has said: "I believe that there is such a thing as a Jewish genius..." Some of these extraordinary achievements are "the results of Jews' efforts to transcend their minority status and to achieve something universal."[6]

These comments are from the lips of someone who is a self-professed atheist.[7] Nevertheless, Soros perceives that the phenomenon of 'Jewish genius' exists.

In the past, Jewish genius has sometimes been associated with greatness in the religious realm, such as young Jewish boys who can memorize the entire Talmud or show similar feats of extraordinary mental skill. Great Jewish religious figures in the past sometimes acquired the title *Gaon*, as in the Gaon of Vilna, a term associated with the idea of brilliance, excellence, and genius. Our analysis looks beyond the religious realm, although it does circle back to an explanation that is rooted in spiritual reasoning. But to get to that conclusion, please read on.

What is genius? Where does it come from?

What is *genius*? Nobody really knows. In the nineteenth century, famed British Jewish Prime Minister Benjamin Disraeli's father, Isaac Disraeli, wrote a book about genius. The elder Disraeli noted that "theories of genius are the peculiar constructions of our own philosophical times." which is most certainly true. Such "constructions" have thus far failed to adequately explain genius; nevertheless, Disraeli's observation still rings true. Every generation constructs its own theories about genius and giftedness, but we still cannot explain where it comes from, nor "teach how to invent invention."[8]

Genius has been defined as a means of demonstrating "the highest form of creativity," as well as "the ability to come up with ideas that are new, surprising, and valuable."[9] The ancients used the phrase *divinum quiddam* – part of the 'divine' within man – to try to capture part of the essence of genius.[10] If we think of mankind as being made in the image of God and not as some accidental cosmic flotsam that just happened to emerge on Planet Earth as *Homo sapiens*, then the idea that genius reflects 'a spark of the divine' makes more sense. The Book of Genesis says that man is made in the 'image of God.' Edmond Halley (after whom the comet is named), penned an ode to Sir Isaac Newton that described the latter's genius as attaining that *"...insuperable line, The nice barrier 'twixt human and divine."*[11]

Renaissance writers used the word *ingenium* (closer to our modern understanding of "ingenious") to describe "an inborn capacity for mental activity, natural talent, innate intelligence, and inherent ability."[12] Indian genius Jagadish Bose once noted that "he took great pleasure in connecting 'many phenomena which at first sight do not seem to have anything in common,'" a comment that another observer characterized as "a pretty good definition of creative genius."[13] James Gleick, author of *Genius,* a biography of Jewish physicist Richard Feynman, remarked about the term *genius* in this way: "What a strange and bewildering literature grew up around the term *genius* – defining it, analyzing it, categorizing it, rationalizing and reifying it."[14] Although we cannot explain where it comes from, we most certainly see its manifestations.

In this modern era of reductionism, many have tried to reduce genius and giftedness down to a set of basic elements that can be measured and analyzed. These efforts have failed. If they had succeeded, then the obvious next step would have been reconstructing and replicating them for the benefit of those who had discovered the 'magic formula' of creativity. Attempts to 'demystify' and deconstruct the mystery that surrounds genius have also failed. We don't know how to replicate it.

When Einstein's brain was dissected and preserved after his death, genius-seekers were deeply disappointed to find only some small irregularities. There was nothing decidedly different about Einstein's brain from ordinary brains.[15] The hope that they would make a startling find was a carry-over from the long discredited pseudo-science of phrenology.[16] *Why* was Einstein a genius? We really have no idea, certainly not from examining his brain.

In the past, genius was often viewed by scholars and observers within a religious or spiritual framework. In *Divine Fury: A History of Genius* (2013), Darrin McMahon cites historian Will Durant: "When genius stands in our presence, we can only bow down before it as an act of God, a continuance of creation."[17] One might characterize this as 'thinking God's thoughts after Him' (an irony today, when one considers that many in whom we see genius in the modern era, such as some of our most gifted physicists, deny God entirely). Nevertheless, this spiritual dimension of genius has been a recurring theme through the centuries. Michelangelo's contemporary, Giorgio Vasari, referred to the former as the "divine one," while he characterized Leonardo da Vinci's giftedness as raining down "through celestial influences...endowed by God... rather than created by human artifice." Genius in this sense would be found in "a creature set apart, elected and chosen..."[18]

'Nature versus nurture'

The ancients largely believed that genius was the result of divine inspiration manifested through special spiritual "guides" assigned to connect with certain gifted people at birth. Later, Isaac Disraeli (Benjamin Disraeli's father) promoted the view of the *predisposition* of genius. This predisposition was thought to be inherent in the person so gifted. By the eighteenth century, the view that "nurture, as opposed to nature," had gained enough ground that it was then believed to be "the deciding factor in shaping the human mind."[19]

Today the argument among academics and secular observers flares not over a divine origin for genius (which they reject out of hand) but rather between the two poles of genetics and the environment, or, as it has been more poetically stated, 'nature versus nurture.' Richard Lynn, author of *The Chosen People: A Study of Jewish Achievement and Intelligence*, for example, is viewed as a "strong advocate for the critical importance of high IQs as the cause of disproportionate Jewish achievement..."[20] Lynn also believes that the books and articles that have been written in recent years about Jewish success have neglected Jewish intelligence as an explanation.[21] Another perspective, expressed by authors Amy Chua and Jed Rubenfeld in *The Triple Package*, aver that higher IQ can't "by itself explain Jewish success...IQ without motivation lies fallow. Drive predicts accomplishment better than IQ..."[22]

Sir Francis Galton, a British polymath, is credited with first coming up with the formulation of 'nature versus nurture.' Described as "an odd but brilliant man," Galton developed this idea in his 1869 work, *Hereditary Genius.* Galton sought to catalogue and tabulate the sources of greatness and genius. He was also the first to "try to measure the gradations of greatness."[23]

Two of his followers, Alfred Binet and Lewis Terman, successfully adapted his methods, which eventually led to the development of the "intelligence quotient" or "IQ" tests that we use today.[24] So, whatever you want to say about Galton and his work (and there were some very negative features), he had an enormous influence on what we view as definitions of intelligence.

On the negative side, as a result of his views, Galton also emerged as the father of the modern eugenics movement. He believed that mankind should 'weed out' part of the human race in order to improve the whole. He can rightly be seen as one of the fathers of the view that some groups of people are inferior human beings – the very essence of racism. Eugenics later became a key component in Nazi ideology. But could Galton and others who used his work have possibly conceived of the horrors that were to come as a result of these views?

The world today recoils at every notion of racism, and rightly so. The most horrible things have been done in the name of race, from slavery to the Holocaust. As human beings, we are all the same underneath – the same blood flows in our veins; we are all (or should be) equal under the law, and we are all equal in God's sight. Yet, there are also differences between people. To deny this is to embrace an unsupportable position: for example, many African-Americans excel at various professional sports such as football and basketball, far beyond their statistical proportion in the population at large. Is it 'racism' to note this? No, of course not; it is reality, although not to some multiculturalists and those for whom 'political correctness' trumps truth and factual data.[25]

We take great pleasure in observing and noting the prowess of those who are greatly gifted in the area of athletics. Those who break Olympic records do so as individuals, but in an extended sense, they do so for the whole human race. We all marvel at their achievement, but we also all share in that achievement because *it is a human being* that is doing something on a physical basis that has never been done before.

We need to look at genius and giftedness in a similar way, that is, that there may often be some genetic component involved, but there is a strong reluctance in society today to acknowledge this possibility. This reluctance has clouded our judgment and our ability to see clearly what is right in front of us. If this is true when it comes to talking about genius in general, then dissecting the source of *Jewish* genius and creativity is even more problematic.

There are many theories about genius that beat around the edges. For example, author Eric Weiner, whom, I assume, is Jewish,[26] published a book in 2016 that looks at what he called "the geography of genius."

Weiner considered Galton's thesis and rejects it. He acknowledges that, while "[t]here is no genius gene," yet, when it comes to creative genius, genes are part of the mix." But they are "a relatively small part," he says, somewhere reportedly between 10 and 20 percent, citing unnamed psychologists.[27] And even that small percentage pretty much falls by the wayside in Weiner's view. In analyzing the golden age of Vienna, he asks: "Why were so many of the city's greatest minds Jewish? Does the answer lie in genetics?...Of course not," he answers himself, "The explanation is cultural."[28] He apparently does not want to contemplate the alternative. In his massive first tome on Jewish achievement in 2009, Steven Pease told us that, "[w]hile it can be argued that phenomenal rates of Jewish achievement arose from genes, second-generation immigrant status, or any number of other factors, in the end, those arguments, while interesting, are not compelling." Pease asserted that it was Jewish "culture, born of religion and circumstance that spurred exceptional rates of Jewish achievement."[29] By the time of his second book in 2015, Pease still believed "culture to be the stronger force and better explanation." Nevertheless, he added, "we are beginning to see growing evidence that nature and nurture are not so much dichotomous forces as complementary phenomena."[30] But while culture has a very important role to play, as a full explanation, it also falls short.

Interestingly, the arch-enemy of the Jewish people, Adolph Hitler himself, believed that culture has *nothing* to do with genius. He wrote in *Mein Kampf* that "true genius is always inborn and never cultivated, let alone learned."[31] On the other hand, Hitler's twisted view of genius was related to his own lust for power and his desire to control the destiny of the world; he viewed Einstein's genius, for example, as an enemy force that had to be humiliated and defeated just as any enemy army. In Hitler's mind, *whatever* Jews achieved in life fell into that category (we will examine this attitude in greater detail later in the book).

How does a predisposition to genius lead to creativity? Creativity is reportedly higher in societies that are more open to other cultures. In a quote often but incorrectly attributed to John Adams, second President of the United States, genius has been described as "sorrow's child."[32] This would seem to imply that those who have suffered or gone through pain may find new or unique ways of looking at the world. Cultures with a better sense of humor are reportedly more creative than those who lack it.[33]

Let's look at these factors from a Jewish context: in the Diaspora the Jewish people have been 'on the go' as wanderers for centuries. They certainly have experienced a great deal of sorrow and tragedy along the way. But despite the tragedies and ironies of life, Jewish humor is renowned. Whether these factors have helped cultivate genius, I do not know, but perhaps they have played a role.

While we are considering the views of John Adams, Adams did say something amazing about the Jewish people: "If I were an atheist," he once wrote, "and believed in blind eternal fate, I should still believe that fate had ordained the Jews to be the most essential instrument for civilizing the nations."[34] Clearly, Adams, who was not what one would consider today to be an evangelical Christian, still believed that God Himself had ordained a special role for the Jewish people.

Recognized as a Phenomenon in the Sociological and Intellectual History Literature

While Jewish giftedness and genius are recognized in the professional literature, their acknowledgement is often muted. Jewish pride on this score is sometimes quietly shared within the Jewish community, but it is usually not trumpeted too loudly for obvious reasons. Instead, more often than not the discussion is submerged under the weight of concern that might be aroused should this become a general topic of public discourse.

But it is nevertheless still discussed on occasion. In their book, *Why the Jews? The Reason for Anti-Semitism,* Dennis Prager and Joseph Telushkin have a chapter titled, "The Higher Quality of Jewish Life as a Cause of Antisemitism." They assert that: "In nearly every society in which Jews have lived for the past two thousand years, they have been better educated, more sober, more charitable with one another, committed far fewer violent crimes, and have had a more stable family life than their non-Jewish neighbors. *These characteristics of Jewish life have been independent of Jews' affluence or poverty.*"[35] Prager and Telushkin certainly cannot *prove* such a sweeping assertion, since it would be impossible to gather scientific data for all the communities and nations over the past two thousand years where Jews have lived. Nevertheless, as a *general* observation of the role and place of the Jewish people in most societies throughout history where they have lived, it is probably true. There is no reason to believe that their general conclusion is flawed.

Causing Anti-Semitism?

If we *generally* accept the Prager-Telushkin view as a working thesis, does realization or proclamation of this phenomenon stir anti-Semitism? The authors state: "Of course it is impossible to measure precisely to what extent the higher quality of Jews' lives has been a major cause of anti-Semitism. Few anti-Semites list the Jews' good qualities as reasons for attacking them."[36] Except that that is exactly what famed economist and philo-Semite George Gilder claims: "[t]he source of anti-Semitism is Jewish superiority and excellence."[37]

Perhaps Gilder is right in part, but not wholly so. Anti-Semitism goes far deeper than just Gentile envy and covetousness of Jewish achievement; it has a very dark and often demonic side – one that we will discuss later. While Jewish giftedness and superior achievement in some societies throughout history may have been contributing factors to anti-Semitism, they were not usually the primary causes of it. Ultimately, I believe, that cause has been a spiritual one.

Nevertheless, in 'polite' society today for the most part, drawing attention to Jewish giftedness is something that *just isn't done.* Yes, the phenomenon is sometimes quietly examined in certain journals, academic books and studies, but it is not paraded about in the popular press or in the media. More often than not, it is simply ignored. Gilder describes this state of affairs as reflecting "immense realities that cannot be broached."[38]

Yet they must be broached, and that is what this book attempts to do.

Joseph Jacobs and Galton, The Lotka Curve

One person who started to broach this subject but never finished was Jewish writer Joseph Jacobs (1854-1916). Jacobs looked to Galton's work as inspiration for what he wanted to do in assessing Jewish genius. I came across Jacobs' work while perusing the shelves of Widener Library

at Harvard University in 2015. Jacobs has been described as a versatile
Jewish writer and thinker who started doing research in this area "as
early as 1886."[39] His *Studies in Jewish Statistics* (1891) determined "that
in conditions of relative freedom, the Jews produced more geniuses and
men of eminence, on average, than other peoples."[40]

Steven Pease refers to a 1910 book by Dr. Mendel Silber as the first
"Jewish Achievement" book. Silber wrote that it was then "probably the
only book in which the reader may find a survey of the entire field of
Jewish contributions to the world's progress."[41] Silber's book is more of a
catalogue of achievement, and Jacobs' 1891 work obviously predates that.

In 1919 Jacobs published what he referred to as "Book I," which he
closed with the following words: "The remarkable outburst of Jewish
talent, which has been so striking and characteristic since the age of
emancipation, will form the subject of our next book."[42] But such was
not to be. Jacobs died before being able to continue that work. The back
cover of a modern reprint of Jacobs' work, published ninety years later in
2009, describes his contribution as "A useful study for anyone wishing
to reflect on what the world would lack without the vital elements of
civilization brought to all by the Jewish nation..." Between Jacobs'
work and Silber's book, as well as Mark Twain's comments in 1899 and
Thorstein Veblen's and others' writings, it is clear that as the nineteenth
century ended and the twentieth century began, thoughts about the
special nature of Jewish genius and achievement were beginning to
percolate in various intellectual circles.

Consider for a moment this supreme irony: the Jewish people,
especially after Emancipation, as Jacobs noted, brought forth a burst
of talent to the world – talent that continues to explode today whenever
it has a chance to blossom. But, instead of that reality being celebrated
and used for the benefit of all mankind, the Jews instead were again
demonized as if it were the Middle Ages all over again. During the
twentieth century, they were singled out by the Nazis for dehumanization
and personal destruction. Only now, decades after the Holocaust and
the establishment of the State of Israel have the Jewish people had an
opportunity to begin to recover and to thrive again. We shall examine the
implications behind this further on.

What leads to genius?

The work of Charles Murray has continued the discussion of where genius comes from. Murray asserts: "When you assemble the human resumé" of global historic achievement, "only a few thousand people stand apart from the rest. Among them, the people who are indispensable to the story of human accomplishment number in the hundreds."[43]

What factors brought about greatness and extraordinary achievement among these *hundreds*? Galton tried to find a way to assess that. Murray notes with respect to Galton: "Even though he had been instrumental in creating the modern concept of intelligence, Galton argued that intelligence alone was not enough to explain genius." Instead, what Galton found was that the explanation is tied to a combination of "ability combined with zeal and with a capacity for hard labour."[44] Joseph Jacobs sought to build on this concept in his analysis of the reasons behind Jewish pre-eminence in so many fields.

Not long after Jacobs' death, there was an interesting development in the analysis of defining and measuring genius and greatness, referred to as the science of *historiometry* or *historiometrics*. This was the work of Alfred James Lotka, who developed the so-called *Lotka Curve* to measure pre-eminence in the 1920s.[45] Lotka developed a mathematical formula for measuring greatness that has proven consistent through the years. This is a hyperbolic curve that shows that roughly sixty percent of people in a field who publish a scientific article or have a work of art shown or otherwise contribute to their field will only do one thing during their careers, while, of the remaining forty percent, only a very small number make a large number of contributions to their respective fields, skewing the curve tremendously. This rough mathematical relationship seems to hold across many different fields and types of contributions.[46]

Eric Weiner, mentioned earlier, has another approach, related to his "geography of genius" theory and the existence of so-called urban "genius clusters." Weiner cites the work of Dean Keith Simonton, who has pioneered this aspect of historiometrics. Simonton has been at it for quite a while, publishing a book with Harvard University Press in 1984 titled, *Genius, Creativity, and Leadership: Historiometric Inquiries.*

This view explores culture and geography as primary explanations for genius, looking at the cities of Athens, Hangzhou, Florence, Edinburgh, Calcutta, Vienna and Silicon Valley, each of which experienced its own 'golden age' of genius and creativity. Weiner explains: "Only now...are we beginning to fully understand the connection between the cultural milieu and our most creative ideas." He says that Simonton and a few others "have quietly been developing a new theory of creativity, one that aims to chart the circumstances of genius."[47] With the exception of Vienna, where the story of the city and the story of her Jews are "inseparable,"[48] Weiner ignores any unique Jewish contributions and pre-eminence, preferring to focus on *location* as a key explanation for genius, not ethnicity. He also completely ignores the Veblen thesis on the Jewish people that we will look at later, as well as the more recent views of people like Gilder. Although he cites Charles Murray once with respect to China and lists Murray's *Human Accomplishment* in his bibliography, somehow Weiner didn't find it worthwhile to even mention Murray's amazing section in *Human Accomplishment* on Jewish achievement. Discussing ethnic or tribal genius or giftedness appears to be off-limits for many contemporary writers and researchers, which is probably why Weiner and others take refuge in the geography thesis. While the geography/location thesis is not without some validity (and Weiner does an exemplary job in developing his geographical explanations), it is woefully incomplete.[49]

For example, during Vienna's golden age, "a disproportionately high number of the city's creative geniuses" were Jewish - a number "so large it cannot be ignored," according to the author of *Vienna and the Jews, 1867-1938*.[50] Nevertheless, while there have been locations such as Vienna where Jewish genius flourished and was quite pronounced, Murray, who has looked at the phenomenon both globally and historically, is quite insistent that Jewish pre-eminence is *not* country-specific: "...the hypothesis that Jewish accomplishment is explained by the activity in the countries where they worked fails."[51] In other words, there have been locations where Jews have certainly flourished in large or influential numbers, such as Vienna during its golden age, or academia today in Boston, or the financial sector in New York City, or as producers in Hollywood. But while success can be accentuated by a local and like-minded 'community' of talented individuals, whether Jew or Gentile, what Murray is telling us is that Jewish pre-eminence is *not limited* by such factors; pre-eminence may emerge *regardless of them.*

The Source of Creativity

Various explanations have been offered as sources of creativity and genius. These include "risk-taking" in the creative process, rivalry and competition between geniuses (such as between Michelangelo and Leonardo da Vinci, or seeking to understand our world through a sense of wonder and surprise.[52]

One of those trying to "chart the circumstances of genius," or, at least, creativity, is British author Margaret Boden. In *The Creative Mind*, Boden decries what she terms the *inspirational* view of creativity, which views creativity as being "essentially mysterious, even superhuman or divine." She claims that such a view is "extreme." A "less extreme" view, she says, is the *romantic* view, which claims "that creativity – while not actually divine – is at least exceptional." Boden himself rejects both views. She believes that science will someday understand creativity, even though thus far it has failed to do so. Since creativity is currently unpredictable, she says that developing a scientific understanding of it would have to show "why this unpredictability does not anchor it firmly in the depths of mystery.[53] Exactly right, but she rejects the mystery portion of it. So I suppose if we applied the Boden definition of what constitutes the source of creativity to the thesis of this book, she would lump my view into the *inspirational* camp, since I do believe that God has been directly involved in "gifting" the Jewish people.

Boden also builds on the views of famed Jewish novelist Arthur Koestler, whom we shall discuss later. Koestler, in addition to his well-known novels, published a book about creativity titled *The Act of Creation*. Koestler described the sudden appearance of new insights "as an act of intuition. Such intuitions," Koestler continued, "give the appearance of miraculous flashes," but "In fact they may be likened to an immense chain, of which only the beginning and the end are visible above the surface of consciousness."[54] Boden has sought "to identify some of the 'invisible links' underlying intuition, and to specify how they can be tempered and forged."[55] But those links remain invisible. Clearly, the "science" of creativity and genius is still in its infancy. While Boden, Murray, Simonton, Weiner and others are doing important work in trying to understand it, it still remains largely a mystery. That reality is not going to change any time soon.

Types of Genius

Martin Guttman is an Israeli-born physicist who has developed a 'taxonomy of genius,' as Weiner describes it. According to Guttman's taxonomy, there are two types of geniuses, unifiers and revolutionaries. Unifiers are those who 'connect the dots' from various fields or sources of knowledge in a way that no one before them had done. They see the connections that others have missed. Revolutionaries, on the other hand, "create new dots." Guttman does not view one approach as better than the other; these are just two different types of genius. As we look at various types of Jewish genius, achievement and pre-eminence, I believe that they fall into both categories.[56]

The Aspect of 'Chosenness', Love or Hatred of the Jewish People

Closely tied in with the idea of Jewish giftedness is the concept of 'chosenness.' The Jewish people are often referred to as "the Chosen People," and they have lived with that designation from Biblical days. But, according to Prager and Telushkin, "...among those Jews who continue to believe in chosenness, few ever make reference to it."[57] This is in great contrast to many evangelical Christians and Messianic Jews who see Jewish 'chosenness' as being central to the purposes of God.

The very notion that God has had a special plan for the Jewish people throughout history delights some and infuriates others. Prager and Telushkin assert that "...virtually every modern anti-Semitic movement has referred to Jewish chosenness."[58] Jewish 'chosenness' has been completely inverted by those who hate the Jews into 'de-selection'. Sadly, Jewish author Frederic Raphael sees this as being an inherent part of Christianity: in his view, Jewish humiliation became proof for Christians "that the once Chosen People had forfeited divine favour."

From here it was just a short step to "de-selection...fashioned into they-asked-for-it justification for anathemas, ghettoization, *pogroms* and, eventually, genocide."[59]

Raphael is not entirely off-base. Many people throughout history who have called themselves Christians indeed saw Jewish humiliation as allegedly negating Jewish 'chosenness.' This is a horrible blot on our history. But as terrible as it has been, this view by no means equates to the teachings of the New Testament (the *Brit Chadashah*) – just the opposite.

But it is very, very sad. Raphael cites a passage from atheist Bertrand Russell's 1927 book, *Why I am Not a Christian*, in which Russell for some bizarre reason used the hypothetical annihilation of the Jewish people in order to make a point in an argument (how eerily this hypothetical scenario presaged the Nazis and the Holocaust). As explained by Raphael, Russell posited that, "if it could be proved that killing all the Jews in the world would procure an earthly paradise for the rest of the human race, there was no logical reason not to proceed with their annihilation." By using such a horrible example, Russell countenanced the idea – no matter how improbable it seemed when he said it – that he actually would be willing to give such a notion careful consideration if he was ever presented with this choice. With such reasoning, anything is permissible. The very fact that Russell could come up with such an awful formulation demonstrated (to Raphael at least) that the atheist Russell actually *was* a Christian![60] By such a formulation, Christianity in essence then becomes defined as simply being anti-Semitism. What a terrible and ironic state of affairs.

Yes, someone had to die to bring the world redemption, but it was never intended to be the Jewish people – it was the Jewish Messiah, Yeshua HaMashiach.

Why do some people love the Jewish people and others hate them? Why some do and others don't is a mystery. There is no ready answer to this question other than to note once again that this question has a deep spiritual dimension that cannot be measured or quantified in sociological terms. Beyond all the stereotypes and conspiracy theories and self-hatred and all the nuances pro and con, why some people hate the Jews and others love them really does have one simple explanation: *some love the Jews because they know they are God's chosen people.* They know this truth at a very deep level, or they love the Scriptures and therefore love the Jews, or they appreciate excellence and quality and see it in so many Jewish people who strive for excellence in their respective fields. *Some others hate the Jews in part because the Jews have been termed 'the chosen people'.* These haters rail against that reality either on the surface or deep inside; they refuse to accept it and seek every reason to justify their non-acceptance of that truth - they discriminate against Jews; they kill them, and they often blame the victim for their own hatred and misdeeds.

But no matter how much some haters hate the Jews and try to destroy them - whether the haters and killers are Haman, Hitler, Russian *pogromchiks*, or Islamic jihadists, the Jewish people just won't go away, they just won't die...and worse yet for the anti-Semites – they keep bouncing back and excelling! *This just can't be!* the anti-Semites tell themselves. This reaction is at the core of anti-Semitism.

Some anti-Semitism today is cloaked in 'anti-Zionism'.[61]'Anti-Zionism' is trendy to many because they see the Palestinian people as victims (and, certainly, some Palestinians *are* victims). But this is not just because of Israel's missteps. *It is because the anti-Semitic world needs Palestinian victims in order to justify its desired final destruction of Israel and the Jewish people.*

The Demonic Side of Anti-Semitism

Among all the hatreds of the world, 'Jew-hatred' seems to be in class by itself. In *Why the Jews?*, Prager and Telushkin have a chapter titled "Why Jew-Hatred is Unique." They assert that "Hatred of the Jew has been humanity's greatest hatred."[62] The horrors of the Holocaust would seem to bear that out. The Holocaust was unlike anything that has ever happened in history. The most horrible dimension of anti-Semitism is its demonic side – an irrational, unfathomable hatred toward the Jewish people *just for existing,* exemplified by Hitler and Nazi ideology. This most vicious form of anti-Semitism – one that seeks Jewish *annihilation* – seems to once again be on the rise in our world. As Ephraim Kishon has noted: "...the world has gotten used to this heinous custom of slaughtering Jews, and rarely does it stop to ask itself, 'Seriously! Why?"[63]

Jewish giftedness is related to God's plan for the Jewish people and the redemption of the world. You may not want to think so; you may be in denial. Nevertheless, the 'immense realities' that Gilder referred to *must be broached*, because they concern not just the fate of the Jewish people and the nation of Israel, but, ultimately, the fate of the whole world.

Jewish Ignorance/Denial, *Tikkun Olam*, Philanthropy and Radical Causes

I started this book as a look at Jewish brilliance and genius and explanations for the reasons behind them. Though some see this as a 'given', sometimes the 'smartest people in the room,' so to speak, are oblivious to the phenomenon.

To show that this is so, I will repeat a story involving two Jewish Nobel Prize winners and giants in the world of physics – Murray Gell-Mann and his one-time colleague at Caltech, Richard Feynman.[64] Both have had enormous impact. Feynman's contributions continue to reverberate decades after his death: "It was permitted in connection with Feynman to use the word *genius.*"[65] Friend and colleague Freeman Dyson once described Feynman as "the most original mind of his generation."[66]

Gell-Mann was considered a 'boy genius' - a *wunderkind.* Some have called him "Albert Einstein's scientific successor..."[67] At age eight, his intellectual prowess was said to be "equal to that of most college students."[68] He entered Yale on a full academic scholarship at age 14. According to Gell-Mann's biographer, George Johnson, "For years, particle physicists argued over who was the smartest person in their field: Richard Feynman or Murray Gell-Mann."[69] All of this establishes the credentials of both men as very, very smart people.

Gell Mann and Feynman's Discussion about Hungarians

Gell-Mann was well-known for de-emphasizing his Jewish background. But in one key discussion between him and Feynman on the subject of Jewishness and Jewish genius, it was Gell-Mann who recognized the phenomenon and Feynman who was clueless. In one incident, Feynman was discussing numerous famous Hungarians who had made outstanding contributions to physics, including "Szilard, Teller, Wigner and others." Feynman only saw these men as Hungarian. Gell-Mann looked at him "in mild disbelief," according to one account. "'Don't you know, Dick, that all these Hungarians were Jewish?'"[70] Feynman had no idea. It had never struck him, and he apparently didn't care. (An important aside – and one that would later impact the whole world – these same three Hungarian Jewish physicists were part of the so-called "Hungarian conspiracy" that explained to Einstein the possibility of an atomic bomb and urged him to alert President Roosevelt.[71] Earlier, Teller and Wigner had left Hungary "because they had no chance for advancement" in that country. Teller also later became known as the father of the hydrogen bomb.[72])

Feynman was the kind of person who either largely ignored or else couldn't be bothered about his Jewish heritage.[73] One might think that he rejected his Jewish heritage entirely, but that would not be the whole story either. Feynman just avoided the issue as much as possible.[74] On the other hand, he once expounded on his Jewishness with famed Jewish novelist Herman Wouk, who failed, apparently, it getting him to explore it further.[75] Feynman is said to have turned down an opportunity to be included in a book about Jewish winners of the Nobel Prize, reportedly stating that participating would be an "adventure in prejudice."[76]

In any event, if someone as brilliant and renowned as Richard Feynman was oblivious to or consciously dismissive of Jewish genius and never gave it much thought or attention, this tells us that many other Jews today probably also either ignore or downplay the subject.

Tikkun Olam

*"Being Jewish means striving for **tikkun olam**. "*

DANIEL GILL[77]

Jewish communities are rightly proud of those Jews who make extraordinary contributions to science and the arts or to civilization in general. Even in the scientific arena, many apparently 'do science' as a means of refashioning "the societies in which Jews [have] found themselves....," and a way of serving humanity as well.[78] Much of this can be chalked up to the desire – deep within the hearts of so many Jewish people – to make the world a better place – the words in Hebrew are *tikkun olam,* that is, 'fixing up of the world,' 'repairing' or 'redeeming' it - the desire to leave the world a better place than one found it. A quote attributed to the young Anne Frank, one of the most famous victims of the Holocaust, perhaps best expresses this idea: "How wonderful it is that nobody need wait a single moment before starting to improve the world."[79] The desire for doing *tikkun olam* takes many forms, under all kinds of conditions. The famous Hebrew song by Arik Einstein, "Ani v'Ata," expresses the idea of changing the world together.

Jewish Philanthropy

Conceptions of *tikkun olam* take many forms, but a common thread runs through them – trying to find ways of making the world a better place. One sees it in the arts, in music, and in some cases, in Jewish devotion to science. One also sees it in the countless examples of Jewish philanthropy in the Western world, where, for example, a successful Jewish businessman or family often funds the wing of a hospital or gives a substantial sum to the arts. Some have become renowned collectors in their given fields.[80] David A. Rubenstein, who rose from humble circumstances to become a self-made billionaire, has given tens of millions of dollars to many different projects and causes. He has bought rare documents in order to preserve them for future generations. He is America's foremost "patriotic philanthropist."[81]

Generous Jewish givers are not alone in such philanthropy by any means, but the depth and breadth of their giving to such causes and collections far outstrip what nearly all other ethnic groups do in terms of their percentage numbers in society. Steven L. Pease has noted that "38 percent of America's most generous philanthropists" were Jewish.[82]

In assessing Jewish giftedness and intelligence, author Miles D. Storfer observed that, "...examining the overall record of Jewish accomplishment, *one cannot help but be struck by the extraordinary degree to which the Jewish people have been drawn to occupations in which the emphasis is on improving the human condition, whether in physical, emotional, intellectual, economic or legal terms.*"[83] (emphasis added)

Storfer sees this as what he calls the 'Jewish mission' - seeing in the Jewish people a desire "'To help make the world a better place to live in, in the hope that God will finally say 'You have done well my children,' and will cast down his countenance again to shine upon the human race and reveal himself anew."[84]

Jewish Radicals; Jewish Activism and Idealism; Russian Jews and Communism

Jewish activism and idealism in social causes, sometimes quite radical and revolutionary causes, is also a well-known and well-documented phenomenon. These are Jews who seek "earthly forms of salvation"[85] – a complete inversion of God's intent for the Jewish people. Instead, Jews are often leading such movements. For example, "Jews were...disproportionately represented and were conspicuous as leaders" in the radical movements in the U.S. in the 1960s.[86]

Billionaire speculator George Soros, who settled in America after escaping the Nazis in Europe and made a fortune from the capitalistic systems of the West, has funded numerous extreme radical causes, which he apparently views as part of his "Jewish utopianism."[87]

Jewish Marxist Isaac Deutscher was forced to ask himself in 1968: "Why has the Russian revolution not succeeded, in the course of nearly half a century, in solving the *Jewish problem*?"[88] (emphasis added). That 'problem,' in Deutscher's eyes, was that the Jews of Russia and the Soviet Union had *not* succeeded in fully assimilating into Soviet, or, better yet, an internationalist socialist society, as he had hoped. Lies, propaganda and personal destruction replaced the dreams of a new and better world, such as Russian Jewish writer Isaac Babel, who was murdered in 1940 by Stalin's secret police for being a 'Trotskyist' (a code word at the time for 'Jew').[89] Deutscher himself, who rejected his Jewish roots, still had a strong commitment to a form of *tikkun olam*. He wrote: "..if the search for an identity" – in this case, finding a Jewish identity – "can help the

Jewish intellectual in his struggle for a better future for the whole of mankind," then that search might be justified.[90]

Deutscher was born into a Hasidic Jewish family in the small Polish village of Chrzanow, located only ten miles from what later became the massive Nazi death camp at Auschwitz. Young Isaac was extremely gifted, a child prodigy who became a rabbi at the tender age of thirteen and was the top student in his Hasidic Jewish sect. He was considered to have "an uncommon ability for abstract thinking." But he later abandoned his Hasidic Jewish faith and became a fervent socialist, joining the Polish Communist Party and embracing the Soviet Union – until he was expelled from the Party. Later, David Ben-Gurion himself sought him out in Israel.[91]

The desire to build a socialist utopia where Jews would be treated fairly was a dream that ultimately failed. With the exception of groups like the Jewish Bund (the Jewish Workers' Party), most Jews in the Soviet Union wanted nothing to do with their Jewishness – they wanted to cast it off or ignore it entirely. But they could not – the anti-Semites among their fellow Communists wouldn't let them. Virulent anti-Semitism in the Soviet Union made it nearly impossible for Jews to simply cast off their Jewish identity and become fully assimilated into Soviet society.

This failure by Soviet Jews to fully assimilate was a development that one could view as a means that God used *to help fulfill His promises to preserve the Jewish people.* Despite their rebellion and even shaking their fists at heaven in denunciation of the God they no longer believed in, God Himself, who is always true to His Word, preserved them as a people. A few generations later, in the latter part of the twentieth century, Russian Jews would emerge in the forefront among Jewish people from around the world who have come to faith in Jesus as the Messiah.[92]

God had 'the last laugh,' so to speak, with regard to men's plans to ignore Him or to walk away from Him to build a successful 'New Communist World' without Him.

The Communist Experience
and the Jews of the Soviet Union

Prominent Soviet Jews like Trotsky, Zinoviev and Kamenev, and others were some of the key movers and shakers of the Russian Revolution. Outside of the USSR itself, "Soviet Russia commanded the sympathy and support of many Jewish radicals." (1) Strange as it seems now, during the heady days of the Revolution, many Russian Jews flocked to and were even welcomed into the ranks of the secret police and military forces. (2) They made up some of the most dedicated early adherents and leaders of the Revolution. At the start, these Jews truly believed that they were building a New World and a New Man in which their Jewishness would no longer be a factor but would quietly disappear into the mists of time. Meanwhile, they there was, they thought, a bright Communist future around the corner – a New World (another version of *tikkun olam*!). Former Soviet Jewish dissident Natan Sharansky (now Israeli Minister of Jerusalem and Diaspora Affairs) once was one of them and describes the desire to build *Homo sovieticus* [the new Soviet Man]. Jews in Russia and Ukraine had already become assimilated and had left Judaism and the *shtetl* of the Pale of Settlement far behind them. Yet their desire to change the world, as Sharansky shares in the book of essays, *I Am Jewish*, was nevertheless "a very Jewish aspiration..." These men and women wanted to be a Communist-inspired "light to the gentiles" – in the form of the working class. They wanted to "mend the world..." However, they couldn't have been more completely wrong. As Sharansky notes: "The Jews who led the Bolshevik Revolution believed that rubbing out their Jewish identity was the way to redeem the world." But things turned out in just the opposite way: "Instead of being a light to the gentiles, they brought a great darkness on the world." They ended up lending "a hand to one of the cruelest regimes mankind has known." (3)

Over time, a new form of the old Russian anti-Semitism, now a new Soviet anti-Semitism, put an end to any Jewish leadership in the Communist state. Soviet Jews who had wholeheartedly committed themselves to building this new world began to see that it was constructed on lies and death. By then, anti-Semitism had reared its ugly head once again. They were deeply disillusioned but had no way out.

The new anti-Semitism later became so severe that the Soviet authorities would not even permit the acknowledgement of that portion of the Holocaust that occurred on Soviet territory *as being directed at Jews just because they were Jews.* Whether at Babiy Yar in Kiev or the killing-field at Berdichev, the 1.5 million Soviet Jews slaughtered by the Nazis on Soviet territory were just 'Soviet citizens' victimized by the Nazi regime, not *Jewish* victims in Soviet eyes. Even in death they were denied their identity. The Communists regime did

everything in its power – even the use of brutal force – to deny this *Jewish* aspect of the Second World War. Despite all past hopes and efforts, Jews once again became pariah citizens, second-class members of the socialist 'utopia' they had put so much faith in.

In another historic twist, despite all the hatred, opposition and discrimination against them during both the Russian Tsarist period and later in the post-Revolutionary Soviet period, Russian/Soviet Jews still managed to be disproportionately represented among Russian significant figures during the period 1870-1950 by a ratio of 4:1! (4)

1. Stephen J. Whitfield, Jewish Voices of Jacob, Hands of Esau: Jews in American Life and Thought (1984), 81.

2. N. Efron, Chosen Calling: Jews in Science in the Twentieth Century (2014), 102. According to Richard Lynn, by 1934 Jews made up 63% of senior officials of the NKVD/OGPU secret police. (R. Lynn, The Chosen People: A Study of Jewish Achievement and Intelligence (2011), Table 15.7. Jews in the Soviet Union 1926-1939", 222).

3. Natan Sharansky, cited in the I Am Jewish book of essays (2004, 2015), 32-33.

4. Charles Murray, "Jewish Disproportional Representation Within Countries," Human Accomplishment, 281.

Jewish Activism Today

Jewish support of radical causes has a long history and continues to this day in various forms. Why are so many Jews drawn to radical causes? I think the answer is that, no matter how much some causes are discredited, no matter how catastrophically some social experiments have failed, no matter how destructive these causes have been on the lives of tens of millions of people, so many Jewish activists tell themselves: '*We* can still succeed where all others have failed; we know best.' This is misguided, and, since it is also very often involves shaking one's fist at God, it is doomed to destruction. At the same time, though, there is a headstrong aspect to this attitude that reminds one of......none other than the Jewish patriarch Jacob himself, he who 'wrestled with God and prevailed'!

Today, Jewish activism takes myriad forms in various countries and social movements and on all sides of the political spectrum. The motivation is to try to make the world a better place.

There is no lack of trying, nor a limited variety of means for attempting to re-shape the world. But common to nearly all of them – except for some of the most radical and rebellious forms - is a Jewish sense of shared values, "a passion for justice," as one observer has put it. This concept of 'repairing of the world' (which defines *tikkun olam*) has become rooted in the championing of "*mentshlekayt* – a commitment to human decency and mutual respect." This, for many, this has become "the essence of Jewishness."[93] And even some of the most radical forms are still viewed by their adherents as belonging to a Jewish tradition.[94]

This is what Jews of all ages and backgrounds – as well as Gentile men and women of good faith – have thirsted for for centuries – justice, decency, and respect – not just for themselves but for all of society.

Striving for Excellence, Unlimited Optimism

I believe that a striving for excellence by many Jewish people in so many fields is closely related to the notion of 'repairing the world,' to making the world a better place, to improving mankind. Author George Gilder emphasizes this Jewish quest for excellence in *The Israel Test*: "The facts are clear," he writes: "What makes Jews unique is their excellence." He goes even further: "On a planet where human life subsists upon the achievements of human intellect and enterprise, Jews are crucial to the future of the race."[95]

That is an amazing assertion. It sounds similar in some ways to what famed Jewish theoretical physicist and self-proclaimed atheist, David Deutsch of Oxford, one of the founders of quantum computing, said in his

2011 book, *The Beginning of Infinity* - not about Jews per se - but about human beings in general. Born in Israel in 1953, Deutsch is considered by one observer to be "one of the most daring and versatile thinkers alive."[96] Deutsch has a philosophy of optimism that human beings can fundamentally change almost anything we put our minds to, that "our values and our objectives can continue to improve indefinitely" and that society and human institutions are capable of "unlimited improvement" – there is no inhibiting 'original sin' holding mankind back according to Deutsch's worldview. *If* mankind can only dispense with such fetters, he believes, the sky – literally – is *not* the limit: we could "be exploring the stars by now, and you and I would be immortal."[97]

Deutsch has many crazy ideas – he thinks mankind could be controlling the Sun (when we can't even control the weather?!), but my point is that, putting aside his atheism and his rejection of the concept of sin, his fundamental belief in the *possibilities* of human intellectual capital harnessed toward a particular goal is infectious and inspiring. I believe that this attitude is a God-given quality – though, as noted, Deutsch leaves God out of the equation entirely.

Gilder takes this attitude of optimism about what is possible a step further – unlike Deutsch, he doesn't focus on the human race as a whole *but primarily on the Jewish people themselves.* As a card-carrying American WASP (White Anglo-Saxon Protestant), Gilder believes that the Jewish people are best equipped to make the breakthroughs in knowledge and creativity to make the world a better place or to fundamentally improve the quality of life for all mankind (This type of philo-Semitism, by the way, rankles many Jewish intellectuals, who dismiss it as misguided to refer to a unitary body of people called 'the Jews' that is otherwise so diverse in background and talent. At the same time, these same critics themselves often employ the same terminology when it suits their purposes, so their critique carries no merit on those grounds).

Gilder is quite pessimistic if such a course is *not* followed, that is, if the Jewish people are *not* permitted to work on behalf of mankind, or if the state of Israel is destroyed. He paints the situation in very stark terms: "Survival of the [human] race depends on recognizing excellence wherever it appears and nurturing it until it prevails." For the human race to succeed, this situation "depends on passing the Israel test."[98] (for those who believe the Scriptures, the story ends differently, but Gilder's point is well taken).

But I can answer Gilder's question regarding his 'Israel test' (Gilder also does not include God in his equation of how Jewish intellectual capital and genius can positively change the world). The world has already made its choice, and the world has 'flunked' the 'Israel test' – it is presently on a path to let Israel be destroyed. As Jewish author Frederic Raphael has written, "Israel has become the Judas state."[99]

Israel is now in a constant battle with the rest of the world for legitimacy (except in the United States and a few other countries). It is continuously being treated as the world's pariah state that must be punished or destroyed. If my secular friends can suspend their disbelief just for a moment, this development is, I believe, a fulfillment of Scripture, where God says that the nations of the world will turn against Israel (Zechariah 14). But this does not make it any less painful to see it happening before our eyes.

So at a time when Jewish (and, specifically, Israeli) ingenuity and creativity are poised to help with many of the most intractable problems the world faces, the world appears ready to once again turn its back on the Jews. It certainly is not prepared to embrace Israel at the level that Gilder says is both urgent and necessary.

I believe that it is God who has placed this driving desire to improve the world very deep upon the hearts and souls of the Jewish people. It is an important part of God's calling upon them, whether they recognize it or not. Wanting to fix the world is a common human trait for any person who looks beyond his or her own selfish desires and needs. It is a noble and virtuous goal. Jewish people seem to have that trait or characteristic in greater depth than most people. It emanates from an understanding that the world is broken. One aspect of this concept emerges from the Jewish book of mysticism, the Kabbalah, not the Scriptures, based "upon a kabbalistic notion that viewed the world as a broken vessel...."[100] The idea is that, "By working to perfect ourselves, perfect our soul, and serve society, we each contribute in our unique way to the perfecting of the world. This is our duty and our calling as human beings."[101]

But there is a conundrum here. *Tikkun olam* does *not* have a Biblical origin.[102] Instead, the Bible instead makes clear that *we* are the broken ones, that *we* have to be the ones to get fixed first before we can 'fix the world.' As my good friend and Jewish believer in Jesus, Steve Herzig, has written in *More Jewish Culture and Customs*, "the idea of helping God fix the world is entirely manmade, appealing to the well-intentioned but misinformed….[T]he concept…is not found anywhere in the Jewish Scriptures."[103] From its kabbalistic roots it was later transformed and embraced by the Jewish Reform movement. From there it has now pervaded the entire Jewish ethos in our world today.

This does not mean that the innate desire for *tikkun olam* is wrong in itself, only that setting it as a first priority is misguided and leads to a completely wrong-headed approach from what God expects of us.

History Has a Purpose and It Is Going Somewhere: The 'Story' of the Jews

In his book, *A History of the Jews,* author Paul Johnson asks: "Is history merely a series of events whose sum is meaningless? Or is there a providential plan of which we are, however humbly, the agents? No people has ever insisted more firmly than the Jews that history has a purpose and humanity a destiny."[104] Paul Johnson can make that last statement with authority and be absolutely correct, but it is also true that many secular Jews today completely reject such a notion – or, indeed, at a minimum are embarrassed by it.

The continued existence of the Jewish people — *Am Yisrael* — points us to this fact that *something* has intervened in history to miraculously keep the Jewish people alive (and sometimes thriving) despite the worst persecution and atrocities imaginable being carried out against them. Why do they still exist as a people? This very fact, given all the exigencies of our world, has intrigued and challenged thoughtful men and women through the ages.

Nikolai Berdyaev (1874-1948) was a former Russian Marxist who was deeply intrigued by this question. It eventually drove him to abandon atheist Marxism. In his book *Smysl' istorii* (*The Meaning of History*), he wrote:

> "To Jewry has belonged a completely exclusive role in engendering an awareness of history, in an exerted sense of historical destiny, namely by Jewry contributing to the global life of mankind the beginning of [what is called] 'the historical'.... Jewry has a special significance in history. The Jewish people are, predominantly, a people of history, and in the historical destiny of this people is felt the inscrutability of God's destinies....

Berdyaev continued by saying that in his youth he was guided by a materialist view of history, which he attempted to confirm "by applying it to the destinies of peoples." This approach, however,

> broke down in the case of the Jews, where destiny seemed absolutely inexplicable from the materialistic standpoint... The survival of the Jews, their resistance to destruction, their endurance under absolutely peculiar conditions and the fateful role played by them in history: all these point to the particular and mysterious foundations of their destiny."[105]

Frederick the Great's Sneering Question

Leonhard Euler (pronounced 'Oiler') (1707-1783) is considered to be "one of the greatest geniuses mathematics has ever known."[106] What many biographical accounts of Euler skip over, however, is the fact that he was also an ardent evangelical believer. Euler was invited by Frederick the Great (1712-1782) to come to the royal court in Prussia. He did so, and while his mathematical gifts were honored, both Frederick and arch-anti-theist Voltaire mocked Euler for his Christian beliefs.[107] Euler was not alone in suffering this harassment – apparently other believers in Frederick's court also had to endure ridicule for their faith. But knowing how Euler was treated by Frederick despite his brilliance helps set the stage for the following anecdote: at one time Frederick turned to someone in his court (not Euler) who was a Christian believer and demanded a simple proof for the existence of God. We don't know for sure who that person was – the exact facts of that person's identity are somewhat murky.[108] In the end, though, it doesn't really matter who specifically answered Frederick - what matters is the answer that was given. One can imagine the scene: the sneering king and the royal crowd of fellow skeptics and unbelievers waiting upon the answer this person would give to the royal question, 'Can you give me a single proof for the existence of God?'

That person replied simply, "The Jews, your Majesty," and the room was silenced.[109]

"One of the World's Great Wonders"

Whether or not one believes that there has been a 'providential plan' in the history of mankind, or of the history of the Jews in particular, many would still agree with Simon Schama that 'the story of the Jews' has been "one of the world's great wonders."[110] The father-daughter duo of two self-identified Jewish atheists, Amos Oz and Fania Oz-Salzberger, writing of the pervasive influence of Jewishness in our world today, proclaim: "Our names, words, concepts, and ideas resurface everywhere today…We seem to have touched everything…" They add that the "annals of the Jews contradict the facile assertion that history is written by the winning side. Even when they lost," they point out, "and lost terribly, the Israelites, and then the Jews, took great care to tell the stories themselves."[111] Max I. Dimont, in his book, *The Indestructible Jews*, considered one perspective on Jewish history and the Jews' impact on the world as "a manifest drama motivated by ideas."[112] But it has been much more than that.

My thesis on Jewish gifts goes beyond the view of the *general contributions* made by the Jewish people to Western civilization – an idea captured in Thomas Cahill's 1998 delightful book, *The Gifts of the Jews*. In that book, Cahill called the Jews "the inventors of Western culture" and "the progenitors of the Western world."[113] He was not incorrect to say that, but I think that the reality of global Jewish contributions actually goes far deeper.

I believe that the Jewish people have been gifted in a way that defies logical (or natural) explanation. This does not mean that they are 'better' than anyone else – only that they are gifted, as well as driven. This 'giftedness' certainly does not apply to every individual – far from it. It is, rather, a corporate gift bestowed on the Jewish people *as a whole*. When the Scriptures speak of *kol Yisrael* (all Israel), or when there are references to 'all Israel' with respect to the modern-day state of Israel today, it is this corporate existence that we have in mind.[114] The Scriptures speak of a time when "all Israel will be saved" (Romans 11), and this also refers to "saving *all of Israel in a corporate sense.*"[115] (emphasis in original) Even Sir Isaac Newton "had no doubt that Romans 11 spoke of the ultimate conversion of the Jews as a *nation,* and not simply as individuals."[116]

In this post-Holocaust world, we may hear the phrase in Hebrew, *Am Yisrael Chai!* – 'the people of Israel live!' This is not referring to the individual Jewish person; rather, it is a proclamation of Jewish corporate identity and existence. Similarly, the land promises made by God to the Jewish people under the Abrahamic covenant were made "to the corporate family or nation of Israel."[117]

This idea of corporate Israel is very important, as we shall see later.

Three Main Themes

I develop three main themes in this book:

- The extraordinary giftedness of the Jewish people on a *corporate* basis in the arts and sciences and an assessment of how their giftedness has resulted in enormous benefits for mankind.
- The 'Calling of the Jews' – the spiritual dimension of how the Jewish people have been 'set apart' for a special role in history; this also strongly supports the notion that history is *going somewhere* and is not simply an accumulation of random events. But how and why this happens is a mystery to many. The great philosopher Hegel himself, who sought to unlock the meaning of history, was dumbfounded when he came to the history of the Jews: "I am not able to understand it," he wrote. "It does not fit with any of our categories. It is a riddle."[118]
- The Jewish people remain *special* in the eyes of God based on His covenant with the descendants of Abraham, Isaac and Jacob. Their history and destiny are directly tied to the future of the world.

Author Rob Richards has written that God's covenant with Abram (who would be renamed Abraham) included four elements with respect to the children of Israel: they would be "a *People*," they would have "a *Place*," they would have "a *Purpose*," and these promises would exist "in *Perpetuity*."[119] As J.C. Ryle wrote in *Coming Events and Present Duties* in the nineteenth century, the Jewish nation is "the only nation in the earth to which God was pleased to reveal Himself."[120] As King David himself exclaimed, "What one nation in the earth is like Your people, even like Israel, whom God went to redeem to Himself for a people, and to make Himself a name, and to do great things for you....?" (2 Samuel 7:23) This covenant is between God and *the Jewish people as a whole*, "rather than between God and individual Jews."[121] Jewish believer in Jesus Adolph Saphir in 1881 preached that the Jews "will always remain a separate nation till Jesus comes again. Neither adversity nor prosperity can alter this." This is because "God has chosen them to be his witnesses. There they stand – a miracle stereotyped among all the nations of the earth – showing forth the truth of God."[122]

Saphir also said that, "To them [the Jewish people] pertain the promises; promises which embrace the Gentiles, and which are full of exultation and joy over the prosperity and peace of the world, are given by Israel's prophets."[123]

In his 2006 book, *God's Plan for Peace in the Middle East,* Dr. Douglas W. Kittredge has written: "God has made the Jews of utmost significance, and to diminish their place in history is to resist the Creator God of the Bible."[124] It could not be clearer than that – diminishing the place of the Jews in history *is to resist the Creator God of the Bible!* Understanding that purpose and significance is to begin to comprehend God's heart for the world.

Who are the Jews?

'Who are the Jews?" This question has been argued and disputed for millennia. The Jewish people themselves cannot answer it to their satisfaction. The timeless joke, 'Where there are two Jews, there are at least three opinions' certainly applies here. Born of a Jewish mother? Have at least one Jewish grandparent? Orthodox rabbis who seek to certify Jewish marriages in Israel have one definition; Hitler had another. The Nazis, who sought to expunge all traces of Jewishness wherever they could be found, were much more expansive in their definition. If there was a whiff of Jewishness about, they would search it out and destroy it if they could. There was no ambiguity with the Enemy. Steven Silbiger asserts that the Jewish people "can best be understood as a tribe."[125] The Hebrew word *Am* – most often translated as "people," can also be translated "tribe" or "nation." Having said that, all of us who are serious about this topic recognize that there exists a multiplicity of Jewish cultures and ethnic groupings around the world, not just one monolithic set of people. Besides the major division of world Jewry into Ashkenazi, Sephardic,[126] and Mizrahi Jewry, there are great numbers of ethnic Jewish communities of all kinds. The massive work titled, *Cultures of the Jews*, edited by David Biale, catalogues these many cultures, their differences from and influences upon each other, including Afghani, Egyptian, Iraqi, Bukharan, and Yemenite Jews.[127] In the end, though, despite all their variety and diversity, there is still just *one* 'people of Israel' (*Am Yisrael*).

The Origins of Ashkenazi Jewry, Sephardic and Mizrahi Connections

A group of geneticists at Hebrew University in Jerusalem, based on the DNA samples of a large number of Ashkenazi Jews, concluded that Ashkenazi Jewry may have descended from as few as 500 family lines in Europe as a result of an alleged "genetic bottleneck that occurred 500 years ago," reduced from an earlier purported 1,500 family lines. (1) This is put forward as a theory of selection for higher IQs among a disproportionate percentage of Ashkenazi Jewry vis-à-vis the population as a whole. But the genetics story is also unclear, since the "origins of Ashkenazi Jews – the great majority of living Jews – remains highly contested and enigmatic to this day." According to another study, "the Ashkenazim have undergone severe founder effects during their history, drastically altering the frequencies of genetic markers and distorting the relationship of their ancestral populations." (2)

Steven L. Pease has done an extensive study of the recent literature related to genetic studies among Jewish populations in his 2015 book, *The Debate Over Jewish Achievement: Exploring the Nature and Nurture of Human Accomplishment.* He states that "[t]he genetic data also appear to show that Ashkenazi and Sephardic populations are much closer genetically than was thought just a few years ago... The recent genetic research says that most Jews retain a high level of shared genetic inheritance... [from the time of the Babylonian conquest approximately 2,600 years ago]" and across "the full geographic spread of the Diaspora..." The Human Genome Project and subsequent research have clearly shown the genetic links between Ashkenazi Jewry and their Sephardic and Mizrahi counterparts. (3)

The Cohanim are the descendants of Aaron the High Priest, Moses'

brother. An important genetic study of Ashkenazi and Sephardic Cohanim, first reported in the science journal *Nature* (January 2, 1997), showed a particular genetic marker (YAP-) in 98.5% of the Cohanim tested. A collection of additional chromosomal markers related to the Cohanim is now called the Cohen Modal Hapoltype (CMH). According to Rabbi Yaakov Kleiman, "The finding of a common set of genetic markers in both Ashkenazi and Sephardi Cohanim worldwide clearly indicates an origin pre-dating the separate development of the two communities around 1,000 CE...' The rate of variation of mutations among these Cohanim has been assessed to yield "a time frame of 106 generations from the ancestral founder of the line," or around 3,300 years. Thus, we see a strong correlation between Ashkenazi and Sephardi Jews, and the Cohanim predating both of them. (4)

1. See Charles Murray, *Human Accomplishment: The Pursuit of Excellence in the Arts and Sciences, 800 B.C. to 1950,* citing the work of geneticist Ariel Darvasi at Hebrew University (292, 607, fn. 31).

2. Marta D. Costa, Joana B. Pereira, Maria Pala, et al. "A substantial prehistoric European ancestry amongst Ashkenazi maternal lineages," *Nature Communications* 4 No. 2543. 8 October 2013. www.nature.com/ncomms/2013/131008/ncomms3543/full/ncomms3543.html

3. Steven L. Pease, *The Debate Over Jewish Achievement* (2015), 3, 90.

4. Rabbi Yaakov Kleiman, "The Cohanim – DNA Connection," Aish.com, http://www.aish.com/ci/sam/48936742.html?tab=y

Rejecting This Thesis: The Jews are Not Really Jews?!

I have always thought very highly of Arthur Koestler (1905-1983). A famed Hungarian Jewish novelist and intellectual who later settled in Britain, he was a former Communist who became one of the world's best-known *anti*-Communists.[128] Koestler's own life story reads like something out of a spy novel. He was author of the very famous works, *Darkness at Noon* and also *The God That Failed* – "two books vital," according to one observer, "to the defeat of communism among intellectuals."[129]

His non-fiction work, *The Thirteenth Tribe,* published in 1976, examined the alleged origin of Ashkenazi Jewry.[130] Its central thesis was that there should be no real basis for anti-Semitism, since modern-day Jews are not really Semites *and therefore not really Jews at all*, but are allegedly descended from a Turkic tribe called the Khazars. In other words, *'Don't hate us; we're not really Semites after all.'*[131]

The thesis as such is not serious,[132] but for a time it was all the rage in many Jewish circles. And it *still* won't die among some Jewish intellectuals – I recently came across an oblique reference to it in Amoz Oz's and Fania Oz-Salzberger's 2012 book, *Jews and Words*.[133] In fairness, however, scholars believe that many Khazars did convert to Judaism, and, even though there is no genetic evidence linking the Khazars to modern-day Jewry, they may certainly have had some impact.[134] But to say that the Jewish people today are *not* Semitic but are merely descended from this obscure Turkic tribe is absurd.

Of much greater concern, though, this "Khazar myth," as it is sometimes called, has now been taken up by some of the world's vilest anti-Semites (as well as left-wing anti-Zionists) as a means of seeking to de-legitimize Israel: in other words, if the Jews of today are not really Jews, then they have no legitimate claim to the Land of Israel. In a 2007 article in JewishPress.com, author Steven Plaut stated: "It would be hard to exaggerate how widespread the misuse of the Khazar myth is among those seeking to delegitimize Israel and Jews today." Plaut continued, "A recent investigation showed nearly 30,000 websites using the Khazar 'theory' as a bludgeon against Israel and Zionism."[135]

When *The Thirteenth Tribe* first came out I was a graduate student at Harvard specializing in Russian studies. Various Jewish friends of mine at Harvard at the time seemed quite taken with the book, a response I found puzzling. Although I rejected the basic thesis of the book, I did find some items of interest in it, especially with respect to comments he had made about Iran. I was especially interested in Iran (Persia) in the context of the prophecy about Gog and Magog in the Biblical book of Ezekiel.

8 MONTPELIER SQUARE,
LONDON, S.W.7.
01-589 6700.

March 21st, 1977

Dear Mr. Melnick,

To the best of my recollection the sentence about Gog and Magog is in Zeki Validi, but the book has been returned to the library and I cannot give you the page reference.

I cannot remember any source reference to Gog and Magog other than those quoted in "The Thirteenth Tribe".

Yours sincerely,

A. Koestler

Arthur Koestler

Letter to the author from Arthur Koestler, March 21, 1977, regarding a source for a key passage of interest in Koestler's *The Thirteenth Tribe* (1976)

Koestler made some unreferenced comments about Iran that I had never seen before. I wrote to him asking about one of his sources referred to in *The Thirteenth Tribe*. I received a response, but not the response

I was looking for. Instead of answering my question about his source, Koestler said that the book he had used had "already been returned to the library" and that he could not provide a reference page (this was also in pre-Internet and pre-email days).[136] While no doubt that was technically true, it sounded like a dodge. I was shocked that someone of Koestler's stature would respond in such a way. I sought out one of the top Iranian scholars at Harvard, explained the situation to him and asked him if *he* were aware of such a source. He was not. I was stupefied. How was this possible? (I was still quite naïve at the time). The Harvard Iranian scholar just shrugged his shoulders and made a cynical comment to the effect of 'What else did you expect?'[137]

Some of my idealism died that day. But, to be charitable, perhaps Koestler's skill as a novelist won out in this instance over his non-fictional research and he got too carried away with his theme. According to his biographer, his health was also beginning to falter around this time.[138]

But, putting Iran and the question of the Khazars aside, the deeper question is, why would a famous novelist with the stature of a man like Koestler even write such a book? What motivated this former Zionist activist to try to find a way to explain away the ethnic legitimacy of his Jewishness?

Jewish 'Self-Hatred'

The answer to that question could fill a separate volume. Koestler was a complicated individual, but this attitude seems similar in certain ways to some Jews' rejection of their Jewishness and to the troubling phenomenon known as "Jewish self-hatred." This is a phenomenon that most Gentiles do not have the slightest notion about.

Theodor Lessing wrote a famous book on this topic in 1830 titled, *Der juedische Selbsthass*, described as "psychological analysis of Jewish intellectuals who suffered self-hatred, a malady that had once afflicted Lessing himself."[139]

In more recent times, Jewish intellectual historian Sander Gilman wrote an entire book on this theme. He believes that Jewish self-hatred conceptually "is valid as a label for a specific mode of self-abnegation that has existed among Jews throughout their history."[140] Another author has said, "Indeed, it would seem that a modicum of self-hatred has become *de rigueur* for the modern Jew."[141]

This reality seems especially true for many Jews on the Left politically and especially those who are radicals. Robert S. Wistrich examined this phenomenon, and, while "acknowledging that self-hatred 'can exist [both] on the Right or the Left,'" he determined that, among Jewish revolutionaries, self-hatred is primarily "a malady of the Jewish Left..." Such Jews have sought "to transcend the stigma of Jewishness," and "passionately and dogmatically adopted the messianic vision of revolutionary Marxism."[142] Charles Silberman, writing in *A Certain People*, assessed Jean-Paul Sartre's view of the matter in Sartre's 1946 book, *Anti-Semite and Jew*. Silberman notes that Jewish intellectuals are "particularly susceptible to this kind of self-hatred...because for them becoming an intellectual was not just an occupation or vocation." Rather, it was 'an avenue of flight' "from the taint of being Jewish."[143]

Regarding this phenomenon, famed author George Eliot wrote of those "who must walk among the nations and be known as Jews, and with words on their lips which mean, 'I wish I had not been born a Jew, I disown any bond with the long travail of my race, I will outdo the Gentiles in mocking at our separateness'..."[144] Silberman adds: "...it was the rare Jew who escaped some measure of self-hatred or feeling of inferiority altogether."[145]

Sometimes this disavowal of Jewishness or something similar also leads to blaming the Jews themselves for their own misfortunes.[146] Or it leads some Jews becoming radicalized or passionate defenders of various "-isms" (such as Marxism or Freudianism) as a means of deflecting attention away from their Jewishness while obliquely defending themselves from defamation. John Murray Cuddihy wrote an entire book on this subject in 1974 titled, *The Ordeal of Civility: Freud, Marx, Levi-Strauss, and the Jewish Struggle with Modernity.*[147]

There is also a strange psychological connection between Jewish self-hatred and anti-Semitism, one that I cannot really begin to explain. But it is nonetheless real and has been described by one observer in a way that would almost be funny if it weren't so sad: "The thin and not always so clear line between self-hatred and anti-Semitism is suggested by the adage, so typical of the modern Jew's ironic self-awareness, 'an anti-Semite hates the Jews more than necessary'."[148]

This sad but real phenomenon manifests itself in various ways from time to time in different people. Those who have this sense of 'self-hatred' and 'self-loathing' over things Jewish or are confused or ashamed of their identity *will most likely reject the main thesis of this book, which is that the Jewish people are special in God's sight and have a special purpose.*

Yet whether individual Jewish people accept this calling or not, they are nevertheless still enveloped by it. As Israeli Messianic leader Eitan Shishkoff has written regarding Israel's calling: "We [as Jews] can try to dodge it. We can attempt to deny it. But we can't escape it."[149]

There is a level of rejection that goes even deeper, fed by deep anger and bitterness against God. This is the theme of a future book on Jewish atheists that I am working on, so I will only briefly touch upon it here. A large impetus for this book came about when I became aware that some Jews, as they have for some many other fields, had ironically become the leaders of various atheistic organizations and movements in a complete inversion of their intended Biblical role.

I must say that it took me a long time to begin to understand this phenomenon. Some secular Jews are extremely repelled by the very notion or even suggestion that the Jewish people are somehow *special.* Yes, they may see and acknowledge Jewish achievement, but the idea that it might involve anything beyond hard work, good contacts, and a bit of luck is offensive to many. The idea that *God* is somehow involved is considered an utterly reprehensible notion to such people.

I understand that attitude, even if I believe it is sadly mistaken.

Jewish Reticence

Beyond that, there is simply reluctance on the part of many Jews to talk about this topic in general. Steven L. Pease, when he was compiling evidence for his first book on Jewish achievement, remarked that "[o]ne of the more interesting aspects of writing this book was the remarkable ambivalence of so many Jews about the notion of discussing their disproportionate performance."[150] Even back in 1920 in his book, *Jewish Contributions to Civilization*, Joseph Jacobs observed that "The Jewish origin of many professional, scientific , and artistic celebrities is often unknown and sometimes concealed even by themselves..."[151]

Philo-Semitism

Before going further in presenting the thesis of this book, I must first address the issue of *philo-Semitism*, to which I plead guilty. Philo-Semitism is not just a sentiment or an attitude; it is usually derived from a worldview (such as a Biblical worldview) or a careful observation of reality and personal experience (as in George Gilder's philo-Semitism).

One observer asserts that "the philo-Semite loves Jews more than is warranted, while the anti-Semite hates Jews more than is necessary." Both views, it is claimed, "see the Jew as Other."[152] There is some truth to that statement. Attitudes toward the Jewish people have often swung between these two extremes. This has been referred to as the "booster-bigot" trap. This "trap" either puts the Jewish people on an unrealistic pedestal (the boosters), or there is hatred, deep suspicion or dislike of the Jewish people (the bigots). According to David A. Hollinger, this dichotomy either "channels discussions of Jews in comparison to other groups into the booster's uncritical celebration of Jewish achievements" on the one hand, or it manifests itself in "the bigot's malevolent complaint about Jewish conspiracies."[153] Hollinger believes that what sets the 'trap' for either boosters or bigots "is the mistaken idea that a given group [has] possessed an enduring cultural essence grounded in blood and history, implanted in each of its individual members and capable of having an unmediated impact on any object it encountered." This view he terms *essentialism*.[154]

I do not subscribe to the 'essentialism' as described by Hollinger, but only because of the straw-man argument that I see in his phrase, *"implanted in each of its individual members."* I emphasize again that the 'specialness' of the Jewish people is a *corporate* gift, one that may manifest itself in some individuals but not necessarily in everyone who is Jewish. Otherwise, one could never say anything about the Jewish people as a whole without ascribing Hollinger's "essentialism" to each and every

Jewish person in the world. But in that case, phrases such as *Kol Yisrael* ("all Israel") or in *Am Yisrael Chai* ("The people of Israel live!") would be devoid of meaning. But that is an equally ridiculous proposition.

One can accept the fact that the Jewish people are special in some way without bringing this argument or claim down to the level of the individual. Otherwise, one is in denial of the obvious. But let's put aside this zero-sum approach for the moment. What I present in this book looks at Jewish pre-eminence, but it also includes a sobering evaluation of the original purpose (and, in a sense, the current misuse) of that pre-eminence. This is based on the principle that, 'To whom much is given, much is also required.'

Jewish 'Specialness': An Uncomfortable Thesis for Many

What some Jewish readers will find uncomfortable in my book – and perhaps a number of Gentiles, too – are these joint attributes of Jewish *specialness* and *chosenness*. Some reject it with vehemence – authors Chua and Rubenfeld declare the "utter brazenness of the idea – that there is only one God, maker of all the universe, and He has chosen *us* (not *you*, or anyone else) as His people..." They say that this very notion "remains to this day a special burr for many."[155]

Sanford Pinsker also captures some of this feeling of unease. He cites Saul Bellow's novel *Herzog* in his review of Sander Gilman's book, *Smart Jews*. Gilman refers to Bellow's use of his character Moses Herzog to comment on the "extravagant claims about Jewish 'specialness' that are always part of the philo-Semite's agenda."[156]

There is a lot packed by Bellow into that one phrase put into the mouth of his character Herzog. The very *idea* of Jewish specialness is considered by some as "extravagant," based on "claims" (not reality, apparently), and also "always" part of an "agenda."

Applying Pinsker's admonition to myself and this book, I am not sure what "agenda" readers may think I have in this book beyond what I clearly state as its thesis – that such a phenomenon as corporate "Jewish giftedness" – *does*, in fact, exist.

To cite facts about Jewish achievements under various cultural and historical conditions and to draw inferences from those facts is not an *agenda* in the negative sense that such a connotation usually implies. It is instead both a scholarly and a spiritual endeavor to get at the *truth*.

But this is more than just an uncomfortable thesis. Even Jewish author Steven Silbiger, in his book, *The Jewish Phenomenon: 7 Keys to the Enduring Wealth of a People*, writes that, when his book first appeared, it was greeted "with great hostility in the Jewish community and the politically correct press."[157] So I would not be surprised if my view is greeted with the same reaction – at least by some. Others, I hope, will have more open hearts and minds.

The Pursuit of Excellence and the Jewish Dimension

In the end, I believe that all who sincerely believe in and cherish *excellence* on its own terms – especially if we consider the quest for excellence to be a virtue – will be philo-Semitic. Instead of envy and hatred, they should hold admiration in their hearts toward those who excel, whatever their background or ethnicity. And as the evidence accumulates in their own personal experience that the *preponderance* of those who excel are often Jewish, that admiration may begin to turn to wonder and curiosity.

George Gilder in *The Israel Test* chronicles his own fascinating journey in this area and how he 'flunked' his initial 'Israel test' while a student at the exclusive Phillips Exeter Academy. As a young man, Gilder made a disparaging remark one day about there being 'too many New York Jews' at Phillips Exeter. He made this comment to an older girl whom he very deeply admired who at the time was helping mentor him in Greek (she had been hired by his parents as a tutor in order to help George obtain a diploma in Classics). This young woman responded by informing the young Gilder that she herself was "a New York Jew." Gilder was mortified and says that that event was a turning point in his life.[158]

PART I:

JEWISH GIFTEDNESS

CHAPTER ONE

Jewish Brilliance and Genius

Small in Number, Yet So Influential!

I talian Jewish chemist Primo Levi, a survivor of Auschwitz, once compared the Jewish people to the chemical gas argon. He wrote a book titled, *The Periodic Table*. The opening chapter of that work "hesitantly compares the almost invisible trace of argon in the atmosphere to the Jews in humanity.... Jews are also about five times rarer than argon."

Levi's 'Jew-argon' analogy is witty and perceptive, but as he himself acknowledges, it is not altogether valid. This is because argon is inert, and "In stark contrast to argon, inertness is not a typical Jewish trait..." Instead, "[t]throughout history, it has been the fate of Jews to lurch periodically from being seen as troublesome impurities, to being nurtured as valuable catalysts."[1]

But in the end, it is the breadth and depth of Jewish contributions relative to their numbers that is so amazing.

One study that looked at Nobel Prizes concluded that "In the sciences and literature, Jews were disproportionately represented during 1901-1950 by a ratio of 6:1." By 1951-2000, that ratio doubled again, to 12:1, "rising substantially in every prize category, even when calculated by a method that understates the per capita Jewish contribution by several-fold. This trend is consistent with the hypothesis that Jewish accomplishment up to 1950 was still being held back relative to its potential."[2] Besides such concrete results, George Gilder further avers that, "in any rivalry with intellectual dimensions, disproportionate numbers both of the challengers and of the winners will be Jewish."[3] In his book, *The Golden Age of Jewish Achievement*, author Steven L.

Pease presents an even more stunning statistic: "The rate at which Jews earn Nobels is higher today (27 percent) than before the Holocaust (14 percent) when their proportion of the population was greater."[4]

Harvard Days

When I was a graduate student at Harvard in the late 1970s, I will never forget two young Israelis who lived in my dorm for a short time and were considered geniuses in mathematics. One of them – who was then, I believe, still in his teens - was reportedly offered either a professorship or tenure at Harvard, an unheard-of development at the time. I don't remember their names or how their stories turned out, only that the two of them had not yet even served their required time in the Israeli Defense Forces. It was astonishing.

Over the years, stories of the Jewish *wunderkind* or child prodigy in this or that field are so numerous as to be almost routine, both in the arts and sciences.[5] We will look later at the arts. To start, we will consider Jewish genius in the sciences, especially physics, as well as mathematics.

University Quotas: There Are Too Many Brilliant Jews!

Jewish brilliance and genius in the areas of math and science have been especially well-documented in modern times - so much so that sometimes academic departments or admissions officials have even devised ways of trying to limit the number of Jews in their programs or else be overwhelmed with too many qualified Jewish students. This has sometimes been the case irrespective of culture or political system. This occurred at Harvard, for example, in the 1920s during the Lowell Administration, when then President Lowell "was disturbed by the 'Jewish problem'." Since 1900, Jewish student enrollment at Harvard had risen dramatically from 7 to 21.5 per cent, and by the 1920s, it was spiraling higher. Lowell decided that *something* needed to be done at the admissions process level to keep the 'problem' under control.[6] Lowell's plan, however, was initially derailed when it was publicly leaked and challenged by a Jewish student.[7] The President's Commission on Higher Education reported in 1948 that Jewish students in the U.S. still did "not have an equal opportunity" when it came to higher education.[8]

While universities should have liberty to set their own policies for determining what number or kinds of students should be admitted to fill a limited number of available spots (the idea of *numerus clausus* – "a closed number" of available positions), overt, systematic, and pre-determined discrimination is another matter. In this respect, "One sad fact of that era [in the early twentieth century] was that Harvard, Yale, Princeton, and other schools had institutionalized discrimination against Jews, limiting the number of Jewish students or faculty."[9] Yale, in fact, was "the subject of one of the most rigorous, scholarly treatments yet completed of academic anti-Semitism and of the pressures finally brought against it..."[10] For a time between 1919 and 1932, New York University instituted a special "personal and psychological test" whose real purpose – according to intellectual historian David Hollinger, was "to enable NYU to more easily reject Jewish applicants."[11] Princeton at one point was "regarded as a very difficult Ivy League school for Jewish admission and tenure," but now is believed to have at least 15 percent Jewish representation.[12]

Sadly, though, in the present era, a new form of educational bias has emerged: Asian-American students now face many of the same types of discrimination that Jewish students once did.[13] Asians are 'the new Jews'. According to Amy Chua and Jed Rubenfeld in their book, *The Triple Package,* "...hypersuccessful Asian American teens are outperforming other groups on standardized tests and in admissions to elite universities." They further state that "some believe that there is an implicit 'anti-Asian admissions bias' in the Ivy League."[14] While the universities have denied it, the evidence is mounting.[15]

In a similar way, in the 1970s under Communism, many highly qualified Jewish students who applied to the renowned math department of Moscow State University were turned away simply because they were Jewish. That department was the most prestigious of its kind in the former Soviet Union and home to possibly "some of the brightest mathematicians in the world."[16] But its leadership (or the authorities) considered the acceptance of too many Jews to be highly 'undesirable.' Those in charge sought or were told to find creative ways of rejecting the number of Jews accepted by making up what were referred to as especially difficult *'Jewish'* math problems. Jewish candidates were given their exams in different rooms than the other students. According to one account, these rooms were morbidly referred to by some as the 'gas chambers' – those who didn't make the cut felt that their career prospects were then greatly limited. A person tasked by the authorities to develop some of these special 'Jewish math problems' published her account of this discriminatory practice in a 2011 paper titled, "Jewish Problems" - a title with a clear double meaning.[17] At one point, Jewish students were also reportedly being barred from the physics department of Moscow State University.[18] Before that, there had been the famous *Zhdanovshchina* campaign by the Soviet Communist Party against so-called 'cosmopolitanism,' a coded term of the times that suggested "ties to an international Jewish conspiracy." Jewish scientists, and especially Jewish theoretical physicists, were near the top of the list for repression before the Communist ideological and Russian nationalistic witch-hunt came to an end.[19]

But most of this terrible discrimination under Communism came later. In the early years of the emerging Soviet Union, a great number of Jews embraced the goals of Soviet Communism. This was before they came to realize that their efforts to build an elusive socialist utopia were based on lies. For a time, Jews flourished in a number of fields, including physics, where they made enormous contributions, including names like: Abram Ioffe, Yakov Frenkel, Matvei Bronstein, Igor Tamm, Leonid Mandelshtam, Semion Shubin, Yuli Khariton, Fedor Galperin, as well as the shining stars of the Soviet nuclear program, Lev Landau and Yakov Zel'dovich, and Zel'dovich's protégés, Isaak Khalatnikov and Evgeny Lifshitz.[20] And there were many more. These were the men "who established and ran some of the most important science institutes of their day" in the former Soviet Union, turning "Soviet science – above all, physics – into the international powerhouse that it became…"[21] Given the opportunity, they rose to the top – until their overwhelming presence or over-representation became too much of an embarrassment or a threat, or both, to the authorities.

But Why?

Looking beyond the obvious issues of anti-Semitism and discrimination is the unasked question: why are some Jews so brilliant in math and science that a given society had to devise special exams in order to keep them from advancing? Why indeed?! Put another way, why do some brilliant Jews still rise to the top of their respective fields in both free capitalistic societies and oppressive socialistic ones? Does that phenomenon not invite both our wonder and deep curiosity as to what is at work here?

Just a Modern Phenomenon?

One might try to make the argument that the phenomenon of Jewish brilliance is simply a modern development, a temporary or isolated 'fluke' of history. I don't believe that that is the case, but this must be explained.

The flourishing of Jewish giftedness in the modern era only became possible when Jews were finally emancipated and allowed to enjoy the legal advantages and opportunities of free societies. As soon as the political, legal and social fetters against them began to be removed, there was a concomitant emerging growth of disproportionate Jewish representation among significant world figures across a multitude of fields. This is an empirical fact. We know that Jews began to "have a high rate [of representation of becoming significant world figures] even in 1800-1850." This was the case across numerous fields where general achievement could be measured. It is astonishing to see the correlation of this development with the advent of Jewish Emancipation.[22] This also correlates to the emergence of what is broadly referred to as the Jewish Enlightenment, or *Haskalah*, which led to modernization among portions of European Jewry.

My prediction is that this trend will become stronger as time goes by, unless the world first descends into utter chaos and destruction. If more Jews had had greater freedom and opportunity in the past, we might have seen even more Jewish contributions emerge in earlier centuries. But there was no meritocracy in most countries, and many Jews were barred from those professions where they could excel, or otherwise it was often financially or socially impossible for them to pursue such careers.[23] That is actually putting the case mildly. At various times from at least the 5th century onward, if Jews were not being demonized in the countries in which they settled, they were often still barred from universities or from holding public office. For example, in 1434 under the Council of Basel, Jews were barred from even obtaining university degrees. Through the centuries, during various outbreaks of intense *Judenhass* (Jew-hatred), Jewish property was often expropriated, Jewish children were taken from their parents to be forcibly raised as 'Christians', and Jews were forced into exile or even murdered simply because they were Jews.[24] The record of Gentile nation oppression of the Jewish people through the centuries is abysmal. Given the circumstances, it is remarkable that Jews were able to achieve anything at all.

In Charles Murray's grand scholarly sweep chronicling great human achievement and excellence throughout history - *Human Accomplishment: The Pursuit of Excellence in the Arts and Sciences, 800 B.C. to 1950*, he makes this revealing assertion about why the world did not see more Jewish contributions prior to the nineteenth century: their "sparse representation in European arts and sciences" through the beginning of the 19th century was due to the fact of the "Jews' near-total exclusion from the arts and sciences. Jews were not merely discouraged from entering universities and the professions, they were often forbidden by law from doing so."[25] That is crucial for our understanding. After those barriers were lifted, there was an explosion of talent across many fields of science, art, music, literature, and philosophy – something that Murray refers to as "the sudden emergence of Jewish significant figures."[26]

This is a very, very important point. It may be difficult for us to comprehend today what it must have meant for untold thousands of Jews who had so much to offer, so much that they wanted to contribute, but whose hopes and dreams were stillborn. They had nowhere to go, nowhere to blossom outside of the synagogue.

When we think of the modern era, keeping in mind post-Enlightenment Western civilization, our era has witnessed the growth of democracies where Jews *could* excel, free from the restrictions of the past. I would include Jewish stellar achievements in the early Marxist Soviet Union as being an extension of Western post-Enlightenment, since, despite later discrimination and persecution, in its early days the Soviet Union granted Jews new freedoms and a level of equality that they had scarcely ever experienced in the Diaspora. In short, as Steven L. Pease has noted in *The Golden Age of Jewish Achievement*, "In any meritocracy, Jews excelled."[27]

My Thesis

What we are witnessing today in the form of Jewish genius, brilliance and drivenness is not a fluke – it will continue as long as Jews can live and thrive in freedom.[28]

That is the thesis of my book. To support my view, I must go back in history, to the destruction of the Second Temple in 70 AD, and to the subsequent worldwide dispersion of the Jewish people.

I contend that, in God's eyes, according to the covenant, the Jewish people were to remain a light to the nations even after their dispersion. But Judaism as it was then constituted could not fulfill that task and became ever more distant from its original purpose. Instead, rabbinic Judaism became more insular and isolated than ever before, placing more and more rules and restrictions on the Jewish people in the post-Temple period. These rules and restrictions – as they came to be defined in the Talmud, the 'Oral Law,' and other extra-Biblical sources – drifted farther and farther away from the Word of God as contained in the Hebrew prophets. Many of these became almost unrecognizable from what the Bible actually commands or teaches.[29]

The Impact of "Jewish Emancipation"

In this sense, the post-Enlightenment break-up of the Jewish Pale of Settlement (where Jews were able to practice Judaism in their own insular, rabbinic-dominated communities but where they had little impact on the world at large) *also meant that Jews were now fully free to pursue their own giftedness in an atmosphere of freedom.*[30] This is another reason why many Jews from the Pale were later attracted to radical causes – such causes offered them a complete break from

Orthodox Jewish traditions and restrictions (except for those who chose to remain within those communities).

Thus, not only anti-Semites and anti-Semitism prevented Jewish people from achieving their potential and exercising their full gifts and abilities – so did Orthodox rabbinic Judaism. In other contexts, Jewish liberation from the latter is referred to by scholars as the "Jewish Emancipation." Emerging Jewish contact with modernity in an atmosphere of freedom produced major contributions for the world but also fiery ideologies, the subject of Cuddihy's previously mentioned book, *The Ordeal of Civility*. Cuddihy has contended that secular Jewish intellectuals spoke out of "the predicament bequeathed to them by Jewish Emancipation and modernization."[31] Jewish attraction to radical causes was also, in part, a reaction to Gentile civilization – a way out of the "predicament" noted by Cuddihy.[32]

Only after Jews had experienced some degree of freedom from both the immediate dangers posed by anti-Semites as well as from the daily strictures of Orthodox Judaism within the Pale of Settlement or within Jewish ghettos did they have any serious chance to succeed and flourish in non-religious fields, or for their gifts to become more apparent and more widely manifested within society at large.

It is also important to note that Jewish success in a given country has not necessarily been tied to larger percentage *general* success in those countries that have been studied. The statistics show that Jewish pre-eminence began exploding disproportionately in the mid- to late-nineteenth century thru the present - *irrespective* of what was occurring among non-Jews in those countries where Jewish global significant figures found themselves. In the post-Emancipation period, Jews who were becoming pre-eminent or significant world figures in the countries in which they lived did so in most cases *not because their countries themselves were necessarily becoming more pre-eminent,* and 'a rising tide lifted all boats,' so to speak. On the contrary, their pre-eminence appeared to occur independently.

The evidence of this phenomenon has continued to rise steeply in nearly all assessed fields, according to experts who establish standards for measuring human achievement. Jews were finally thriving in a general atmosphere of greater freedom and opportunity. Incredibly enough, from the period 1870-1950, the country with the highest ratio of Jewish to Gentile significant world figures, after controlling for population, was Germany, at 22:1![33] This is really quite astonishing. As we shall later see, Nazi ideology was a reaction, in part, to the very notion that the Jewish people were *naturally* gifted and could be pre-eminent in so many fields and walks of life. For anti-Semites, *there had to be some other explanation* – involving either trickery or a worldwide conspiracy of some kind.[34] The Nazis violently rejected the idea that the Jews were corporately gifted as a people. They responded to such an idea with demonic fury, even though for civilized Germans, the evidence of this phenomenon within Germany itself was demonstrable in the generations leading up to World War II. Throughout the nineteenth century "and through World War I, Germany was a success story of growing Jewish opportunity and assimilation into German high culture."[35]

Globally, the disproportionate ratio of Jewish Nobel Prize winners in the sciences and literature during the period 1901-1950 was an amazing 6:1. Nevertheless, the data also imply that that figure might have been even higher if not for continuing unexpurgated discrimination against Jews during that timeframe. From 1951-2000, when anti-Jewish discrimination was finally overcome in the West, the number of Jewish Nobel Prize winners worldwide skyrocketed to a 12:1 ratio, "even when calculated by a method that understates the per capita Jewish contribution by several-fold." That trend "is consistent with the hypothesis that Jewish accomplishment up to 1950 was being held back relative to its potential."[36]

Brilliance in Physics – Not Just Einstein

When allowed to be free to pursue the best that is in them intellectually, Jewish genius in the areas of mathematics and physics has changed the world. Jewish brilliance is especially striking in the area of physics, which has its own special place among the sciences. Richard Feynman himself, one of the Jewish physicists examined here, put it this way in his famous Caltech *Feynman Lectures*: "Physics is the most fundamental and all-inclusive of the sciences, and has had a profound effect on all scientific development." It is "the present-day equivalent of what used to be called *natural philosophy*, from which most of our sciences arose."[37] Even the Nobel Committee sees physics as pre-eminent: the prize in physics is always presented first among the Nobel prizes in science.[38]

The best known physicist of the modern era was Albert Einstein (1879-1955), who introduced the theories of general and special relativity, helped usher in the nuclear age, and made many other enormous contributions to science along the way.[39] Einstein inspired the image of the "good genius" upon popular perceptions of what a genius is supposed to be.[40]

But there are many more examples: Einstein was certainly not the exception, even if he is best known. Feynman himself was considered one of the greatest minds in theoretical physics to have ever lived: "the most brilliant, iconoclastic, and influential physicist of modern times."[41]

Jewish physicists such as Steven Weinberg, Sheldon Glashow, Murray Gell-Mann and David Deutsch have made major contributions to our knowledge of physics, including some of the most significant scientific discoveries in recent history.[42] Another example is physicist Wolfgang Pauli, discoverer of the 'exclusion principle'. Before the discovery of the exclusion principle, it was unclear how the elements of the periodic table existed. Pauli explained how a "multitude of possible chemical combinations" could exist, "and hence all material substance, living and non-living. This was a fantastic achievement."[43]

Pauli was considered to have a genius comparable only with Einstein, while Jewish Nobel Laureate Max Born once said that Pauli "was possibly even greater than Einstein."[44] Pauli did not even know that he was Jewish until he attended university.[45]

Ushering in the Nuclear Age

As noted earlier, the so-called "Hungarian conspiracy" of the three Hungarian Jewish physicists Szilard, Teller, Wigner conceived of the *idea* that the construction an atomic bomb might be possible. They convinced Einstein of this possibility and urged him to write President Franklin Roosevelt.[46] Because of his immense fame, a warning from Einstein was not something that Roosevelt could ignore. The warning struck its mark, and the Manhattan Project, under the guidance of General Leslie R. Groves, began. Groves sought a genius leader to head the project full of other brilliant physicists and mathematicians.[47] He found that such a leader and administrator in Jewish physicist J. Robert Oppenheimer.

J. Robert Oppenheimer (1904-1967), who directed the development of the atomic bomb at Los Alamos, was a child prodigy.[48] He graduated summa cum laude from Harvard and received his PhD two years later in 1927 in quantum theory from the University of Goettingen.[49] Later he also directed the Institute of Advanced Study at Princeton.

Hitler's war against the Jews led to a flow of Jewish refugees to the West – some of whom had amazing gifts and insights. This flight to the West became "indispensable to the Western triumph."[50]

For example, "[t]wo of the most crucial steps in the early development of the atomic bomb came from papers by German Jewish refugees in Britain: Peierls and Frisch in March, and Simon in December 1940..." Sir Francis Simon, born into a Berlin Jewish family in 1893, won the Iron Cross during World War I and was decorated by the Kaiser himself. But none of that mattered by the time the Nazis came to power. The Simons succeeded in leaving Germany for England and settled in Oxford. Their home became "a haven for other Jewish exiles in Oxford." Simon did highly important work on the development of the atomic bomb, was knighted and was elected a Fellow of the Royal Society.[51]

Another Jewish scientist who worked with Oppenheimer at Los Alamos was Victor Weisskopf, who came from a Viennese Jewish family. After the war, Weisskopf went to MIT, where he taught later Jewish Nobel Laureate Murray Gell-Mann.[52]

The head of the theoretical division at Los Alamos was German-born Hans Bethe, a refugee from Nazi Europe whose mother was Jewish. His genius 'sidekick' was none other than Richard Feynman, mentioned earlier with Gell-Mann.[53] After the war, Bethe won the Nobel Prize in Physics.[54] Philip Morrison, who was later a colleague of Feynman's at Cornell, was another Jewish physicist at Los Alamos. At one point during the war, Morrison famously "carried the atomic bomb's plutonium core...in the back seat of an army sedan."[55]

And then there was celebrated Danish physicist and also Nobel Prize winner, Niels Bohr. Bohr – the great debater with Einstein over the nature of reality - helped launch the nuclear age. Bohr had a Jewish mother but grew up in the Danish Lutheran Church. While still a teenager, he rejected Christianity for atheism. Whether he had any strong personal sense of his Jewish heritage is unclear, but his Jewish roots were sufficient for Hitler's purposes. Bohr eventually fled Denmark for Sweden to escape the Nazis and from there flew in a British bomber to England, finally making his way to Los Alamos to help work on the atomic bomb.[56] He merited a substantial entry in the *Dictionary of Jewish Biography*. He later met with Israeli Prime Minister David Ben Gurion in 1962 when he returned to Copenhagen after the war.[57]

Nearly "the whole of the early drive and research into the atomic bomb was powered by refugee scientists from Germany, Austria and Hungary, as well as scientists from Britain, most of them Jewish."[58] This has been called the 'Quantum Exodus' – the title of a book by Gordon Fraser. The phrase is a clever play on words and also on history because so many of the scientists who were beginning to research the quantum world were exiting Europe because of the Nazi threat. The elite group that gathered at Los Alamos under intense secrecy has been referred to as "the most exclusive club in the world."[59] At the same time, the Nazis themselves might have succeeded in producing the bomb first, had the situation been somewhat different. They set up the so-called *Uranverein* ("uranium club" or "uranium society") under the German Army Ordnance Research Department. How far did they actually get? – the full answer is still unknown. Despite intense efforts to obtain the answer to that question – even including months of detention of the leading German scientists in Britain and secret bugging of their conversations – the answer "is still not known with certainty."[60]

It is tempting to look back and speculate on what 'might have been' had Hitler never come to power in Germany. Without these Jewish geniuses and their intense collaboration because of the existential threat of annihilation from the Nazi war machine, would the so-called 'nuclear age' have turned out quite differently? Would the Nazis have succeeded if conditions had been altered? Once it became clear that Germany would be defeated in the war and did not have its own bomb nearly ready, Szilard and some others who had been instrumental in developing the U.S. atomic bomb began petitioning authorities *not* to use it against Japan, but to give a demonstration instead of its terrible destructive power. One key group of scientists who didn't want the bomb used against Japan was headed by James Franck, "a Jewish physicist from Germany who had come to the United States to escape Hitler...."[61] But the die was cast, and their views went unheeded. The bomb was dropped on Hiroshima on August 6, 1945. Standing as I did in 2014 in the spot right under where the bomb exploded nearly seventy years earlier, one is struck at how 'normal' life is today in that part of Hiroshima, once the scene of such terrible destruction.

A world with few or no nuclear weapons, no Holocaust, and perhaps even with no emergence of the State of Israel,[62] is difficult to imagine today. All of these three developments, occurred in part or emerged as a result of the horrific reign of Adolf Hitler and the Third Reich. One of the Jewish scientists who worked on the bomb, Isidor I. Rabi, wrote that it "was fear that made this peace-loving country [the United States] lavish such huge sums of money on the rapid development of the bomb." There was great concern "lest the enemy get it first." He reminisced about when he was "in New Mexico, seated in the room with some of the top scientists there." They were trying to figure out how advanced the Germans might be in developing the nuclear bomb themselves: "What did the Nazis have? Who were the Nazi scientists? We knew them all..." Had the Nazis been cleverer than they had been? "What then? We finally arrived at the conclusion that they could be exactly as advanced as we were, or perhaps further."[63] This was the driving force behind the development of the bomb. For better or worse, the nuclear age that finally came to be was largely made possible by Jewish geniuses at a time when the world faced a time of utmost peril.

The Development of the Computer; Genius in Mathematics

In the area of computer development, Jewish recipients are very highly over-represented as a proportion of the population as awardees of the Alan M. Turing Award in computing. The same situation applies with respect to the highly prestigious Fields Medal in mathematics.[64] There is no Nobel Prize for mathematics, so the Fields Medal is in some ways a substitute for it: "There have never been Nobel Prizes for mathematics, but the list of outstanding Jewish mathematicians is equally impressive."[65] These have included names such as Stanislav Ulam (who also was a key figure in the development of the nuclear bomb), as well as Witold Hurewicz and Jerzy Neyman, who were developers of mathematical set theory and topology.[66] A quarter of the winners of Fields Medals have been Jewish.[67]

Jewish Women of Genius

When considering Jewish genius, we must also consider the role of women. Given pervasive external Gentile prejudice against them for being both female *and* Jewish, as well as internal traditional Orthodox Jewish restrictions, smart and ambitious Jewish girls had two powerful strikes against them before they even started. Nevertheless, as Amos Oz and Fania Oz-Salzberger have pointed out, despite these challenges, some Jewish women of genius, such as Bruria, overcame all obstacles to be considered Talmudic sages. Bruria must have been "an exceptional genius," they write, to have prevailed under all these circumstances.[68]

Freed from the fetters from the past and given new freedom and opportunity, we have perhaps only recently begun to see Jewish genius emerge among women as they have the opportunity to flourish in various fields. One of those bright lights was Emmy Noether, but there have been others, such as British biophysicist Rosalind Franklin and medical scholar Rahel Gotein Straus. And then there is the case of Lise Meitner, who was only "the second woman to receive a Ph.D. in physics from the University of Vienna, and in many opinions well meriting a Nobel Prize."[69] As an Austrian Jewish woman living and working in Berlin, she had to escape Germany when stripped of her citizenship during the war. Many believe this cost her the Nobel Prize in Physics. In late 1938, she had a unique insight "so revolutionary, so powerful, and so contrary to accepted wisdom," according to one account, "that it rivaled those of Einstein and Newton." Her new way of thinking led directly to "an overarching idea that would literally change the world." Walking in the snow in the Swedish countryside with her nephew, Otto Frisch, she worked out the mathematics that explained the idea of nuclear fission.[70]

Emmy Noether

Born in Bavaria in 1882, Emmy Noether has been called "the first woman mathematician who can unhesitatingly be described as truly great." She has been dubbed 'the Queen of Modern Algebra.' Einstein said of her: "in the judgment of most competent mathematicians, Fraulein Noether was the most significant mathematical genius since the higher education of women began."[71] Noether's insights and contributions were so profound that physicist Victor Stenger once stated that, if more people understood mathematics and physics, "Noether would be considered one of the foremost heroines of the twentieth century."[72]

John von Neumann

The Hungarian-born American mathematician John von Neumann is considered to have been one of the most brilliant mathematicians of all time. The eldest son of a Jewish banker, von Neumann "was a mathematical prodigy."[73] He was "the main person originally responsible for the theory underlying electronic computer development," making him "one of the fathers of modern computing." He also was one of the key mathematicians who worked on the atomic bomb at Los Alamos.[74]

Even though von Neumann's name is not a household name as Einstein's, the two men knew each other very well. George Gilder even says that "von Neumann was the paramount figure of twentieth century science because he was the link between the pioneers of quantum theory and the machines that won World War II" and the Cold War "and that enabled the emergence of a global economy tied together and fructified by the Internet."[75] Von Neumann's impact on our modern world was nearly incalculable.

Jewish Nobel Prize Winners in Physics and Other Notable Achievements

Albert Abraham Michelson (1852-1931) was "the first American Nobel laureate, in any field," which was in Physics. He received the Nobel Prize in 1907. Michelson also served as the President of American Physical

Society, President of the American Association for the Advancement of Science (AAAS) and President of the National Academy of Sciences. Einstein once characterized Michelson "as an artist in science..."[76]

Georges Charpak was born in Poland and moved with his family to France. During World War Two he became part of the French Resistance, was captured and sent by the Nazis to Dachau. Because Charpak "did not look Jewish, [he] came out alive." Many years after the war Charpak was awarded the 1992 Nobel Prize in Physics.[77]

Other Jewish Nobel Prize winners in Physics include: Gabriel Lippmann (1908), James Franck (1925), Gustav Hertz (1925), Otto Stern (1943), Isidor Isaac Rabi (1944), Felix Bloch (1952), Igor Tamm (1958), Emilio Segré (1959), Donald A. Glaser (1960), Robert Hofstadter (1961), Lev Davidovich Landau (1962), Julian Schwinger (1965), Dennis Gabor (1971), Brian David Josephson - jointly with two others: Ivan Glaver and Leon Esoki (1973), Benjamin R. Mottelson (along with Aage Bohr), Peter Leonovich Kapitza (1978), Arno Penzias (1978), Sheldon Glashow (1979), Leon Lederman (1988), Melvin Schwartz (1988), Jack Steinberger (1988),[78] Jerome Isaac Friedman (1990), Martin L. Perl (1995), Frederick Reines (1995), David Lee (1995), Douglas Osheroff (1996), Claude Cohen-Tannoudji (1997), Zhores Alferov (2000), Vitaly Ginzburg (2003), Alexei Abrikosov (2003), David Gross (2004), H. David Politzer (2004), and Roy Glauber (2005).[79] Saul Perlmutter shared the prize in 2011 for his work on supernovae.[80]

Besides Nobel Prize winners, there have been many other outstanding Jewish physicists. Jewish-born Abram Fyodorovich Ioffe, for example, was considered the "dean" of physics in the Soviet Union during the 1920s and 30s.[81] Other famous Jewish physicists today include Ralph Alpher, David Bohm, Brian Greene, Alan Guth, and Lee Smolin.

One of the most important institutions in physics and advanced scientific topics in the world, the Institute for Advanced Study (IAS) in Princeton, New Jersey, had Jewish founders and donors.[82] Einstein, Niels Bohr, von Neumann, Wolfgang Pauli, J. Robert Oppenheimer, Murray Gell-Mann and many others of the world's most brilliant people worked or had some close association with the institute. Famed physicist Edward Witten has been a professor at the Institute since 1987.

In 2012, Witten was the recipient of the $3 million dollar Fundamental Physics Prize, given by the Russian Jewish high-tech investor, Yuri Milner. Although "raised in a Jewish family...[Witten] doesn't take religion seriously," but he does care about Israel.[83] According to an article in *Haaretz*, he said: "I like to say that in my life, apart from the family there are three passions – physics, tennis, and Israel."[84]

Original and unique contributions to physics by Jewish scientists, theorists and scholars exceed every other nationality on earth by a huge margin. That is an indisputable empirical fact – even if we limit ourselves to merely counting Nobel Prizes as a measure.

Medicine

Jewish doctors and Jewish medical specialists are so widespread in Western society today as to represent the stereotype. During the medieval period, even though they only made up 3-5 per cent of the overall population in those regions, Jews reportedly made up some 50 to 60 per cent of all physicians.[85] This was the case despite the intense discrimination that Jews often faced.

The modern era has witnessed large numbers of Jewish recipients of Nobel Prizes in Medicine. These include Willem Einthoven, who created the electrocardiogram (EKG) and received the Nobel Prize in 1924, Baruch Blumberg, who found the vaccine for hepatitis B and won the Nobel Prize in 1976, and Baruj Benacerraf, who developed transplant immunology and won the Nobel Prize in 1980.[86]

Vitamins were discovered by Casimir Funk, while the polio vaccine was developed by Jonas Salk, both of whom were Jewish.[87] A 1938 British work by author Cecil Roth titled, *The Jewish Contribution to Civilisation* noted the outstanding contributions of various Jews to medicine, including "[o]ne of the best-known names in modern medicine...Paul Ehrlich, father of chemico-therapy and the greatest biochemical philosopher of all time." Another was "Jacob Henle – the greatest German microscopic anatomist of his day, and one of the greatest anatomists" who ever lived. Henle is credited with being the first to accurately describe "the cellular structure of the skin and of the tissues lining the intestines and other parts of the body: he first investigated the minute anatomy of the kidney," while "his researches on the ligaments, the muscles, the viscera and the vascular nervous system were without number and were of epoch-making importance."[88] In the area of endocrinology, "one the of the greatest names of all is that of Moritz Schiff, a German Jew who taught in Switzerland and in Italy." The founders "and the most prominent workers in the field of otology" – the study of the diseases of the ear – were the Austrian Jews, Ádám Politzer and Róbert Bárány. Bárány received the Nobel Prize in 1914.[89]

Rita Levi Montalcini shared the 1986 Nobel Prize in Medicine for her discovery of the specific protein Nerve Growth Factor. Because of her scientific achievements, Italy awarded her the honor of "senator for life" in the Italian parliament. According to a tribute written after her death in 2012, Levi-Montalcini was "born and raised in a Sephardic Jewish family in which culture and love of learning were categorical imperatives..."[90]

Roth continued his 1938 list with many more names of Jewish recipients of the Nobel Prize in Medicine or others who were responsible for major breakthroughs in medicine, such as Karl Landsteiner, whose "studies on the compatibility of types of blood have made scientific transfusion possible." Finally, Roth noted that "[t]he list must end here, but it might well be continued to a wearisome length."[91]

James Franck and Otto Meyerhof were both Jewish refugees who came to the United States to escape the Nazis. Both were Nobel Laureates. Along with others, they "soon effected hardly less than a revolution in American academic chemistry."[92]

Contributions to Technology

In the area of technology, there are many notable examples of Jewish *wunderkinds* who have changed our world. Here are just a few:

- Jan Koum, co-founder of the WhatsApp company and technology, which Facebook bought in 2014 for $19 billion dollars, has been described as "a rebellious Jewish child" who grew up near Kiev, who had very "little when he immigrated to California with his mother at the age of 16 just after the Soviet Union's breakup."[93]
- Max Levchin, who is also from a Ukrainian Jewish background, is a well-known high-tech entrepreneur and a co-founder of PayPal.

- Andrew Grove, co-founder and chairman of Intel Corporation.
- Google co-founders Larry Page and Sergey Brin both have Jewish backgrounds. Sergey's parents were Soviet Jewish immigrants who left the former Soviet Union in order to emigrate to the West and give their son a future. The first major investor in Google was Sun Microsystems cofounder Andy Bechtolsheim, a German Jewish immigrant himself.[94]
- Larry Ellison, co-founder and chief executive officer of Oracle, is Jewish on his mother's side.[95]
- Mark Zuckerberg, the creator of Facebook, is one of the best-known young Jewish entrepreneurs. He is said to be the world's youngest billionaire.[96]
- Michael Dell, billionaire founder and CEO of Dell Inc., the personal computer giant.
- One extraordinary Russian Jewish high-tech investor is particle physicist Yuri Milner, born in Moscow in the Soviet Union in 1961. He has been stunningly successful as an entrepreneur and venture capitalist. In 2013, *Foreign Policy* magazine listed Milner on its "Power List" – a list of the 500 most powerful people on Earth.[97] As a budding physicist he befriended famed Soviet physicist Andrei Sakharov. More recently, in 2012 Milner established the Fundamental Physics Prize award – a $3 million dollar prize – the highest prize in academia, which far exceeds the monetary value of the Nobel Prize.

The website www.israel21c.org carries many articles on the incredible number of technological innovations and inventions by Israelis.

World Chess Champions and Geniuses

Besides science and technology, many Jews have excelled as world chess champions and geniuses, including Wilhelm Steinitz, Emanuel Lasker, Mikhail Botvinnik, Vasily Smyslov, Mikhail Tal, Bobby Fischer, Boris Spassky, Gary Kasparov, and possibly Vladimir Kramnik, among others. These names have dominated world chess championships since they began in 1886.[98] And then there is the name of Samuel Herman Reshevsky (1911-1992). Reshevsky is shown below in 1920 at the age of eight, beating various chess masters.

SAMUEL HERMAN RESHEVSKY (1911-1992)

Samuel Reshevsky was a child prodigy at chess, eventually becoming a chess Grandmaster. His parents belonged to the Ger Hasidic dynasty in Ozorkov, Poland. After his family moved to the United States, Reshevsky became an eight-time winner of the U.S. Chess Championship. He developed a close friendship with the sixth Lubavitcher Rebbe, Rabbi Yosef Yitzhak Schneerson. At age 70 he defeated the then world chess champion, Vasily Smyslov.

Samuel Herman Reshevsky, chess prodigy, at age eight, defeating numerous chess masters (Source: Public Domain photo in Wikipedia, "Samuel Reshevsky" entry)

Not Just Based on Hard Work

The record shows that a high percentage of Jewish people have a natural affinity for excellence and achievement in the arts and sciences. As author Vox Day wrote in *The Irrational Atheist*, it is an "undeniable fact that Jews possess the strongest intellectual tradition in human history..." He adds that they also "account for a much higher percentage of scientific advancements than would be statistically indicated by the small fraction of the global population they represent."[99]

The percentage of Jewish Nobel Prize winners is incredibly stunning relative to their percentage of the world's population. [100] In physics alone, there have been some 50 Jewish prize-winners, 26% of the world's total in this field. [101] Most would say that their success was due to hard work and had nothing to do with ethnicity. Of course, no one would presume to say that these achievements occurred without enormous effort and hard work. But at the same time, their ethnicity cannot be ignored when we consider the question of *why* so many Jewish scholars and scientists have excelled so dramatically in so many fields.

David Hollinger has also examined the cases of a number of persons who excelled tremendously in their respective fields, only to find out *later* in life that they were Jewish. Or, in some cases, the individuals knew that they were Jewish but never said anything about publicly until decades later. One example was sociologist Robert K. Merton. Merton was a scholar who "did not proclaim his Jewishness" until "half-a-century after he began to produce the magnificent series of papers that rendered him a giant of American sociology." [102] Hollinger adds that "three of the individuals who exercised the greatest influence on the historical, sociological and philosophical study of science in the United States were born to Jewish parents yet lived their lives well outside of communal Jewry." These three were "[Robert] Merton, Thomas S. Kuhn, and the Viennese Karl Popper." [103]

Regarding the question of hard work and persistence versus ethnicity, other ethnic groups have worked very hard as well but not come anywhere close to what Jews corporately have achieved given their numbers in society. According to a *Los Angeles Times* article cited by author Steven Silbiger, "a theory that might explain the contributions of people as diverse as Howard Stern and Albert Einstein" has encountered "a silence in the literature." [104]

Leftist financier George Soros has not been silent on this point. About himself he says, "If there is anything of this Jewish genius in me, it is simply the ability to think critically. To that extent," he adds, "Jewishness is an essential element of my personality and...I am very proud of that." [105]

Chinese Frustration: My Experience at Tsingua University, Beijing

An experience I had in Beijing in 2007 with a Chinese work-colleague puts all of this in sharp perspective. He and I were walking through the campus of Tsingua University at the time. Tsingua is often considered the top university in China. It is nestled amidst a large number of institutes, technology centers and is located not far from one of the greatest technology marketplaces in the world - *Zhong-guan-cun*.

Tsingua is considered to be the 'Harvard of China' and is extremely difficult to get into – only the "cream" of the 'cream of the crop' get in, as my friend related to me. He himself was a graduate of Tsingua and now works in the West in the computer security field. One can only imagine in a country as vast as China what kind of competition exists for those choice academic spots. Microsoft's Bill Gates has a close relationship with the university – he even received an honorary doctorate from Tsingua in 2007.

This background is important in understanding the context and significance of what my friend next shared with me: he talked about the very profound desire within China to have Chinese researchers develop original research and ideas that will lead to Nobel Prizes. Despite the great numbers of highly-trained Chinese scientists and researchers that are graduated each year, that has not yet occurred. Less than half a dozen China-born researchers have received the Nobel Prize in physics, but when they were awarded, the awardees were residing or affiliated with universities such as Princeton, Columbia, or elsewhere in the West. So the 'glory', so to speak, has not gone to China.[106]

Although China has produced a massive number of highly-skilled experts at the PhD level or equivalent, it has still not been able to produce very many original thinkers in scientific fields, despite enormous effort and a huge commitment of resources.[107]

China is definitely increasing its scientific *output* as measured by scientometric standards,[108] but *originality* has remained elusive. My colleague's feelings were not unique to him - this frustration is felt throughout China. As author Eric Weiner noted while visiting the country: "Everything is made in China but nothing is invented here." This is sometimes referred to as the 'innovation gap.' How does a nation or a culture get past that? One Chinese television program put this dilemma in the form of a question: "China has the talent pool, it has the resources...What else does it need?"[109] Originality and creativity are just not happening. This is in sharp contrast to the modern Jewish and Israeli experience.[110] One explanation is that creativity "requires the freedom to question and challenge authority...which is why China has so far trailed us in inventiveness..."[111]

The Golden Age in China

This situation in modern-day China stands in stark contrast to the burst of creativity and intellectual achievement that occurred in classical China, which saw the invention of paper, the magnetic compass, block printing, an advanced system of mathematics, medical advances, and the development of a merit-based examination system for Chinese officials. A flowering of Chinese creativity occurred especially during the Song Dynasty (960-1279). The city of Hangzhou became the 'Florence' of the Chinese Renaissance. Hangzhou's poet-governor Su Tungpo was a Renaissance man "three hundred years before the Renaissance."[112] Joseph Needham's history of Chinese science during the classical period fills seven volumes.[113]

Somewhere along the way, though, China lost the key to creativity and originality.

Why this golden age ended is considered by historian of science Peter Watson to be "one of the most fascinating puzzles in history": "why the Chinese civilisation, which developed paper, gunpowder, woodblock printing, porcelain, and the idea of the competitive written examination for public servants, and led the world intellectually for many centuries, never developed mature science or modern business methods...."[114]

'Capturing' Genius

James Gleick has described China's dilemma and that of other nations as follows: "the nature of genius – genius as the engine of scientific discovery – has become an issue bound up with the economic fortunes of nations." Vast sums are expended trying to capture or tease out this elusive quality, but without much demonstrable success. Despite the "vast modern network of universities, corporate laboratories, and national science foundations" devoted to this question, "the best financed and best organized of research enterprises have not learned to engender, perhaps not even to recognize, world-turning originality."[115]

Transcending Location

There is certainly some value in the 'geography of genius' and golden age theory that Weiner and Simonton promote – that is: 'now you have originality and creativity in a particular geographical location and now you don't,' whether it's Athens, Florence or the Song Dynasty in China. But the Jewish people seem to defy this type of categorizing. Somehow, they transcend it. Great nations and 'golden ages' come and go, but the Jews remain.

CHAPTER TWO

Jewish 'Communicators' and 'Interpreters' of the Human Condition

The 'zeal-in-search-of-a-cause' in so many Jewish hearts and minds manifests itself in a myriad of ways. In the areas of science and mathematics, much of that zeal is turned inward and directed towards trying to explain why the Universe is the way it is. In this role, Jewish scientists, just as scientists in general - especially physicists - seek to serve as 'explainers' and 'interpreters' of reality. What is the universe made up of? How does it work? These questions have inspired generations of those seeking answers to existence. It is part of the human quest for knowledge and understanding that transcends any question of whether one is Jewish or not. Nevertheless, Jews have excelled in these fields beyond any rational explanation. Often they have excelled even when freedom and access were limited. High IQs cannot explain it, nor why so many Jews excel at being among the world's greatest communicators and 'explainers of reality,' if you will. It is an extraordinary phenomenon.

Explaining reality goes even deeper than merely analyzing how the universe ticks. It also means probing the depths of the human heart, understanding who we are as human beings and some of our most profound feelings and desires. In this, we see amazing Jewish contributions to literature, the arts and music.

In the area of famous writers, numerous recipients of the Pulitzer Prize (from both the non-fiction and fiction categories) who have a Jewish background include: Saul Bellow, E. L. Doctorow, Ariel Durant, Norman Mailer, Bernard Malamud, Carl Sagan, Barbara Tuchman, Theodore H. White, and Herman Wouk. Additionally, Joseph Pulitzer himself – the man in whose memory the Prizes were established – also had a Jewish background. Shmuel Yosef Agnon was the first Hebrew writer to receive the Nobel Prize for literature. That occurred in 1966.[1] Other notable names in literature include: Sholem Aleichem, Sholem Asch, Isaac Babel, Franz Kafka, Boris Pasternak, Gertrude Stein, and Leon Uris, among many many more.

Jewish people as a whole are very avid readers. I have seen a statistic on the reported percentage of Jewish purchasers of non-institutional hardcover book sales in the U.S. that is so high that I have not recorded it here (since it seems almost unbelievable).[2] Suffice it to say that Jewish readership of new books is extremely high in the United States. My personal experience with Russian Jewish immigrants is quite similar – they are a highly literate group. Very prestigious publishers with strong Jewish connections include: Bantam, Basic Books, Alfred A. Knopf, Pantheon, Random House, Simon & Schuster, Farrar, Straus and Giroux, and Viking, to cite some of the better-known publishing houses.[3] Alfred Knopf himself, who was "the first American Jew to be hired by a Gentile publishing house" went on to publish through his firm "more Nobel Prize winners than any other firm in the world."[4]

In the arts and music, we see something similar – Jewish musicians who plumb the heights and depths of human expression, often being the most proficient technical masters of their craft in the world. Author George Gilder names "Serkin, Horowitz, Rubinstein, Cliburn, Fleisher, Gibels, Gould, and Ax," and concludes that "Jewish genius [has] dominated the global culture of the piano."[5] And the list goes on and on.

Among world-renowned Jewish conductors, we have Lorin Maazel, Georg Solti, Bruno Walter, Andre Previn, Eugene Ormandy, to name a few. Leonard Bernstein, the former beloved music director of the New York Philharmonic Orchestra deserves special mention. As Howard Sachar wrote, in whatever role he served, whether "as composer or conductor, writer of classical or popular music, champion of Jewish music or pioneer guest conductor of the Israeli Philharmonic, Bernstein...blazed across the firmament as possibly the most renowned musical figure of the late twentieth century."[6]

I have already noted the impact of violinist Isaac Stern on my own life. Among the world's greatest violinists, besides Stern, we could add the names of Joseph Joachim, Jascha Heifitz, David Oistrakh, Nathan Milstein, Pinchas Zukerman, Itzhak Perlman, Yehudi Menuhin, and Joshua Bell. After the Holocaust, given the fact so many of the world's greatest violinists are Jewish, many thereafter refused to play on German-made violins. This resulted in "Italian and French violins eclips[ing] German instruments in prestige and cost" in the latter part of the twentieth century. The rest of the marketplace began to reflect what the greatest Jewish virtuosos preferred.[7]

In "The Story of the Jews" television series, we are told that the great composer Felix Mendelsohn (grandson of Jewish philosopher Moses Mendelsohn) and his sister both had "a prodigious gift." At only ten years of age, Felix was already "writing music that was far in advance of anything that had been seen, of anything that Mozart was doing at that age." In his day, Mendelsohn had an extraordinary impact on the European music scene. "This boy," the commentator noted, "was an absolute whiz."[8]

An amazing book titled, *Violins of Hope: Violins of the Holocaust – Instruments of Hope and Liberation in Mankind's Darkest Hour*, tells the story of famous violinist Ida Haendel, whose "father brought her to Warsaw to study at the Chopin Conservatory" when she was only seven years old.[9]

Bronislaw Huberman (1888-1947), a young violin prodigy from Poland, was one of the greatest violinists who ever lived. The composer Brahms was said to have been moved to tears when he heard the then 14-year Huberman play his famous violin concerto.[10] Because of Huberman's fame and influence, he was able to save "over a thousand Jews from certain death" by getting them to Palestine. They included some of the best musicians in Europe, later forming what would become the Israel Philharmonic Orchestra.[11] In an amazing story, Huberman's famous Stradivarius violin, after being stolen for nearly half a century, eventually came into the hands of another famous Jewish violinist, Joshua Bell.[12]

Music is a different way of 'explaining' or 'interpreting' reality than what scientists do. Expressing that reality through music and seeking to reach beyond our day-to-day world to express the deepest longings of the human soul is also a very Jewish way of doing things.

Art and Jewish Artists

In the area of art, Jewish contributions have been of a somewhat different order. Because of the Biblical commandment against making 'graven images,' as Isaac Deutscher states: "...the *Shtetl* [the Jewish Pale of Settlement]...had its superb cantors and musicians, its bards, poets, and composers of folk tales; but it had no painters or sculptors." [13] But if even if that were the case in the *shtetl*, some scholars question whether the commandment was really interpreted that broadly within traditional Judaism in earlier centuries, asserting that is a "misconception" to believe "that Jewish culture was hostile to the visual arts." [14]

Nevertheless, it is true that, historically at least, we don't see the same level of original Jewish contributions to art as we do in science and music. In the modern era, that situation has been turned on its head. We have, for example, the extraordinary art of Marc Chagall: "...until Chagall, more or less – Jewish images could never stand alone." [15] Chagall is a towering figure in the history of art. There are also the examples of Impressionist and Post-Impressionist painter Camille Pissarro and Russian Jewish landscape master, Isaak Levitan.

But even putting aside the historical Orthodox Jewish religious attitude toward art in earlier centuries, from a practical standpoint - over the last two hundred years or so, how many Jews (unless they came from very rich families) had the luxury of going to art school, setting up and keeping expensive studios, or hob-knobbing with Gentile art elites and potential purchasers of art? Until they had greater financial security and social acceptance, that possibility was out of the question for most Jews. Jewish musicians could play for weddings and other events for money, keeping both Jews and Gentiles otherwise entertained with their music. But Jews historically making money from art? – not so much.

In the modern era that situation has changed dramatically. In modern times we see the Abstract Expressionist movement and subsequent Pop movement in visual art, which were well populated and shaped by

Jewish artists. Much of the work of these schools of art, just like so many areas of science, were greatly impacted by the Jewish presence. The list of famous historical figures in the visual arts who were Jewish is considerable.[16] Chaim Soutine, a Lithuanian Jew who migrated to Paris, was a very famous expressionist painter.[17]

As Steven L. Pease notes in *The Golden Age of Jewish Achievement*, the well-known Phaidon list of great Western art of 500 leading artists, combined with the data presented in Charles Murray's assessment of Jewish contributions, show an "unmistakable" trend: while no Jewish artists were included before 1900, by the time the Phaidon volume was published, more than twenty percent of the artists were Jewish.[18]

Collecting Art

When it comes to *collecting* art, the Jewish presence is not simply considerable – it is often overwhelming! Having achieved a general measure of financial security in the West, Jewish interest and appreciation for art have exploded – especially in the United States. As Howard Sachar explains in his book, *A History of Jews in America*, at one point "so many galleries were Jewish-owned, so many collectors Jews, so many art fellowships Jewish-sponsored…so many museums directed by Jewish curators," that some critics of all this began to refer to the art world as a 'Jewish mafia'.[19]

In Europe during World War II, Hitler and the Nazis conducted the largest mass looting of art treasures in history. Much of this consisted of art treasures stolen from great Jewish collectors such as the Rothschilds, the Bloch-Bauers, and others.[20] According to a report given at the Nuremberg Trials, "21,903 objects taken from 203 private collections were removed, notably from the Rothschild, Alphons Kahn, David Weil, Levy de Benzion, and the Seligmann brothers collections." Twenty-nine transports and some 137 trucks were deployed for this mass looting of art collections that once belonged to Jewish families in Europe.[21] The sheer amount of great art that once belonged to prominent Jewish families in Europe – let alone lesser known works of art that were collected and appreciated by many individual Jewish families but were lost or destroyed during the war is difficult to even fathom. Nevertheless, this gives a glimpse at a terrible moment in history into the breadth and quality of Jewish collections of great art.

And then there is the extraordinary story behind the painting, "The Lady in Gold," recently made into a full-length feature film (*Woman in Gold*). The original painting, done in Austria, was titled, "Portrait of Adele Bloch-Bauer I." It was completed in 1907 by painter Gustav Klimt. The painting belonged to the Bloch-Bauer family in Vienna. During World War II, it fell into the hands of the Nazis. Adele's niece, Maria Altmann, who later settled in the United States, tried to reclaim it. The painting by this time had become extremely famous and valuable. It had been renamed "The Lady in Gold" by a Nazi curator in order to hide the fact that Adele was Jewish. After the war it hung for many years in the Austrian State Gallery. The Austrian government did not give up the painting very easily. After a protracted court battle that went to the U.S. Supreme Court and a panel of arbiters in Austria, Altmann eventually won custody of the painting. It was sold to Ronald Lauder (son of cosmetics industry leader Estée Lauder) for $135 million and was brought to New York. At the time that price represented the most expensive painting ever sold.[22] The Lauder family, who also is Jewish, in 2008 had a fortune valued at around $7 billion.[23]

The Gestapo stole not only the Klimt paintings from Maria Altmann's family but also her father's beloved Stradivarius cello. He died two weeks later of a broken heart.[24]

There are several things that must be said about this story. First is the fact that the Altmann family, then living in Vienna, was devoted to great art and to great music. Second, as in many other areas, the Nazis could recognize value in *things*, such as paintings and musical instruments, even if they had no regard for those who created or sponsored such art or music if they were Jewish. Then we see that, despite all the suffering that the Altmann family experienced at the hands of the Nazis, the Austrian government still did not turn over the painting to its rightful owner, Maria Altmann, without a very bitter legal battle. Finally, Jewish businessman Ronald Lauder used some of his immense fortune to help 'set things right,' so to speak, with respect to the horrible losses that had been suffered by the Altmann family during the Holocaust.

That is our brief look at the modern Jewish contribution to art and art collecting. Beyond science, literature, music and art, Jews have also excelled as 'explainers' and 'interpreters' of the human condition in other areas, such as communicating.

Extraordinary Communicators

As 'explainers' of reality, many Jews have excelled as communicators to the public, which includes a whole host of Jewish entertainers, producers, and directors, and legions of others in the entertainment and creative arts. Regarding creativity in general, George Gilder considers the Jews "the world's most creative people."[25]

Sometimes entire movements may grow around a particular creative genius or entertainer, such as a Bob Dylan, or even the degenerate comedy of a Howard Stern, around whom an entire entertainment medium was built on satellite radio. Or consider composers such as Irving Berlin or George Gershwin (born Jacob Gershowitz), whose music is timeless, or a performer like Benny Goodman.[26]

Or, take for example the quintessential American song of optimism and hope, "Somewhere Over the Rainbow." I never knew until quite recently that this song has a very Jewish origin. It was written by Yip Harburg, whose real name was Isidore Hochberg and who "grew up in a Yiddish-speaking, Orthodox Jewish home in New York." The music for "Somewhere Over the Rainbow" was composed by Harold Allen, whose real name was Hyman Arluck, born a Jewish cantor's son. The Recording Industry Association of America (RIAA) and the National Endowment for the Arts voted "Somewhere Over the Rainbow" as the number one song of the twentieth century.[27]

Of course, not everyone has appreciated Jewish giftedness in music and entertainment. Well-known anti-Semite Henry Ford instead "frequently accused the Jews of causing a decline in American culture, values, products, [and] entertainment..."[28]

Impact on Media and Politics

In the area of profound political thinkers and intellects who have made extensive contributions to Western society, the names of Leo Strauss, Hans Morgenthau, and Hannah Arendt come to mind. Howard Sachar comments that Arendt "became the paradigm of Jewish intellectualism," representing "European Jewry's supreme cultural gift to the New World – the deprovincialization of the American mind."[29]

As 'explainers' or communicators, two of the best-known American interviewers of the modern era - Larry King and Barbara Walters - are Jewish. So is Wolf Isaac Blitzer of CNN fame.

In the world of politics, specifically American politics, there are prominent Jewish commentators and activists along all aspects of the political spectrum. There were famous Jewish radicals from the 1960s, such as Abbie Hoffman and Jerry Rubin, and ex-radicals such as David Horowitz, who understands the Left and Jewish radicalism very well.

Despite generally overwhelming Jewish support for liberal politicians, there are also many famous and highly influential Jewish voices on the politically conservative side - Mark Levin, Michael Savage, and Charles Krauthammer, to name only three. Each has media audiences in the U.S. numbering in the millions or tens of millions. In 2006, Krauthammer was dubbed the most influential commentator in America by the *Financial Times*. One of the most influential political thinkers and writers of the modern era – especially impacting the libertarian movement - was Russian Jewish-born Ayn Rand (Alissa Zinovievna Rosenbaum), who later became an American and author of the hugely popular novels *The Fountainhead, Atlas Shrugged* and others. Rand was founder of the philosophical school of thought known as *objectivism*, which was based on a fierce belief in individualism. Except for her atheism, one may think of Ayn Rand as the complete antithesis of another Jewish political philosopher – Karl Marx. She has been described as "one of the most passionate defenders of capitalism of all time."[30] To give some idea of her influence, one of her best-known followers is the former Chairman of the Federal Reserve system, Alan Greenspan (who is also Jewish).[31]

In the area of giving the public the news of the day, in the U.S. at least, a "disproportionate number" of television news producers are Jewish, according to *The Jewish Phenomenon*.[32] "By the 1970s," as Howard Sachar points out, "the principal television news producers and editors" at the major networks were Jewish.[33] Though many are liberal-leaning, one of the most influential conservative-leaning news sites ever created, The Drudge Report (www.drudgereport.com), was put together by Matt Drudge, the son of Reform Jewish parents and who is reportedly worth $90 million.[34] The late Walter Lippmann was "incomparably the most influential [political columnist] in American journalism."[35]

It must be stated that successful Jewish commentators, entertainers and communicators have achieved prominence due to their own giftedness and hard work, as well as through personal connections. This does not mean there is some sort of 'conspiracy' at work. Nearly every ethnic and social group or career field has its own insider connections networks. Jewish groups have theirs, but so do Arabs, Armenians, the Dutch, the Japanese, the Irish, Lebanese, Russians and everyone else operating in the modern world. Yet the Jews are the ones most often attacked for alleged 'conspiracies' because of their networking or the development of their personal connections. The fact that Jews may excel because of genius, hard work and dedication is usually dismissed out of hand by anti-Semites. For those who despise the Jews, conspiracy theories are often substituted in lieu of an explanation for Jewish talent and brilliance.

Jewish Influence on Comedy and Drama

> *"To be a Jew is to watch with good humor how this planet has treated its Jews, and to remain humorous."* [36]

COMEDIAN JACKIE MASON

Entertainment comedy is a special type of communication – one that reflects on the human condition in both light-hearted, and, at times, profound ways and speaks to the age from which it emerges. Many Jewish people excel as comedians - from the bitter humor of a Bill Maher[37] to the popularity of a Jon Stewart (Jonathan Stuart Leibowitz) with his past Comedy Central show's ridiculous antics,[38] to the comic genius of a Jerry Seinfeld, the Three Stooges, the late Joan Rivers, Mel Brooks, Phil Silvers, Harvey Korman or Don Rickles. Other names include the Marx brothers,[39] Lenny Bruce (born Leonard Alfred Schneider), Jack Benny, Peter Sellers, Billy Crystal, Carl Reiner, Bob Saget, Ben Stein, Gene Wilder, and George Burns, to name a few.[40] We must also include the famous 'Borscht Belt' of comedians that included Milton Berle, Sid Caesar, Jerry Lewis, Alan King, and Buddy Hackett, among many, many more.[41] Then there are those who are able to connect comic genius with music, such as Danish Jewish comedian-musician, Victor Borge. A 1978 study "calculated that four out of five professional comedians in the United States were Jewish."[42]

But the Jewish connection to comedy goes deeper. There is a form of self-deprecating Jewish humor in which Jewish comics poke fun at Jewish stereotypes in a way that says to Gentile audiences, 'We're OK. We may be a little different, but we're OK-different, in that our foibles and quirks, while a little unique and special, are really not all that different from the rest of the human condition.' A great deal of Jewish comic genius is built around the notion that 'funny differences are OK' – they should not be a cause for alarm or suspicion among Gentiles. In that sense, modern Jewish comedy performs a very important service – it helps dilute and wash away many of the anti-Jewish prejudices of the past.

And there is another very important aspect to comedy, especially in light of the historic Jewish experience. In the post-Holocaust world, after reading Elie Wiesel's *Night* about his experiences in Auschwitz, some might ask, 'What is there to laugh at? what is funny?' One could easily choose to dwell on only sorrow and tears and despair.

Yet Jewish humor finds a way to look past tragedy and misfortune and to enjoy life, to even revel in life despite all its troubles. This again is a very Jewish way of looking at things, and this is another reason why, I believe, so many Jewish comics have impacted the culture so profoundly and have been so influential and so beloved by generations of audiences.

In the field of drama, one commentary says that "Jews have played a decisive part in bringing to America the banner of supreme excellence in the field of dramatic arts."[43] Some hid their Jewishness or had it 'hidden' for them by their producers, such as Danny Kaye (David Kominsky). Other famed actors whose Jewishness was not well known included Kirk Douglas, Edward G. Robinson, Lauren Bacall and Tony Curtis.[44] Others in a later generation, such as Barbra Streisand, put their Jewishness on full display.

One name spans the generations – Charlie Chaplin, who, according to one account, expressed "his Jewishness in all the world-famous characters he created for the screen...." Chaplin was "an international phenomenon, the first and only actor who made six continents laugh for more than thirty years."[45] This is a wonderful compliment, except that... Chaplin *wasn't* Jewish! Innumerable accounts of his life state that he *was* Jewish, so the myth continues. Chaplin contributed to the misconception in his own way. Even famed Jewish novelist Sholom Aleichem believed that Chaplin was Jewish, so it is easy to see how this mistaken belief was perpetuated.[46]

One very telling comment, however, preserved by Chaplin biographer David Robinson, does capture something very close – Chaplin's own attitude toward Jewishness, which was very philo-Semitic. He once said: "all great geniuses have Jewish blood in them...There must be some somewhere in me. I hope so."[47]

Broadway: A Jewish Legacy

The Jewish contribution to Broadway is so vast that it is nearly impossible to know where to begin. It is probably fair to say that without the Jewish contribution, Broadway would either not exist or would not be such a vital part of American life and world culture. Besides the enormous contributions of extremely talented Jewish composers, actors and musicians, Jewish investors largely made many Broadway shows and theaters even possible. In a fascinating 2013 documentary titled, "Broadway Musicals: A Jewish Legacy," famed American Jewish comedian Mel Brooks stated: "...We're American. The Broadway musical distinguishes us from every other country in the world," while another Jewish observer has said: "American musical theater is one of the jewels in the American cultural crown." Another said: "That's the Jewish legacy to America, and America's legacy to the world."[48]

A ditty from that show proclaimed: *"...You won't succeed on Broadway if you don't have any Jews."* The show noted the immortal Broadway musicals of Richard Rodgers & Oscar Hammerstein, as well as famed former New York Philharmonic conductor Leonard Bernstein, who was also connected to Broadway. Carol Channing said, "You can name off all the [great] Broadway composers" – nearly all of them were Jewish. Mary Rodgers Guettel – the daughter of Richard Rodgers quipped, "I'm trying to think if there was anybody *not* Jewish." According to the program, "Broadway offered Jewish songwriters a chance to make it in America." And they excelled beyond anyone's wildest imaginations. These included names such as Stephen Sondheim, Marvin Hamlisch, Alan Jay Lerner, Frederick Lowe, Frank Loesser, Howard Ashman, and many more.

It all began with George Jessel and Al Jolson and the 1925 Broadway play and later first 'talking picture' show, "The Jazz Singer." This play and film symbolized the struggle - after Jewish Emancipation - of participating in the larger Gentile culture and later having an enormous impact upon it.[49]

Beyond physical Broadway's impact in New York there has been its larger impact on American and global culture. Jewish composer Jerome Kern is acknowledged as the one person who "single-handedly" developed the American musical. As Steven Silbiger notes in *The Jewish Phenomenon*, one "can hardly see a high school musical production today that was not written by a Jew."[50] Extremely famous and influential American Jewish playwrights include Arthur Miller and Neil Simon. Simon is considered to be "the most commercially successful playwright in Broadway history."[51]

Jewish Producers

Beyond actors and composers, Jewish producers – especially American Jewish producers – have shaped and transformed the culture of the world through their movies. In the modern day, one need only mention the name Stephen Spielberg. But there are many, many more – some names ae better known than others, but all have had a monumental impact on both American and world culture: Born near Minsk in a

Jewish shtetl, the founder of the NBC radio and television networks, David Sarnoff, arrived in America in 1901 around age ten.[52] Sarnoff has been rightly called "the single most important figure behind the creation and development of radio and television."[53]

William Paley created what later became the CBS television network. Besides Spielberg, Steven Silbiger has compiled a list of famed Jewish producers, some of whom include: David O. Selznick, Stanley Kubrick, Oliver Stone, Rob Reiner, and Jerry Bruckheimer.[54] Others include Norman Lear, Sheldon Leonard, Rod Serling, Fred Silverman, Aaron Spelling, David Susskind, and many more.[55]

Jewish giants in the entertainment industry who have made an almost incalculable impact on our culture and on global culture have included: Warner Brothers (Harvey, Albert, Sam and Jack), Harry Cohn (Columbia Pictures), Bob and Harvey Weinstein (Miramax), Jeffrey Katzenberg (Dreamworks), Michael Eisner (Paramount, Disney). Even most of the founders of the great studios were Jewish: Columbia Pictures by Adolph Zukor, Universal Studios by Carl Laemmle, Twentieth Century Fox by William Fox, and MGM by Louis B. Mayer and Samuel Goldwyn.[56] Sumner Redstone (Sumner Rothstein) created a massive media empire through acquisitions, later taking over Twentieth Century Fox and Columbia Pictures, and establishing the media and publishing giant Viacom. In 2008 his fortune was estimated at over $5 billion.[57]

What Does All This Mean?

Does all this mean that young Jewish boys and girls, given the right circumstances and opportunities, would all grow up to be academic leaders, musical virtuosos, great entertainers, or Nobel Prize winners? Of course not. The very idea sounds absurd even as I write it. I am reminded of the storyteller Garrison Keillor's joke about the children of his fictional Lake Wobegon, where 'all the children are above average.' Keillor's amusing fiction about how Lake Wobegon parents view their children breaks down in the real world, where the law of averages applies, and this applies to the Jewish people like any other people group: there are certainly plenty of uneducated and unmotivated Jews, just as there are plenty of dumb and unmotivated Gentiles of every description and background! *Of course* not all Jews are brilliant. *Of course* not all African-Americans are great basketball players. *Of course* not all Irishmen drink beer to excess. But there is a reason for stereotypes, and that reason is that, very often, there is some generalized truth behind them.

The average Jewish person in the world is about the same as the average Gentile person when it comes to hopes and dreams, talents and abilities. Expectations and differences vary by culture and generation, and we are all one human race. What I *am* saying is that I have come to believe that there is a *corporate giftedness* that has been bestowed upon many Jewish people as a blessing from God because of their 'chosenness' (or whatever else one wants to call it). This 'giftedness' somehow transcends pure hard work, social connections or cultural norms, as important as all of those are to worldly success. It is something that is also a mystery, although its manifestations are clearly observed.

CHAPTER THREE

Explaining (or not) Jewish Pre-Eminence

Jewish pre-eminence in so many fields has often baffled, intrigued or infuriated those who have observed it or used it as a pretext for their various hatreds.

Henry Ford, whose virulent anti-Semitism had a deep influence on Adolf Hitler and the Nazi Party, posed the issue in terms of *power* in his four-volume set of previously published articles titled, *The International Jew* (originally published between 1920-1922): "We meet the Jew everywhere in the upper circles, literally everywhere where there is power... How does the Jew so habitually...gravitate to the highest places? Who puts him there?..."[1] Ford and other opponents of the Jews throughout history have promoted fears of 'dark' conspiracies when there were none; nevertheless, these anti-Semites readily observed that the phenomenon of Jewish influence and achievement was *real*. While Ford wrote of Jewish gravitation toward "power," we usually do not see that in the political sense – as in the direct use or control of power. Rather we often see Jewish men and women of influence *impacting* the exercise of power, such as serving as presidential advisors – in recent years, names like Rahm Emanuel, David Axelrod, Jack Lew, Janet Yellen and Lawrence Summers. In past American political history, a famous name that comes to mind is former U.S. Secretary of State Henry Kissinger. Kissinger had tremendous influence over former President Richard Nixon and U.S. foreign policy. Or we might consider the influence of Jewish neo-conservatives in the administration of former President George W. Bush, or the close friendships and influence of Jewish advisors Lanny Davis and Sidney Blumenthal on the Clintons.

Putting aside the anti-Semites' fascination with conspiracy and power themes, the key point is that through time Jewish thought-leaders and activists have exercised enormous *influence* on those who actually wielded that power.

Is There Any *Reasonable* Explanation for Jewish Pre-eminence?

Raphael Patai in his book, *The Jewish Mind*, asks: "...what are the factors which can be considered responsible for these special Jewish talents?" Patai was specifically looking at certain sciences and medicine, but his question can be applied to other fields as well.

Patai concludes that this is a very difficult question to try to answer: "In many cases the factors responsible for the emergence of special Jewish talents eludes us; in others, we can only venture more or less informed guesses as to their nature."[2] In looking at Jewish influence on culture, Paul Buhle asks, "What explains the impact of Jews on popular culture?" His unconvincing answer: "Jews happened to be in the right place at the right time, and kept on being there."[3] (The last two words of Buhle's comment remind me of one of my favorite movies, "Being There," starring Jewish actor and comedian, Peter Sellers, who also played the beloved character "Inspector Clouseau" in the *Pink Panther* film series[4]).

Regarding the Jewish impact on the sciences, one "explanation of Jewish achievements in science has been that an enduring tradition of learning, and a love of learning, led Jews in droves to seek the advanced university degrees that lay the groundwork for scientific genius." Others have seen "the key to Jews' successes in science as arising from the Talmudic tradition of disputation."[5]

Author Ioan James has written: "There may be no simple answer to the old question of why Jewish people have been so successful, particularly in the closely related fields of mathematics and physics, but various theories have been advanced in the literature."[6]

A 2001 paper presented by David A. Hollinger at the annual meeting of the American Association for the Advancement of Science posed this question: "Why have Jews been demographically over-represented by factors of six and even ten or twelve in some departments of the leading universities of the United States...?"[7]

In his 1963 book, *The Scientific Intellectual: The Psychological and Sociological Origins of Modern Science* – revised in 1992 – author Lewis S. Feuer readily acknowledged the phenomenon: "Jewish eminence in scientific achievement…reflected itself in their frequent honors as Nobel Prize laureates. The percentage of Jews among the laureates has been far greater than their proportion among the European and American populations." But why? Feuer continues: "There have been various theories to account for Jewish eminence in the sciences beginning in the nineteenth century."[8]

We shall examine each of these theories in turn.

Veblen's Thesis

Feuer notes that one of "the best-known of the theories that have been advanced to account for the high Jewish contribution to science is the one Thorstein Veblen set forth in his essay, 'The Intellectual Pre-eminence of Jews in Modern Europe.'" This seminal piece appeared in the March 1919 issue of the *Political Science Quarterly.*[9]

Veblen's essay has been characterized as "one of the most adamantly philo-semitic treatises ever written by a gentile." It remains, according to one observer, after "more than eighty years…the most influential analysis of Jewish intellectual creativity."[10] One of the reasons that Veblen's thesis has been so popular is that it attempted to explain "not simply intelligence, but something more specific: the successful use of intelligence in science and scholarship in the rigorous, methodical study of the world." It was in large measure "a specific intellectual style, a habit of thought," in Veblen's view, that enabled those who had it "to have a better perception of the world as it is…" Veblen then "tried to show why Jews were more likely than other people to have this style."[11]

Before getting into Veblen's thesis more specifically, one must first ask whether this question has been one that has been comprehensively considered and examined in modern Jewish/Judaic studies. The answer is a resounding *no.* As one observer has noted, "this is not a topic that has inspired much creative insight or research in contemporary Jewish studies…" The reason is because, among other things, "it cuts too close to neuroses of the field and the egos of its exponents."[12] This is precisely why some Gentile scholars have picked up the torch instead – to try to fill the vacuum of an explanation.

"Alienation" as an Explanation?

Veblen's primary theory regarding Jewish achievement was related to the concept of *alienation*, the idea "that the fertility of Jewish science rests on the fact that the Jew is what is called today an 'alienated' intellectual."[13] This alienation, combined with skepticism and estrangement, was associated with "the partial liberation of Jews from traditional Judaism and Jewish communal life."[14] Another way of expressing this was having an "outsider mentality," which "allowed Jewish people to work outside the mainstream and create new ideas, inventions and businesses."[15] Eric Weiner has written that a "glance at some of history's greatest discoveries and inventions demonstrates the power of the outsider." Both Einstein and Freud saw themselves as outcasts who needed to prove themselves, according to Weiner.[16] More recently, Dean Keith Simonton, who has studied the sources of genius, offered a similar explanation for Jewish achievement and distinction. "This phenomenon," he wrote, "probably has many sources, including the superior family environment found in Jewish homes. Nevertheless," he continued, "not the least of the developmental factors is the marginal position Jews have in Western culture."[17]

Veblen asserted that this alienation could turn a given Jewish person "into a skeptic, a dispassionate inquirer, a complete follower of scientific method..." Feuer has been critical of the Veblen alienation thesis, asking: "Does Veblen's drama of the Jewish scientific intellectual really conform to the facts?" His answer is no: "[I]t scarcely explains the fecundity of Jewish scientific work." He cites the example of Italian Jewish scientists: "The least 'alienated' Jewish community in Europe, the Italian, was proportionately the most vigorous in its scientific contribution."[18] Israeli historian Shulamit Volkov has also done careful empirical research that turns Veblen's alienation theory on its head.[19] Noah Efron, in writing on Jewish participation in twentieth century science, asserted: "If Veblen's Jews were connoisseurs of alienation, those portrayed in these pages wished for nothing so much as to escape alienation, to fit in."[20]

Here's an irony, though, regarding the alienation thesis, captured by two authors who looked at the Jewish impact on modern American culture: "How can Jews be seen simultaneously as cultural outsiders – a minority seeking integration into the American mainstream – and as the ultimate insiders – a group with decisive, 'disproportionate' influence over a nation's cultural sensibilities?"[21]

Veblen got another area precisely wrong. His alienation thesis was closely tied to the image of the 'wandering Jew' – the image of a community and individuals that are stateless, unable to put down real roots because of persecution. This state of mind contributed to Jewish giftedness and creativity, in Veblen's thinking. As Richard Lynn has characterized it, Veblen predicted that "Jews would cease to be creative if and when they acquired their own homeland in Israel and were no longer rootless wanderers."[22]

Hollinger writes that "Veblen was so enamored of the persona of the detached critic" – vis-à-vis the Jewish community – "that he gave short shrift to the possibility that a sustaining social community, with a coherent culture, might promote rather than retard intellectual creativity."[23] So, does the Jewish *community* itself help to foster Jewish brilliance and creativity? Of course it does to an extent, but that is hardly a startling insight (other than the fact that Veblen did not include it among his own explanations). But this can be said of nearly any culture where there is positive reinforcement. We might consider the Vietnamese diaspora community, for example, or the Greek community or any number of other cultures or ethnic or religious communities. Nearly all have traditions and cultural mores that can serve to stimulate creativity among some of their more talented or industrious members. Yet this in no way adequately explains Jewish genius or pre-eminence.

Feuer's Thesis

How does Feuer himself explain Jewish scientific pre-eminence?: "It is possible," he says, "…that the Jewish reverence for learning tended through the centuries to result in a genetic selection which favored the reinforcement of intelligence."[24] This is an argument without merit, since "reverence for learning" is not a trait that can be passed genetically. But reverence for learning can be a very strong community trait: Among Ashkenazi Jews from Central and Eastern Europe, "[e]xplanations of the causal dynamics vary, but they all start from one indisputable, consistent fact about traditional Jewish life: the extraordinarily high value attached to learning."[25] On the other hand, there are those like Charles Murray who believe that an elevated Jewish IQ is a key explanation for Jewish accomplishment, or at least a primary building-block needed for accomplishment, combined with qualities such as "imagination, ambition, perseverance, and curiosity." These latter qualities, in his view, are "decisive in separating the merely smart from the highly productive." Interestingly, Murray also "suspects that elevated Jewish intelligence was (a) not confined to Ashkenazim and (b) antedates the Middle Ages...." He asserts that "a strong case could be assembled that Jews everywhere had unusually high intellectual resources that manifested themselves outside of Ashkenaz and well before the period when non-rabbinic Ashkenazi accomplishment manifested itself."[26]

Raphael Patai in *The Jewish Mind* commented that the quality of the Jewish home environment is crucial to Jewish intelligence: The Jewish home was and is "a place in which learning is highly valued," and this esteem for learning remains "an age-old Jewish trait." Historically, this esteem began very early. As Amoz Oz and Fania Oz-Salzberger relate in *Jews and Words*, early exposure to the written word for Jewish boys used to begin "at a staggeringly young age...from the age of three to the age of thirteen." This attitude extended back to (at least) Mishnaic times, they write, and has been shown to be an "astounding constant of Jewish history." They contend further that "words that came from books" actually came to define the Jewish family, no matter how poor they might have been, while Jewish parenting "had, [and] perhaps still has, a unique academic edge."[27]

The Jewish commitment to education is largely unparalleled in the modern age, but it is not unparalleled in history. For example, during the period known as the "Scottish Enlightenment," education in much of Scottish society was not "just a means to professional credentials or social advancement. It became a way of life."[28] That is certainly true of many Jewish communities today, especially Ashkenazi Jews. Among many

American Jews, the goal often is to achieve the best education possible, given a family's resources.[29] Concurrent with this deep Jewish reverence for learning has been the understanding, "intuitively grasped by the millions of East European Jewish immigrants who arrived in America" prior to the introduction of quotas in 1924, that "the road to intellectual achievement led through the gates of academic professions."[30]

An Astonishing Percentage

In his 2002 essay on this theme, David Hollinger proposed expanding the definition of Jewish achievement beyond what Veblen did to include the areas of business, finance and law (areas that Veblen ignored in his analysis of Jewish achievement). In doing so, he came up with a very interesting list of closely matching percentages. The percentage of Jews who became American recipients of Nobel Prizes over the previous 30 years was an astounding 40%, according to Hollinger's reckoning. Additionally, "the percentage of Jewish partners in the leading law firms in New York and Washington" at that time was "also 40%." Thirdly, "the most recent list of the wealthiest Americans" at that time showed that "40% were of Jewish descent."[31] What are we to make of these percentages that are so incredibly disproportionate in Jewish representation to the general American population? There is no simple answer. And it is not merely our own generation - this was a phenomenon noted by Mark Twain in his day, when he commented that the contributions by Jews "to the world's list of great names on literature, science, art, music, finance, medicine, and abstruse learning" as something that was "way out of proportion to the weakness of ... [their] numbers."[32]

The percentages noted by Hollinger show that Jewish preeminence and disproportionate in representation[33] extend far beyond the areas of science and academic scholarship - something much broader appears to be at work here.[34] These data also demonstrate that the Veblen thesis of the 'alienated' or 'detached' Jewish intellectual or scientist, working away in solitude to come up with creative or original ideas (we might have the image in our minds of Albert Einstein in the Swiss patent office, for example) – is wrong, or at least is woefully incomplete as an explanation. Hollinger concludes: "Even if detachment and alienation are assumed to be good qualities for a career in science, they may not be necessary for success as a Hollywood producer or an investment banker."[35]

Exactly. The Veblen thesis on the reason for Jewish pre-eminence is inadequate in trying to explain the full scope of this phenomenon. It is much wider and deeper than Veblen imagined or was even willing to consider.[36]

Ioan James took up the question in his 2009 book, *Driven to Innovate: A Century of Jewish Mathematicians and Physicists.* In a section titled, "Secrets of Success," James cited Patai's *The Jewish Mind.* In trying to understand the sources of Jewish achievement, Patai emphasized factors such as the Jewish home environment, the pressures of Gentile persecution, the "religio-cultural tradition of considering learning the highest value," concentrated urban living, and other factors.[37] Patai also cited the comments of Joseph Jacobs, who, on the issue of Jewish brilliance in philology, stated that it was "in part due to their [the Jews'] frequent change of country..." But if that were the case, as Patai asks: "If polyglottism leads to eminence in philological research, why have no other polyglot peoples, of whom there is no dearth, produced outstanding philologists?"[38] Why indeed.

Lynn's Jewish "Achievement Quotients" (AQs)

Richard Lynn has developed what he calls Jewish "Achievement Quotients" (AQs) to describe outstanding Jewish success and accomplishment "as the percentages of outstandingly gifted Jews in relation to their population numbers" compared with percentages of Gentiles vis-à-vis those populations numbers.[39] These "AQs" are based on various studies that looked at outstanding persons of European background. One set of studies was conducted by Colin Berry and published in 1999. The first timeframe was from 1830 to 1879 and the second from 1880 to 1930. Jews were highly over-represented during both timeframes, spread out across numerous fields. Of the 1,352 individuals covered in these assessments, 220 were Jewish. The average AQ for the first timeframe was 8.7. This 8.7 number means that Jews were 8.7 times *over-represented* beyond what should be expected. The AQ factor then nearly doubled to 16.6 during the second timeframe from 1880 to 1930.[40]

Lynn also takes the comparable research of Charles Murray from two other timeframes, 1870 to 1950 and from 1951 to 2000, and comes up with a Jewish AQ for those periods of 6.0. He concludes that "the Jewish Achievement Quotients in the two centuries from 1800 to 2000 are reasonably consistent, lying between 6.0 and 16.6." As Lynn elucidates, there are numerous reasons why there may be variances in these two quotients.[41] The important point is not the variance itself but the fact that over-representation is so striking and well-documented, whether we accept either figure.

From Australia to Britain to Italy

Lynn went on to develop AQs for Jewish over-representation in other parts of the world for various timeframes in the twentieth century based on various studies and assessments. A 1979 assessment of 370 leading Australians, for example, showed high Jewish AQs in the areas of politics and media (6.2), academics (26.8), business (10.7), etc.[42] In the United Kingdom, an assessment of Jewish membership as Fellows in the extremely prestigious Royal Society went from an AQ of 1.7 in 1901 to a high of 13.3 in 1985 to 8.0 in 2005, trending higher and higher over the last half century or so.[43] In Italy, a review of Nobel Prizes during the twentieth century showed four Jews receiving Nobel Prizes (24%) out of a total of 17 Italian Nobel Laureates. Jews made up only a very tiny 0.075% of the population during this timeframe. This results in an absolutely stunning AQ of 320![44] Again, it is not the actual figures that are important as much as the trends that they represent and most of all the consistency of those trends across numerous nations and societies.

Jewish Success in Finance

The 10.7 AQ for Australia cited above is just one example of the well-known fact that Jews are very well represented in business and finance occupations around the world. While there are certainly plenty of poor Jews in the world, Jewish success in finance is so well-known that it has become a stereotype – both negative and positive, depending on the circumstances and who is doing the stereotyping. The negative stereotype was captured in Shakespeare's creation of the character Shylock – a pejorative view that has dogged the Jewish people for centuries.

Anti-Semitic propaganda, such as the counterfeit "Protocols of the Elders of Zion," claimed that Jewish "conspiracies" were behind the reason why vast fortunes have been made by some Jewish financiers and entrepreneurs. As authors Amy Chua and Jed Rubenfeld have noted, "it's generally much harder to talk about Jewish wealth than that of any other group." This is because "[e]xaggerated or even patently false claims of Jewish economic 'control' have in the past led to discrimination, ghettoization, and some of the worst atrocities in history."[45]

This topic must be approached with great sensitivity, but at the same time, some are so sensitive about it as avoid discussing it entirely. That also is an incorrect response. We must seek to understand what is right in front of us.

Jewish "Agility of Intellect" and Success in Finance

One can, I think, trace some Gentiles' envy for Jewish success in finance back to Biblical times and Laban and his sons' envy over the success and abundance of Jacob's flocks in Genesis 31. Haters of the Jews have traditionally attributed Jewish success in finance to underhandedness or conspiracies of some kind. But as George Gilder points out, the real reason is more an "agility of intellect" in the financial sphere – an agility that we see demonstrated in many other fields as well. As he writes, "In this most intellectual of capitalist endeavors Jews throughout history have excelled." (1) Elsewhere he asserts: "At the heart of anti-Semitism is resentment of Jewish achievement..." (2)

1. George Gilder, *The Israel Test* (2009), p. 165.

2. George Gilder, "Capitalism, Jewish Achievement, and the Israel Test," *The American*, July 27, 2009. http://www.discovery.org/a/11771

In reality, Jewish success in finance is due to numerous factors, but perhaps the most important one is the "agility of intellect" that Gilder refers to. In developing Gilder's view further, I believe that this "agility of intellect" extends not only to a better grasp than most people have of what is possible in the financial sphere, often combined with the courage of risk-taking necessary to make it possible. All three factors are necessary to achieve success.

There have also been enormously successful and influential Jewish economists, such as Arthur Burns, Paul Samuelson, Alan Greenspan and Milton Friedman. Great Jewish economists of the past include Henry Morgenthau, Jr., David Ricardo, and Ludwig von Mises, to name a few. Of the Nobel Prizes awarded in economics, Jewish recipients make up more than 35% of the total.[46] Many of the most successful hedge fund managers are Jewish, including Carl Icahn, Jim Simons, Steve Cohen and Bruce Kovner.[47]

Capitalism

While meant as a great positive attribute, this phenomenon – the close association between Jewish success and finance - has been viewed by some Jews as an historical albatross around their necks.[48] This is quite understandable. As noted, the Jewish people have been blamed both for being successful at capitalism and also blamed (by the Nazis and others) as being the agents of *anti*-capitalism.[49] For those who hate them, they cannot win no matter what they do.

Famed American historian Henry Adams, grandson of John Quincy Adams and great-grandson of America's second President, John Adams, reflected a deep-seated anti-Semitic attitude toward the Jewish people and finance. Adams was about as 'Establishment' as one could get for his times and had every advantage, yet he bitterly decried his era and blamed "the Jews" for his own misery, despite all his worldly success and acclaim. In July 1896 he wrote to a friend that he lived "only in the wish to see the end" of those times, "with all its infernal Jewry." He said that he wanted to "put every money lender to death, and to sink Lombard Street and Wall Street under the ocean.... We are in the hands of the Jews. They can do what they please with our values..."[50]

Silbiger's Thesis – "Jewish Mothering!"

One American Jewish author – Steven Silbiger – has put forward his own thesis on why Jews excel when given the opportunity. He leaves explanations like "alienation" in the dustbin. For him, the explanation is *Jewish mothering*! Citing the work of sociologist Zena Smith Blau in her 1974 study, *The Strategy of the Jewish Mother*, Silbiger believes that Jewish child-rearing practices, though "…largely overlooked…have had a profound impact on Jewish-American success." Silbiger, citing Blau, says that Jewish mothers in her study cultivated "a strong ego structure" in their offspring." This, they assess, contributes to "a strong belief in their own ability to achieve success in the classroom and eventually in their careers."[51]

At first this sounds like a reasonable thesis, but good parenting is hardly unique to Jewish families (while there are certainly plenty of Jewish families that are completely dysfunctional). The same might be said for how the first-born son is often treated in, say, traditional Chinese culture or in many single-children families in many other cultures. Family culture, as Eric Weiner, author of The *Geography of Genius*, notes, "can either cultivate creativity or squelch it." So, family culture is important, but it still does not explain Jewish pre-eminence.

Cultivating a strong ego structure might be a contributing factor toward helping explain some success (although it can also potentially bring problems as well), but it hardly begins to explain originality and creativity. At the same time, "high expectations and high standards" are placed on many Jewish children (one is reminded of Google co-founder Sergei Brin's hypothetical but all-too-real comment from his father about why a school in Israel had not achieved *all* the top spots, not just some!). These attitudes are strongly reinforced outside the family: "the entire [Jewish] community pushes the 'achievement' message…"[52]

Blau's research also found that many Jewish mothers pampered and spoiled their children and that the parenting style she observed most often "was accompanied by volatile exchanges between mother and child." Instead of direct discipline, this led to more nagging on the part of the mother. Jewish fathers were more reserved in their parenting, while "a father's silence created just as much discomfort" as the mother's nagging and "actually resulted in quicker compliance."

There is also a heart-breaking note in all this. With respect to success and the independence granted to many Jewish children by their parents as part of the price of achieving it, "Children are expected to repay their parents by achieving the success their parents wanted for them," but they often use that success to make sure that their *own* children – the next generation – are just as successful or more so. But this can mean that by then the grandparent's generation is largely abandoned as the cycle of life moves on. Silbiger notes, "whole neighborhoods in Florida and New York City are filled with such [abandoned elderly] parents."[53] This, sadly, is often the Jewish experience – it is one of the heavy costs of drivenness when it comes to trying to be as successful as possible.

Silbiger's "Keys" or Principles of Success – Useful But Inadequate

In addition to his views on Jewish mothering, Silbiger believes that Jews (especially Jews in America) have succeeded because they have applied certain principles to their lives and work and how they approach money. He contends that the "the factors that work together to create Jewish wealth…can be applied to individuals and groups from any background." What "secrets of success" have they learned?[54]

These "secrets" include, among others, cultivating knowledge, taking care of one's own, having an entrepreneurial spirit, developing one's verbal skills, and related factors that he covers in his book.[55] The principles he outlines all make sense, and applying them would undoubtedly improve both the lives and lot of most people or groups who follow them. But other groups and cultures throughout history have practiced similar principles. None of them has succeeded like the Jews.

So, while Silbiger's effort to capture universal principles for other groups and individuals to follow is interesting and useful, his thesis that any group employing them will succeed like the Jews fails. There certainly is no evidence that applying these or similar principles will lead to breakthroughs in original thought that may change the course of civilization. Yet achieving such breakthroughs is exactly what Jewish thinkers and professionals have done time and again when they weren't being hounded from one country to the next.

In fact, I would go so far as to say that a partial attempt by some Gentiles historically at fulfilling Silbiger's thesis has actually led to a form of anti-Semitism. Even without a book like Silbiger's that attempts to guide people along certain principles, some Gentiles in the past already have 'played by all the rules,' so to speak, but still not been very successful. But then they have perhaps looked at their Jewish neighbors who *have* succeeded and wondered, '*What do they have that I don't have?*' – and they don't see any answers that they can comprehend. Thus, some of these Gentiles conclude that some other unseen force must be at work – *a Jewish conspiracy!* – that allowed some Jews to succeed where they themselves - their Gentile counterparts – failed or fell short of the goal. That form of anti-Semitism is as old as the hills, but who has ever been able to adequately explain it? It is covetousness, certainly, and jealousy as well, but it is the *mystery* of Jewish success that confounds so many.

In the end, the title of Silbiger's book itself is an apt refutation of his thesis with respect to simply applying certain principles and finding success as a group or individual. Yes, applying such principles as he recommends may improve some people's lives and are very useful. But they in no way guarantee the extraordinary levels of success achieved by so many Jewish people in those societies where they have been able to pursue their hopes and dreams with complete freedom of opportunity. That level of success is indeed '*the Jewish phenomenon.*' No other culture or people group even comes close.

Steven L. Pease's View – A Possible "Fading" Golden Age of Jewish Achievement?

Two books by author Steven L. Pease take a somewhat different perspective – at least with respect to the future. The first was titled, *The Golden Age of Jewish Achievement* (2009) and the second, *The Debate Over Jewish Achievement* (2015).

As the title of his first book makes clear, Pease sees Jewish achievement in the modern era as a "golden age." However, near the end of that book he has a chapter titled, "A Fading Golden Age?" He believes that "demography, apathy, and dissipation of [Jewish] cultural values are all serious threats" to keeping this "golden age" alive. This appears to stand in complete contrast to Gilder's views in *The Israel Test* – if anything, reading Gilder, one gets the impression that Jewish achievement, especially in Israel, is only in its incipient stages and may be ready to reach even greater heights. "The real case for Israel," he writes, "is as the leader of human civilization, technological progress, and scientific advance."[56]

I certainly would side with Gilder's view over Pease's when it comes to assessing the future. In my view, there is every indicator that Jewish accomplishment and influence are growing, not receding. While hatred against Israel and anti-Semitism are on the rise in our day, they have not yet altered this course.

A Falsification Test – Finding Genius and Excellence Elsewhere

For the skeptics, we now need to apply a *falsification test* to this thesis about the preeminence of the Jewish people. The evidence that Pease provides in his two books, a review of the scholarly literature of previous generations, coupled with what Gilder has presented about technological advancement in Israel, should be overwhelming to most critics. Nevertheless, a falsification test is in order.

A falsification test is one of the hallmarks of the scientific age and is well-known to any competent scientist (although it must be added that not all so-called scientists are competent – some wouldn't recognize a falsification test if it hit them squarely between the eyes!). If one example or piece of data can show that a specific thesis is not true, then it can be said to have been *falsified*, or to have been shown to be false.

The falsification test that I will construct for our case is quite straightforward, and it is based on this assertion: "The Jewish people are a special and unique people on the face of the Earth. When, given periods of peace and stability, and especially, freedom, as a group they excel and often prosper, even in the face of discrimination over a period of centuries."

This thesis about the Jewish people might be falsified *if it can be shown that any other nation or people group* **consistently** *rises to eminence, influence and excellence over the centuries - despite often fierce opposition and persecution from their adversaries - whenever given the smallest opportunity to pursue their hopes and dreams.*

The key words of this falsification test are *consistently* and *over the centuries.* There have been numerous societies and people groups which have excelled and made major contributions to mankind's treasure store of knowledge and culture and who have fought back against adversaries to achieve a limited time of greatness. We might consider the extraordinary culture and erudition of Athens in the age of Socrates and the birth of democracy.[57] Athens, it is said, "produced more brilliant minds – from Socrates to Aristotle – than any other place the world has seen before or since (only Renaissance Florence came close)."[58] But then it was over. "Classical Greece' lasted 186 years, but the real flowering of creativity was a mere 24 years. The great period of the Scottish Enlightenment did not even last half a century and then it was over.[59]

Next, we can consider the Roman Empire during the age of Horace, Virgil, Ovid and Cicero and Roman contributions to law, classical learning and engineering feats. This was followed by the Golden Age of Florence and the Italian Renaissance and names like Leonardo da Vinci, Michelangelo, Raphael and Leon Battista Alberti.[60] Or we could consider the French golden age in Paris during *La Belle Époque*, or the Scottish Enlightenment in the eighteenth century, with luminaries such as Adam Smith, David Hume, Thomas Reid, James Clerk Maxwell, James Watt, William Thomson (Lord Kelvin) and Alexander Graham Bell, to name a few.[61] The Scottish Enlightenment "led to a flowering of education, literature, and science in Scotland"[62] and had a monumental impact on the ideas about government that eventually became the United States of America.

As Arthur Herman explains, "Before the eighteenth century was over, Scotland would generate the basic institutions, ideas, attitudes, and habits of mind that characterize the modern age."[63] The title of Herman's

2001 history of the Scottish Enlightenment - *How the Scots Invented the Modern World: The True Story of How Western Europe's Poorest Nation Created Our World and Everything In It* - sounds presumptuous in the extreme, and it is, but only the subtitle. A close reading of the book shows that, regarding his primary thesis – that the Scots invented the modern world - Herman is largely correct. Interestingly, Herman himself is apparently Jewish.[64]

The Scottish Enlightenment was a period of greatness and extraordinary contributions – a fact that, until recently, has not received adequate attention from modern historians. Sir Walter Scott, for example, created the historical novel and made possible a generation of great writers – names like Jane Austen, George Eliot, Charles Dickens, Leo Tolstoy, and Victor Hugo - who followed in the path he blazed.[65]

For most Scots during the eighteenth century, as with most Jews today, being educated meant "more than just a means to professional credentials or social advancement. *It became a way of life.*" Further, "despite its relative poverty and small population, Scottish culture had a built-in bias toward reading, learning, and education in general. In no other European country did education count for so much or enjoy so broad a base." [66] However, this focused desire and drive within the Scottish culture and ethos was limited to a specific time in history. It certainly does not exist in Scotland today. Similarly, the periods of greatness of Athens, Rome and Florence are relics of the past – there is no greatness or genius in those places today that can in any way compare with what existed before.

Attributes that nearly each of these epochs shared was "a sophisticated culture…[a] keen sense of understanding, [a] flourishing art and literature…self-confidence, [a] regard for truth and the importance of intellectual criticism, and, most important, an appreciation of the humane side of our character."[67] Blossomings of culture have sometimes occurred where there was an atmosphere of freedom and where merit, creativity and excellence were cherished and rewarded. And it was precisely where those traits were cultivated that one saw the rise of *virtue* – a word rarely heard today but one about which volumes were written in the past. This, in turn, could lead to something we call a *virtuous cycle*

– a phrase that has been used in a variety of contexts, but I use it here to describe why certain civilizations have excelled for a time.

But only *for a time*. As one scholar of the *ideas* that have propelled intellectual history and civilization has noted, "[t]hroughout history certain countries and civilisations have glittered for a while, then for one reason or another been eclipsed."[68] Plato's observation that "What is honored in a country will be cultivated there" seems particularly apropos in this context. [69]

In the American experience, authors Amy Chua and Jed Rubenfeld posit what they call "The Triple Package," a set of attributes that they attach to various highly successful ethnic groups in America: a superiority complex, combined with a sense of insecurity, and what they call "impulse control" – which means controlling one's impulses for instant gratification, and also showing discipline, perseverance, and self-restraint. The "fusion of superiority and insecurity…together… tend to produce a goading chip on the shoulder, a need to prove oneself or be recognized." They aver that "Jews have had a chip of just this kind for basically all of recorded history," or at least since the Bar Kokhba revolt.[70]

The question posed by our falsification test is, can any of the examples cited or others be applied *consistently* to show that any one specific people group, nation or location where genius or excellence flourished for a while did so *consistently* - and in spite of persecution and major interruptions, such as wars and economic calamities? In other words, is there any other nation that has *consistently* come back again and again to flourish and excel, when allowed to do so? History demonstrates that the answer to that question is a resounding *no*. The Jewish people are the only people group that fills that bill.

This fact has not gone unnoticed by keen observers of history and culture.

Mark Twain noted the Jewish phenomenon of survival and overcoming and wrote about it in 1899, long before the Holocaust and before the great bulk of discoveries and contributions noted in this book were ever made. Twain wrote of Jewish longevity and overcoming all the odds, but he also hinted at giftedness and the special contributions that the Jewish people have made to mankind's history: "[The Jew] has made a marvelous fight in this world, in all the ages; and he has done it with his hands tied behind him...the Egyptian, the Babylonian, and the Persian rose, filled the planet with sound and splendor, then faded to dream-stuff and passed away; the Greek and the Roman followed, and made a vast noise, and they are gone...The Jew saw them all, beat them all, and is now what he always was, exhibiting...no slowing of his energies, no dulling of his alert and aggressive mind. All things are mortal but the Jew; all other forces pass, but he remains. What is the secret of his immortality?"[71] "Immortality," as Mark Twain used it here refers to the Jewish people's 'staying-power' despite all opposition – even with their "hands tied" behind their backs. Why are the Jews even still around, he queries? What is their secret? No other nation or people group has succeeded in this way, nor even come close.

Mark Twain's question resounds ever more strongly in our post-Holocaust twenty-first century. If what he observed in 1899 was true, how much more so now! The falsification test *fails*.

Just a Mystery?

In 2014 Noah J. Efron published a book titled, *A Chosen Calling: Jews in Science in the Twentieth Century.* In looking at the various theories and explanations for Jewish pre-eminence, he reasoned that, "Almost a century has passed since Veblen asked what accounts for the remarkable preeminence of Jews in Western science and scholarship and offered his answer." Rather than plateauing or subsiding during that time, "Jews' preeminence [instead] grew to a degree that Veblen himself never could have predicted."[72] While "alternative explanations of the phenomenon," he continued, "have been offered since Veblen, and while there is likely some truth to several of them, just as there is some truth to Veblen's theory, *the success of Jews in modern science remains almost as mysterious today as it was a century ago...*"[73] (emphasis added). Author Paul Mendes-Flohr has stated: "The disproportionate number of Jews among... intellectuals – individuals of critical dissent and cognitive originality – of Western society *continues to intrigue* the student of Western culture."[74] (emphasis added)

"Continues to intrigue...."

Are those the very best explanations that observers can provide for this undisputed phenomenon? Steven Pease concludes: "I think we can safely say" (can we?) "that while genes and IQ contribute to the Jewish potential for disproportionate achievement, culture contributed both to the natural selection process for those traits and the outsized expression of those talents in the behavior of individual Jews."[75] Elsewhere he presents the argument that *Jews have thrived because they have learned survivor skills over centuries of persecution...* This argument states that "Incredible hardships over much of 4,000 years resulted in natural selection of the best and brightest."[76] So Pease and others invoke 'natural selection' as a partial explanation. When in doubt, fall back on Darwinism!

The 'Best Arguments'

Here then are some of the best arguments that sociology and scientific analysis offer in trying to explain Jewish preeminence in so many fields of endeavor. Jewish pre-eminence has allegedly emerged from: *alienation and detachment, home environment (Jewish mothering!), concentrated urban living, high esteem for learning within the Jewish community (including marrying scholars), the early drive for literacy, genetics and high IQs, natural selection and survivor skills as a result of persecution, self-help networks, guilt from parents as a motivator, and occupational choice.*[77] Other arguments that can be added include: *overcoming insecurity, whether that insecurity emanates from anti-Semitism or other reasons;*[78] *a superiority complex combined with insecurity;*[79] *a need or drive to excel in order to have status within the Jewish community but also protection and recognition in a Gentile world.*

Each factor has probably had some impact, but even taken together, they are all still woefully inadequate. Those who have put forward these explanations are clutching at straws, and I think, deep down, many of them know it even if they won't admit it. This is because they have nowhere else to go and nothing else to go on. They have done the best they can, since the alternative for them – admitting that God has had something to with it – for many of them transcends the realm of human logic and reason.

In 2010, *New York Times* columnist David Brooks, responding to Steven Pease's first book, *The Golden Age of Jewish Achievement,* simply concluded, "No single explanation can account for the record of Jewish achievement."[80] Pease has published an extensive "Chronology of the Debate" in his second book, listing dozens of sources that touch on the nature/nurture discussion.[81]

But they all fall short, in my opinion, in explaining the *ultimate cause* and *origin* of Jewish achievement, success, and, oftentimes, genius. They touch around the edges. Observers can point to high IQs, Jewish cultural mores, the desire that many Jews have to 'prove themselves' to a larger Gentile world, and other supposed 'explanations'. But all of these 'explanations' remain deeply unsatisfying as a full answer.

At a certain point, if they're honest, most serious observers must throw up their hands and ultimately admit that they can't really explain *why* this phenomenon both exists and persists – it just does.

Since no *comprehensive* and *demonstrable* answer has emerged from secular sources as to why Jewish pre-eminence exists, perhaps there is another explanation – one that has thus far eluded geneticists, cultural observers and scholars of intellectual history. This book puts forward just such a thesis - one that will be embraced by some readers while it appalls others.

That thesis is this: that the Jewish people are *special,* that they are *chosen* and that they have been given extraordinary gifts by God Himself. That is one of the things that sets them apart from the Gentile world.

In one sense, trying to *disprove* such a thesis – even if it was never verbalized directly by Hitler and his minions - was part of the demonic rage behind Nazi ideology.

A "De-mystified" Approach?

But all this sounds "mysterious" and discriminatory. Why would God choose one particular group of people over every other people group in the world? I have a simple answer for that – ***because He did!*** The Hebrew Bible and the New Testament together proclaim this simple message – that though God cares for all the peoples of the world, He also *chose* to have a special relationship with the children of Israel.

This idea of mystery is very upsetting to some. David Hollinger, for example, "argues that we need a demystified approach to the study of Jewish overrepresentation, according to which we would analyze Jewish intellectual pre-eminence alongside, rather than in isolation from, Jewish pre-eminence in other callings, including the arts, the service professions, and finance."[82] He apparently wants to de-couple the analysis of what we are examining from the very idea of a transcendent explanation – the possibility that there is something beyond us that is 'mysterious' about all this.

It is indeed "mysterious" but not mystical. Is it a "mystified approach" to look at the simple words of Scripture, what they promise and what they describe, and to consider how those promises have been fulfilled empirically and therefore hold that they are true? I don't think so. I think it is as sober and level-headed a conclusion as one can work out. But, just as Hitler could not stand to have the Jewish people serve as a witness against him and his worldview, neither can many people stand to have the Scriptures serve as a witness on behalf of the Jewish people and against those who hate them. The latter reject the very notion out of hand - it is abhorrent to them.

But it is nonetheless true.

CHAPTER FOUR

Responding to the Idea of Jewish 'Specialness': From the Anti-Semite to the Jewish Liberal

Responding to the Idea of Jewish Specialness and Pre-eminence

God's blessing upon the Jewish people remains in place even if some Jews do not even believe in Him, let alone obey Him. God is a God of covenants, and His covenants are irrevocable, despite what mankind does or doesn't do in response.

One of the manifestations of that blessing as I am presenting it in this book, is, I believe, a giftedness given to the Jewish people that includes Jewish pre-eminence. Some, in fact, might see it as both a blessing *and* a curse in some ways, but we will discuss that aspect later.

For now, we will look at responses to the very idea of Jewish specialness and especially to the concrete examples of achievement and success.

Jewish achievement and success evoke different responses: consternation, even jealousy and rage in some, but wonder in others. For those historically who have responded with extreme consternation and concern over Jewish success, as previously noted, this has often led to conspiracy theories of all types, reflecting the view that the Jews could not possibly have achieved what they did 'fairly,' that there must be some sort of unfair advantage. This was certainly the thinking behind the creation of the forgery, "The Protocols of the Elders of Zion," which seems to have an unending shelf-life among anti-Semites.

The myth of a global Jewish conspiracy has been a key component behind most forms of anti-Semitism. We shall examine this in more detail in a moment. First, however, we must acknowledge that, while anti-Jewish conspiracy theories are false, there is also a meta-narrative underneath some of them that deserves a thoughtful response.

What do I mean by this? It is the fact that, despite all the attacks and persecution throughout history, some Jewish people have done very well and have been extremely successful. The Rothschilds, for example, come to mind right away. Even to write about this is to potentially give credence to a negative stereotype, which I certainly do not want to do. But we also cannot ignore the reality of this phenomenon in world history, nor its impact.

A more recent example than the Rothschilds is the incredible rise of the Jewish oligarch billionaires in the former Soviet Union in the wake of Communism's demise. This group includes both Russian Jewish oligarch-businessmen as well as high-tech investors who became immensely wealthy after Communism's fall. They include names such as billionaire high-tech investor Yuri Milner and Mikhail Prokhorov, a leading Russian industrialist and owner of the Brooklyn Nets, as well as billionaire businessman Lev Leviev. A 2007 article in *The Guardian* stated that, "of the seven oligarchs who controlled 50% of Russia's economy during the 1990s, six were Jewish: [Boris] Berezovsky, Vladimir Gusinsky, Alexander Smolensky, Mikhail Khodorkovsky, Mikhail Friedman and Valery Malkin."[1]

These are just some of the best known names. There are many more.[2]

Anti-Semites want to imagine that there was some sort of global Jewish 'conspiracy' at work that allowed so many of these Russian Jewish oligarchs to rise to great prominence and wealth, but there was not. There are numerous explanations for the rise of the Jewish oligarchs in post-Soviet Russia and Ukraine - these could fill a separate volume.[3] I wrote about this phenomenon in a special edition of the journal *Mishkan* in 2011. In it, I noted that "when the shackles of Communism were thrown off and capitalism came to Russia and the rest of the former Soviet Union, some of these men were like kids in a candy store – they thrived under the new opportunities afforded them." Some emerged at the top, while many "other Russian Jews ended up at the bottom of the financial pyramid…"[4]

The point is that it was not any conspiracy that brought this about but the working out of history and, in part, the emergence of the phenomenon of Jewish giftedness that this book is all about.

But the anti-Semite is locked into conspiracies no matter what, while his ideological opposite, the modern liberal (including many liberal Jews), also rejects or ignores the idea of Jewish specialness and pre-eminence but for entirely different reasons.

We will look now at both anti-Semite and liberal responses to the idea of Jewish pre-eminence. Coming from completely different sides of the spectrum, neither group knows what to do with the phenomenon of Jewish pre-eminence and the reality behind it: anti-Semites cry 'conspiracy,' while liberals try to sweep it under the rug and pretend that it isn't there.

The Anti-Semite's View

For the anti-Semitic conspiracy theorist, the world stage has already been set and the 'fix' is in - the Jews, in his mind, are behind it.

When it comes to explaining Jewish eminence in so many fields, for example – such as leading to the awards of so many Nobel Prizes – a Gentile friend of mine who loves the Jewish people once shared with me a discussion he had with an anti-Semite on this very topic. The anti-Semite curtly rejected the distinction that so many Jewish people have achieved in winning Nobel Prizes and similar awards: 'Jews sit on all the committees' that award the prizes, he exclaimed to my friend.[5] So much for an objective assessment from an anti-Semite. But what else would we expect, really?

For the anti-Semite, the Jewish people are already condemned no matter what the reason: if they excel or gain prominence, wealth or fame, it is because they allegedly obtained some advantage 'unfairly'; but if these same or other Jews are brought low or suffer severely, it is because (in the eyes of those who are envious or bitter against them) 'they deserved it', 'they brought it on themselves', 'they are cursed', or any number of endless excuses and false rationalizations by those who already hate or despise the Jewish people. For those who hate them, the Jews can't win no matter what they do.

The Liberal View: Starting with Response to The Bell Curve

On the complete other side of the spectrum from the anti-Semite is the modern-day liberal. Liberalism today, at least among intellectuals and policymakers, unlike the classical liberalism of previous generations, is often marked by its intolerance of other points of view and its demand that others adhere to what is deemed 'politically correct' or acceptable. For many, it also reflects extreme secularism. Liberalism was once a great label that has been hijacked by more radical forces who have jettisoned the noble liberal traditions of the past. When I think of great Jewish liberals from the past, the names of Isaiah Berlin or former U.S. Associate Supreme Court Justice Felix Frankfurter, come to mind. But in this book when I use the term "liberal," I am *not* speaking of past generations of true liberals, Jewish or Gentile. Those generations have passed.

Modern liberalism, "progressivism" (or whatever we want to call it) is repelled by the notion that the Jewish people could have any special inherent quality as a race or as a people group that allows them to excel. Many liberals are especially appalled by the idea or publicly stated claim of Jewish superior intelligence or achievement in comparison with other people groups (even if that reality is quietly acknowledged privately or internally). One has only to look at how the 1994 book, *The Bell Curve*, by Richard J. Herrnstein and Charles Murray was greeted by liberals. Many responded with predictably ferocious antagonism to what the authors presented.[6] Their thesis was attacked from every conceivable angle. Many apparently found the implications completely repulsive, and they either savaged or just dismissed them out of hand.

Many liberals found passages like the following especially odious: "Jews – specifically, Ashkenazi Jews of European origins – test higher than any other ethnic group. A fair estimate seems to be that Jews in America and Britain have an overall IQ mean somewhere between a half and a full standard deviation above the mean, with the source of the difference concentrated in the verbal component...." As if this weren't 'bad' enough, the authors then had the audacity to relate their findings on IQs to Jewish levels of achievement in society: "These test results are matched by analyses of occupational and scientific attainment by

Jews, which consistently show their disproportionate level of success, usually by orders of magnitude, in various inventories of scientific and artistic achievement."[7]

But, despite liberals' rejection, it is still hard to ignore hard data. In 1954, "a psychologist took advantage of New York City's universal IQ-testing to identify all 28 children with measured IQs of 170 or higher." Of those 28 students who registered 170 or higher, 24 were Jewish.[8]

The Gilman Rejoinder: It's Just an "Image"

Cultural historian Sander L. Gilman looked at a variety of responses to Herrnstein and Murray. I don't know if Gilman is a 'liberal' or not as I define that term here, but his views would certainly be welcomed by many liberals. Regarding Hernstein and Murray, Gilman wrote that "Jewish savants [saw] the matter very differently" from some of their non-Jewish counterparts.[9] Gilman himself surely did. In 1996, he wrote in *Smart Jews: The Construction of the Image of Jewish Superior Intelligence*: "The myth of Jewish superior intelligence has its origin in the age of biological racism."[10]

So, apparently it's all a 'myth' in Gilman's eyes. He savages those who, like this author, believe that there is a special giftedness of the Jewish people, even with respect to the question 'Who are the Jews?'

Gilman appears to have little patience with those who share my point of view: "A careful examination of the literature on Jewish superior intelligence," he writes, "reveals that a unitary category of 'the Jews' is always imagined."[11]

His attitude assumes that those of us who refer to 'the Jews,' imagine them as a "unitary category,"[12] to use Gilman's phrase, implying that we are blindly ignorant of the many differences and cultural fractures that exist within the global Jewish community. If I am understanding Gilman correctly, this is absurd on its face and false in my view. Yes, there are those who write about 'the Jewish people' broadly without making any distinctions, but does that mean that we are unaware of such distinctions? Not at all.

Meanwhile, I might add, *everyone* who writes about 'the Jewish people' or 'the Jews' is therefore guilty of the same error.

To be thoroughly consistent – to even use the term 'Jewish' at all is to "imagine" a unitary category! We are therefore "imagining" a unitary category whenever we speak of "the Jews" in *any* context, or when anyone seeks to describe a Jewish *this* or a Jewish *that.* By this reasoning, one can never really escape the "unitary category" complaint in speaking of "the Jews"!

But such a conclusion is as ridiculous as it is inconsistent. *Of course* there are distinctly *Jewish* things in the world, and there are many different kinds of people who identify themselves as "Jews" who come from many different cultures and backgrounds, just as there are various categories of 'Dutchmen,' 'Buddhists,' 'gamers' or 'good swimmers,' or any other number of groups of ethnic or religious or sociological categories of people.

Gilman's complaint against those of us who write about this topic in seeing the Jewish people as "a unitary category" is empty and without merit.

Gilman simply does not want to admit the obvious. It is the question of Jewish superior intelligence itself that apparently rankles him as much as those who write about it.

Freud's Perspective

The title of Gilman's chapter on the "image" of Jewish superior intelligence describes this as "A Problem Still."[13] Interestingly enough, one person who - if he were still around - might argue with Gilman would be Sigmund Freud. When challenged once over the question of whether Jews were "a superior people," he replied, "I think nowadays they are...When one thinks that 10 or 12 of the Nobel winners are Jews, and when one thinks of their other great achievements in the sciences and the arts, one has every reason to think them superior."[14] Now, I don't agree with Freud's characterization of the Jewish people as "a superior people" in absolute terms – since I believe all people are equal in God's sight and Jews are not "superior" because some are gifted - but at least Freud 'got it' with respect to Jewish giftedness and pre-eminence.

Martin Peretz, then editor of *The New Republic*, noted that "a population which listens to Midori or Itzhak Perlman is likely to produce violinists from among its children," while the opposite is also the case.[15]

True, but which came first? Someone had to begin to appreciate or play good music in order to start the cycle and then perpetuate it from generation to generation.[16]

Achievement Under Attack

And that brings us to the final dimension of the liberal response to Jewish achievement and pre-eminence. To even acknowledge publicly that it exists is anathema to many liberals. At a minimum it makes many uncomfortable. Some would rather destroy or obfuscate opportunities where Jews can excel – in comparison with other groups – than allow the disparity to shine a light on those who do not measure up, as conservative African-American scholar Thomas Sowell explains.

Sowell, a Senior Fellow at the Hoover Institution, put his finger on this attitude in an August 2014 column titled, "Achievement under attack." Rather than celebrating the extraordinary achievements of some of New York City's elite public high schools – like Stuyvesant, Bronx Science and Brooklyn Tech – liberals want to erase the high admissions standards developed at those schools. All three of these schools have produced Nobel Prize winners, with five Nobel Prize winners in physics coming from Bronx Science alone! Instead of celebrating these achievements and hoping for more, some liberals have dubbed the Stuyvesant school, for example, as "a free prep school for Jews."[17]

Such schools exemplify the very opposite of the socialistic egalitarian views of many so-called 'progressives'. Achievement, pre-eminence and success are the enemies of such 'progressivism'.

Thus, liberals are conflicted and Jewish liberals especially so. They want to achieve; they want to be successful, *but they cannot shine a light too brightly on that success or else it goes against the grain of everything they believe about egalitarianism* – trying to give everyone equal opportunity and hoping that someday there might be equal outcomes.

Some liberals would readily sacrifice the potential for greater achievement on the altar of political correctness. This comes in the form of closing the doors to poor Jews of promise whose families may not be able to afford to send them to special private schools – rather than subsidize public schools which they believe have a too high (and, thus, 'unfair') admissions standard that other groups can't meet.

While the net result of lowering those standards may eventually mean fewer Nobel Prizes coming from such schools in the future – if and when they become 'dumbed down,' this is irrelevant to many radical progressives and liberals, for whom ideology, not achievement, is paramount.

Thus, while anti-Semites see 'conspiracy' when it comes to Jewish achievement and success, many liberals see 'unfairness'. Neither group can readily acknowledge the reality of what really is, since in both cases this would go against their core beliefs.

Not Wanting to Wear their Jewishness on their Sleeves

Another liberal reaction has to do with avoiding Jewish identity. Following the end of the Second World War, there were two primary streams impacting Jewish identity: one was the establishment of the State of Israel out of the ashes of the Holocaust; the second stream was somewhat contradictory to the first – it was the attempt and the desire to 'disappear' into the new world and just be evaluated on merit and achievement, not on ethnicity or religion. The French existential philosopher Jean Paul Sartre caught some of this mood when he expressed the sense that "many Jews throughout the West sought to be treated where they found themselves as *human beings* rather than Jews…"[18]

Israel is an Embarrassment to Some

The State of Israel is an embarrassment to some liberal Jews. This explains why some fraction of liberal Jews and Jewish radicals wish that the State of Israel would simply just 'go away.' The more that Israel is viewed by the world as an alleged 'pariah state,' the more conflicted and messy their own personal identities become. Some are conflicted, but they don't want to have to defend Israel; others would rather just join in with the chorus of condemnation.

With regard to those holding anti-Israel feelings, George Gilder asks, are such persons exponents of "excellence and accomplishment or of a leveling creed of frenzy and hatred?"[19]

This completes our look at critical responses to the thesis that the Jewish people have a corporate giftedness or blessing.

CHAPTER FIVE

Jewish Existence - Surviving the Odds

"The very survival, not to speak of the disproportionate influence, of this tiny group of people is a remarkable mystery."

ALAN DERSHOWITZ[1]

More Than Pre-Eminence

We have been focusing so far on Jewish giftedness and pre-eminence as a phenomenon. But it is much more than that. The *very existence* of the Jewish people itself – in the face of so many enemies and so many attempts throughout history to destroy them – is a marvel. There is no other way of describing it.

Marked for Destruction

From the destruction of the Second Temple in 70 AD until the re-establishment of the modern State of Israel in 1948, the Jewish people have been 'on the run,' so to speak. Dispersed throughout the world, persecuted, despised, ghettoized, conscripted into the military, forced to convert – every manner or means imaginable has been employed to knock them down, humiliate them, defame them, and, when none of those methods worked well enough for their persecutors - to destroy them - from the pogroms of Russia to the Nazi ovens of Auschwitz. Even centuries before the horrific slaughters of Bogdan Khmelnitsky's hordes against the Jews in 1648-1649 (which included some of the worst attacks in history against the Jews prior to the Holocaust), the Jews of Belgium (to choose one smaller subset of world Jewry) were completely wiped out between 1337 and 1370. As noted in the *Jewish Encyclopedia*, "so completely was the work of destruction done that scarcely a trace of their existence has remained."[2]

The Jewish people should not be around. Yet they survived all of this and at certain points in history even thrived.

I believe that the nations of the world will be judged for how they have treated the Jewish people throughout the centuries. As Messianic Jewish believers Haya and Menachem Benhayim once noted in *Bound for the Promised Land*: "We can see how nations and systems based on hatred of Jews time and again have been severely judged by God: ancient Babylon, medieval Spain, Czarist Russia, Nazi Germany. Do people ever learn from history?"[3]

There is a judgment coming. As the prophet Zechariah wrote, "For thus says the Lord of hosts, 'After glory He has sent me against the nations which plunder you, for he who touches you, touches the apple of His eye.'" (Zechariah 2:8)

But for now let us focus on the amazing *fact* of continued Jewish existence despite every hardship and form of opposition, despite the many dictators and empires throughout history that have sought to either assimilate or annihilate them.

A "National Vitality"

As J.C. Ryle noted nearly a century and a half ago, "Dispersed as they are, there is a principle of cohesion among them which no circumstances have been able to melt." Ryle continues: "Scattered as they are, there is a national vitality among them which is stronger than that of any nation on earth."[4]

A national vitality?! In many ways, this succinct phrase, *national vitality*, captures many of the attributes that I am trying to describe in this book. It means more than mere existence: the Jewish people have not just survived – including survival of the worst mass genocide in history, the Holocaust itself – given even the slightest degree of freedom and safety, they have *thrived*.

This is a phenomenon that has intrigued many observers throughout history – long before the issue of global pre-eminence emerged and certainly before the Holocaust took place.

Surviving the Odds

Rev. John Charles Ryle (1816-1900), the first Bishop of Liverpool in the Church of England, acknowledged the amazing continued existence of the Jewish people through the centuries. Writing in 1867, he stated: "I assert then that the Jews are at this moment a peculiar people, and utterly separate from all other people on the face of the earth..." This people, he continued, have been so "often fiercely persecuted and vilely treated. Yet to this moment they continue a distinct, isolated and separate nation, far more than any nation on the earth. Now how shall we account for this extraordinary state of things? How shall we explain the unique and peculiar position which the Jewish people occupies in the world?" How is it that this people "is neither destroyed, nor crushed, nor evaporated, nor amalgamated, nor lost sight of, but lives to this day as separate and distinct as it was when the arch of Titus was built in Rome?"[5] How indeed?

Adolph Saphir wrote in 1864: "...defying every climate and difficulty, and surviving all persecution, they live to witness to the truthfulness and power of God. Every effort has been made to destroy them, to take away their energy, their property, their influence; they have been cramped, despised, tortured and massacred, but they have only outlived their persecutors, but their energy has not been crushed, their intellect not dimmed, their determination not conquered, and their physical and mental vitality not diminished. That they exist is a miracle; but that they are what they are is still more wonderful...in every branch of thought and modern civilization-life they have shown themselves quite able to compete with any nation."[6]

No More Than an Historical Accident?

Nevertheless, many Jewish secularists today simply accept continued Jewish existence as a given, one that is merely an accident of history. Some "see no mysterious necessity, historical or divinely ordained, for the Jews to have come such a long way."[7] How people like Amos Oz and his daughter, Fania Oz-Salzberger, can write such a thing is beyond me. But they are atheists. They purposefully choose not to see any "mysterious necessity, historical or divinely ordained" not only for the Jews surviving but for also having "come such a long way."

If you want to take the Oz-Salzberger view that none of this – Jewish survival and success – is really that astonishing in terms of having existential meaning, well, then, you might as well put this book down now.

But if you think there might be something more to this than just an ongoing combination of fortuitous events, year after year, century after century, then read on. It is a phenomenon that many other observers throughout history have noted – people like Mark Twain, who obviously made his comments long before the establishment of the modern state of Israel and who from his perspective was not pushing any Biblical connotation to what he observed during his lifetime about the Jewish people.

Israel's existence and the Jewish people's continued survival in the face of otherwise insuperable odds – from Haman to Hitler – is a fact of history that begs for an explanation. It is, in fact, more than a phenomenon – to put it in modern scientific terms, it is a *singularity*.

CHAPTER SIX

Another View of the Holocaust

Author's Note: Whole libraries of volumes have been written about the Nazi era and the Holocaust. I offer in this chapter one perspective of a side of Nazi ideology that I believe goes beyond Aryan racism and merely scapegoating the Jews, and extends further to the heart of why Jewish *influence* was viewed by the Nazis as something that had to be rooted out of society if the latter were going to 'succeed' (in their minds) in their demonic and perverted plan of world domination. There is, of course, much more that can be said about this - I only scratch the surface here as to how this theme might relate to the question of Jewish giftedness and the power of abstract thought, building on some of George Gilder's thoughts about the Holocaust. I would be most interested in discussing this thesis further with scholars of the Holocaust and the Nazi period for additional perspectives pro and con. I rely heavily on the authenticity of the Table Talk stenographic record of Hitler's purported talks with some of his closest advisers for drawing some of my conclusions here.

Overview

We have already discussed some of the views of famed economist George Gilder. Gilder's admiration for the giftedness of the Jewish people seems to know no bounds, although he sees these gifts in purely economic and intellectual terms, not in any spiritual sense – nevertheless, the spiritual side of this phenomenon seems to hang in the background, although Gilder was unwilling to touch on it.

But that approach actually strengthens my overall argument, leaving the *reason* or *explanation* for Jewish pre-eminence unanswered, simply acknowledging its existence as a fact of reality.

The Holocaust through Gilder's Eyes

Gilder's view of the Holocaust takes an unusual twist. Most people view the Holocaust as an unspeakable tragedy in the history of mankind, which it certainly was. No value can be placed on the lives lost, while the depths of Nazi depravity and cruelty against millions of innocent men, women and children cannot be fathomed.

Yet Gilder takes us into one more aspect of the Holocaust that fewer have considered – he ponders *what might have been*. He puts it this way: in the Holocaust the world lost six million of "its most creative and productive citizens." It "was incomparably more destructive than other modern genocidal acts not because of the diabolical evil of the Nazis but because of the unique virtues and genius of its victims."[1] That is an extraordinary assertion; I believe that Gilder is wrong in how he constructs the argument - it should be a 'both-and' statement. The Holocaust was indeed "incomparably more destructive than other modern genocidal acts" *because of* the diabolical evil of the Nazis *and because of* "the unique virtues and genius of its victims."

Because of the special ethnic nature of the genocide, neither can the annihilation of millions of lives under Communism by Mao, Stalin, Pol Pot and all of their henchmen throughout history compare with the Holocaust.

Even the current unbelievable barbarism of the Muslim fanatics of the Islamic State (ISIS) in present-day Iraq and Syria – with their beheadings, burning of people alive, crucifixions, and other unspeakable horrors – cannot compare with the systematic slaughter of the Jewish people by the Nazis during the Holocaust. Hitler sought *a complete destruction* of the Jewish people just because they were Jews. The bloodthirsty murdering fanatics of ISIS at least sometimes give their victims a choice of conversion to Islam and paying a tax rather than death. During World War II, Jews had no such option.

Nazi Ideology versus Jewish Contributions & Giftedness

In April 1933, prior to the launch of World War II, the Nazis passed the Law for the Restoration of the Professional Civil Service. This law

Another View of the Holocaust

began a purge of Jews "from all public positions" but was later expanded to private institutions as well.[2]

A month later, in May 1933, the world-renowned German scientist Max Planck, who at the time was also president of the Kaiser Wilhelm Society, personally tried to intercede with Hitler on behalf of German Jewish scientists. One of those whom Planck sought to intercede for was world-famous German Jewish chemist Fritz Haber, who won the Nobel Prize in Chemistry in 1918 for inventing the Haber-Bosch process for synthesizing ammonia from nitrogen and hydrogen gases.[3]

Planck held one of the world's most prestigious posts in physics.[4]

Planck saw the damage that Nazi policies were beginning to have on German science as a result of their persecution of Jewish scientists in that country. According to accounts of that meeting (if accurate), Planck told Hitler that there were some Jews who were "valuable for mankind" - speaking of German Jewish scientists, and that they should not be treated in this way. Hitler reportedly flew into a rage and said, "A Jew is a Jew." He then reportedly concluded the meeting by saying: "If the dismissal of Jewish scientists means the annihilation of contemporary German science, *then we shall do without science for a few years.*"[5] (emphasis added) Earlier, Hitler claimed that "Everything" that Jewish scientists in Germany "created they have stolen from us," concluding: "We do not need them."[6]

If there was one idea that was especially repugnant to Nazi ideology, it was this: **that there were some Jewish contributions that were unique and of special importance to mankind.** It was that very concept that Planck was now telling Hitler – that some Jewish scientists' contributions to German science and to mankind in general – were indeed so special that such scientists certainly should not be persecuted but should be allowed to continue their work in peace. Hitler would have none of it – his demonic hatred of the Jews dwarfed all else. Instead, the Nazi propaganda machine went into overdrive denouncing what it termed "Jewish physics," with Einstein as its primary target: "In line with the grand design of Nazi ideology, Jewish physics had to be eradicated from the system."[7]

As far as we know, Hitler did not actually dispute Planck's bold assertion – either reformulated or repeated back to Planck by Hitler himself - that the dismissal of Jewish scientists from German universities might actually result in 'the annihilation of contemporary German science' – at least for a time. That was an amazing acknowledgement. Planck could not have dared to have been so audacious with Hitler if his argument had not been supported by strong compelling evidence to back up such a claim - which it was. But even though Hitler reportedly did not dispute Planck's assertion about German Jewish scientists, it still enraged him. His hatred of the Jews far outweighed anything else. Hitler apparently really thought that within "a few years" Germany could recover from the loss. Leaving the Jewish scientists in place would have been a direct affront to the Nazi worldview in his mind, regardless of the impact on Germany itself.

How did the Nazis reconcile the hard data showing Jewish pre-eminence with the anti-Semitic demands of their ideology? They dismissed it all as cleverness and trickery, denouncing their Jewish victims as parasites who sucked "the blood of [their] host, sapped and poisoned the creative energies of the body that fed [them]."[8] Jewish pre-eminence was dismissed by Hitler and the Nazis as a trick - part of the endless 'cleverness' of the Jews. This was so, even though, "in the aftermath of World War I," Jews began demonstrating "superior performance.... on intelligence tests and IQ exams." But neither this kind of data nor the earnest pleas of men like Planck meant anything to Hitler: he "simply worked around" the evidence, "emphasizing the gulf that separated creativity and original genius from mere intelligence and imitative cleverness." He saw the Jews as representing "evil genius" as opposed to Aryan "good genius."[9]

Ironically, Hitler's attitude on this crucial point cost him his goal of world domination. He was unwilling to compromise in his view toward Jewish giftedness in order to achieve his other goals. If he had, he might have been the first to obtain the nuclear bomb. Instead, as author Brian VanDeMark points out in *Pandora's Secrets: Nine Men and the Atomic Bomb*, the "irony of fate is that Hitler's actions removed the one group of people who would have been able to provide him with the instrument for world dominance he so eagerly sought."[10]

Under Nazi ideology, Hitler was out to prove to his fellow anti-Semites that the Jews were dangerous and destructive to the rest of the world – the very opposite idea from the view that they are 'special' in a positive, constructive sense. Dismissing their unique contributions across multiple fields, he and his fellow anti-Semitic haters chalked up Jewish success to trickery or cunning, not natural talent. Somehow in his mind they had connived their way into whatever success they had achieved.

The Nazis were dedicated to the proposition that Jewish influence was pernicious, not a gift to the world. They were determined to prove people like Planck wrong, whatever the cost in lives and German treasure to make the point. Soon, so-called 'Aryan physics,' supposedly stripped of any 'Jewish influence,' was being taught at German universities.

Nazi chief propagandist Joseph Goebbels compared the Jews to "an infectious contagion" that needed a "radical excision."[11]

For those who could comprehend his goals, in his January 30, 1939 speech before the Reichstag, Hitler made clear his desire to punish and annihilate the Jews. He asserted that they "possessed nothing except infectious political and physical diseases," and that Germany was by then "merely paying this people [the Jewish people] what it deserves." Later in that same speech Hitler referred to the Jews very sarcastically as those "splendid people" – meaning, of course, just the opposite.[12] By this time, if Germans like Planck still advocated for those whom they thought were "splendid people," they certainly could not do so publicly without endangering their own lives or freedom.

Mind over Matter

In acknowledging Jewish giftedness, author George Gilder has observed that the "reign of the algorithm vindicates the monotheist – and capitalist – intuition that the world in the first instance is a manifestation of thought."[13]

Hitler is said to have been "strangely obsessed with the intelligence of Jews" and viewed Einstein in particular "as an adversary and threat."[14] Einstein, in fact, "exposed through his very being the fraudulence of the Hitler myth, predicated as it was on the essential and exclusive nature of Aryan creativity."[15]

To return to the question of German physics and the Jews, in Nazi ideology it was not just a matter of 'recovering' or 're-defining' physics or mathematics in "Aryan" terms – it was also a conscious effort to alter how one approached reality. For the Nazis, life was a struggle between abstract thought versus the Aryan warrior mentality ('mind over matter'), where the Nazis sought through pure force and violence to achieve their goals. They believed that "matter must rule over mind,"[16] which is another reason why Planck's appeal fell on deaf ears. When the Nazis disparagingly denounced what they called "Jewish science," Gilder avers that, in one sense, the "jibe was on target." It's not that there was or is any specific realm of activity that we can say is "Jewish science" – which sounds offensive to the modern ear and is an oxymoron to anyone familiar with definitions in science. On the other hand, Gilder believes that there is a type of thinking about problems in which Jews excel: "The most valorous feats of Jews and the vilest slanders against them arise from this recognition: as the level of abstraction rises in any arena of competition, so does relative Jewish achievement." He sees this as an "anomaly" – one that is "easier to observe" than to explain.[17] Again, we are faced with *mystery.*

Instead of recognizing this, Hitler and the Nazis subscribed instead to conspiracy theories about the Jews. These lies became the essence of National Socialist policy and propaganda. Anti-Semitic conspiracy theories were and remain the precise opposite of accepting the view that the Jewish people are special and gifted. According to the anti-Semites, the Jewish people achieve prominence through cunning and trickery, not giftedness.[18]

The truth is exactly the opposite.

The real truth is that *there is* a natural giftedness, a blessing upon the Jewish people. But this is completely unpalatable to anti-Semites. Instead, they must invent conspiracy theories in order to try to explain away the clear evidence before them. As noted, there are many examples of this throughout history - from the fabricated *Protocols of the Elders of Zion* to Henry Ford's *The International Jew,* to Hitler and *Mein Kampf.*

Finishing the Story

To complete our story on Planck and Hitler's response, the destruction of German physics was not long in coming. In the case of the Göttingen Institute, which was then considered "the cradle of quantum mechanics" and of worldwide importance to science, the institute was soon an empty shell. After the Jewish members of the institute had been expelled, "the Nazi minister of education asked David Hilbert," who was then the best-known German mathematician, whether his institute had really "suffered so much from the departure of the Jews and their friends?" Hilbert replied no, the institute "didn't suffer... It just doesn't exist anymore."[19] The Nazis had destroyed one of the greatest scientific entities in the world in one fell stroke. Their hatred and venom for the Jews far outweighed their pragmatism.

Hitler so hated the Jews that he was out to prove that their removal from society and eventual annihilation didn't matter – he could kill the Jews and eventually make up for what was lost to science and the arts even if the Jews weren't around. In fact, he didn't want a world where Jewish enrichment made any difference whatsoever. He wanted to re-create the world in his own image where Jewish creativity and originality were no longer factors that impacted life and culture. He failed, but the cost of his demented effort remains incalculable.

Nazi ideology was thoroughly dedicated to disproving the thesis that I am presenting here – the very claim made by Planck to Hitler that so enraged the hate-filled dictator – that Jewish contributions were, in certain cases, very special and unique. While the Nazis slaughtered six million in their death camps, they failed to disprove this thesis in any way (in fact, it seems more prevalent now in the 20th and 21st centuries than ever before).

What Might Have Been

The issue goes far beyond just science itself – it goes to the heart of the very enrichment of the world. How many lives were extinguished and burned up in Nazi crematoria, who, had they lived, might have changed the world in extraordinary ways? We will never know...

The Nazis sought to create a 'master race' through force. Their methods were based on exterminating or enslaving everyone they considered racially 'impure'. The Jews were the special targets of their campaign of murder and destruction.

Nevertheless, the Jewish people, despite all the hardships they faced, still represented a threat to the Nazis – the threat of superior achievement. This enraged their enemies. If the record is correct, Hitler did not contradict Planck's assertion about the deleterious impact of Nazi anti-Jewish policy on German science. All the Nazis could do was, first dehumanize the Jews, then isolate them, then begin to destroy them, all the while deluding themselves that they (the Nazis) could replace those Jewish contributions through sheer force of will.

Trying to Remove All Jewish Influence

Despite all of their murderous attacks against the Jews, the Nazis still perceived that the Jewish 'web' of influence on society and culture in Europe was quite pervasive. The fact that Jewish influence on the cultures of Europe could not be so quickly destroyed was a continuing thorn in the Nazi side. According to one scholar: "For Hitler, the struggle against the Jews was indeed far more than a mere instrument of propaganda or a political means to achieve other ends. In his vocabulary, the Jews were constantly likened to vermin...to the germs of a deadly plague, to bacteria or malignant disease..."[20] In other words, Jewish influence was everywhere.

Hitler's strategy did indeed represent more than a political program to gain and expand his power base by scapegoating the Jews – he actually did see Jewish existence and influence as a 'disease' that needed to be removed from society by violent means. The only way, the Nazis reasoned, that they could really remove Jewish influence was to completely annihilate the Jews. But even that was not enough.

The 'Final Solution' only dealt with the monstrous methods of physical annihilation; it still did not fully address the Nazi 'problem' of how to fully extirpate Jewish influence from human culture as a whole. Nevertheless, the latter remained at the heart of the Nazi program: physical annihilation of the Jews and seizure of their property were only the first steps; Jewish *ideas* also had to be removed. Had the Third Reich succeeded militarily, this would have been an eventual goal also. The Jews excelled at abstract thinking more than any other people. This was the polar opposite of Matter-over-Mind.

Nazism as Anti-Christian, Anti-Jewish and Anti-Bolshevik

A future phase in the National Socialist program – after killing the Jews – would have been to destroy what the Nazis saw as Jewish influence in the development of both Bolshevism and Christianity. In the 'Table Talk' stenographic record of Hitler's innermost thoughts and plans – transcribed from 1941-1944 – as part of his long-term strategy, the German dictator clearly intended to eventually eradicate Christianity as well: "The heaviest blow that ever struck humanity," he reportedly said, "was the coming of Christianity." He also said: "Bolshevism is Christianity's illegitimate child. Both are inventions of the Jew." Hitler concluded: "The war will be over one day. I shall then consider my life's final task will be to solve the religious problem."[21] Hitler wanted to eliminate every vestige of Jewish influence in all areas of life, and this eventually would include even Christianity itself because of its Jewish origin.

The late Robert Wistrich, professor of modern Jewish history at Hebrew University and author of *Hitler and the Holocaust*, believed that Hitler and the leading Nazis "were all fanatically anti-Christian, though this was partly hidden from the German public…" Hitler was convinced that "Judaism, Christianity and Bolshevism represented one single pathological phenomenon of decadence…" Wistrich continued: "At the heart of Nazism, despite its cunning pretense of 'positive Christianity,' there was a deep-seated rejection of the entire civilization that had been built on Judeo-Christian ethics."[22]

Hitler asserted that "The notions represented by Jewish Christianity were strictly unthinkable to Roman brains…" Christianity, he believed, "had been responsible for the extinction of the Roman Empire and the destruction of fifteen hundred years of civilization in a single stroke." Wistrich concluded: "It is indeed striking that as he launched the Holocaust Hitler increasingly sought to emphasize the parallels between Christianity and Bolshevism as subversive doctrines destructive of all human culture."[23]

The Wannsee Protocol and Nazi Fears of a Jewish Revival

The Wannsee Mansion outside of Berlin was where the infamous plan for the 'Final Solution' of the Jewish people was hatched.[24] The so-called Wannsee Protocol for the annihilation of the Jews of Europe was promulgated on January 20, 1942. A key section of the protocol is reproduced here in two slightly different translations:

> *"The possible final remnant will, since it will undoubtedly consist of the most resistant portion, have to be treated accordingly, because it is the product of natural selection and would, if released, act as the seed of a new Jewish revival (see the experience of history.)"* http://remember.org/wannsee.html

This same text was translated slightly differently in a 2012 book by Israel Defense Force (IDF) General Elazar Stern titled, *Struggling Over Israel's Soul.* Stern's parents both survived Auschwitz:

> *"Those remaining will have to be given suitable treatment because they unquestionably represent the most resistant segments, and therefore constitute a natural elite that, if allowed to go free, would serve as a nucleus for a renewed Jewish entity."*[25]

Both translations of the protocol look at those Jews about to be destroyed as constituting "the most resistant portion" of the Jewish population. This was absolutely ridiculous, of course, since most of the Nazis' victims were simply frightened people who had been isolated, humiliated, starved, stripped and dehumanized in every way possible before even arriving at the death camps. Acts of courageous defiance against the Nazi were limited and highly controversial within Jewish communities. Although there were many individual and small-group acts of courage and defiance, as well as spectacular efforts – such as the Warsaw Ghetto uprising, the great majority of the Jewish community was passive in the face of the terror that sought to destroy them. That sad fact gave rise to the phrase – 'Never Again!' – that the Jewish people, and especially the people of Israel – will never again allow themselves to be placed in the position of being victims of those who wish to destroy them simply because they are Jews.[26]

Numerous books have been written as to the reasons for this passivity in the face of unrelenting Nazi hatred. It is not my intention to further analyze those reasons here; rather, my desire is to explain that, despite this reaction, the Nazis still harbored the fear that 'the Jews' might somehow still unite and rise up against them.

This observation brings our discussion full circle: Hitler wanted to *force* his ideology onto reality (Matter-over-Mind), and that was all that mattered to him. His view was that the Jewish people had so infected the modern world that only their complete physical annihilation – and the eventual removal of all the ideas and movements they had influenced – would allow the Nazis' ideal Aryan Man prototype begin to emerge.

The Post-Holocaust World

We shall now contrast what the Nazis tried to destroy (the Jewish people) versus what emerged out of the ashes of the Holocaust – the modern-day state of Israel.

Today the storm clouds of anti-Semitism and modern Jew-hatred are once more raising their ugly heads with demonic fury. The haters are back, and little Israel, which was once viewed in heroic terms by most of the world, is more and more being characterized or cast in the role of a 'pariah state'.

Modern-day Israel has its shortcomings, but it is also located in the roughest neighborhood in the world. It is often cited as the only democracy in the Middle East, but it is more than that. Gilder makes the argument that modern-day Israel is the key to the world's survival.

"The Israel Test": What Does It Signify?

As already noted, Gilder's book, *The Israel Test*, is not about spiritual things but about economics and creativity. He argues that Israel holds a special place in the world due to its extraordinary contributions to technology and science. But he goes further. Gilder views "Israel as the leader of human civilization, technological progress, and scientific advance."[27] Some may reject that assertion out of hand, but it would be worthwhile to understand why Gilder makes such an assertion.

The actual idea that Israel could or should be a center for world scientific achievement goes back to Theodore Herzl himself and even predates him. Herzl's messianism and that of many early Zionists took a strong scientific form.[28] The early Zionist founders envisioned a state in Palestine that could positively impact the whole world, especially the developing world, through Jewish contributions to science and human knowledge. There was a sense that "the luster of scientific success added gleam to Zionist aspirations." For many, the image of the Zionist "pioneer-scientist" in the Land inspired many young people and others "caught up in the drama of building a Jewish homeland."[29] Today, Israel "has more engineers and scientists per capita than any other country" in the world and also "produces more scientific papers per capita than any other nation."[30]

The Vision Today: Applying the "Test"

That was then. Much of that original Zionist luster of faith in science is gone, but the results of what those early Jewish pioneers achieved in laying the foundation for a successful state are not. This is where Gilder picks up the argument and forcefully develops it.

He paints the situation in stark economic terms: "What is your attitude toward people who excel you in the creation of wealth or in other accomplishments? Do you aspire to their excellence?" he asks, or do you bitterly resent it? "Do you admire and celebrate exceptional achievement," or do you seek to attack it? It is a struggle "between creative excellence and covetous 'fairness,' between admiration of achievement versus envy and resentment of it."[31] This is the "Israel test," and it is a *moral* test of one's views, according to Gilder.[32]

Gilder further asserts that, in our current age of information, "when the achievements of mind have widely outpaced the power of masses and material force, Jews have forged much of the science and wealth of the era." While this process has occurred in many countries under a variety of circumstances, it is the State of Israel itself which "today concentrates the genius of the Jews." In a broad sense, the "forces of civilization in the world," he adds, "continue to feed upon the quintessential wealth of mind epitomized by Israel." In other words, the whole world has benefited tremendously by the intellectual capital created in Israel. Gilder adds that "Israel's technical and scientific gifts to global progress loom with...majesty over all others' contributions outside the United States." [33]

Jewish observer Yuri Slezkine, who is originally from the former Soviet Union, put it this way: this age, "the Modern Age," he calls it, "is the Jewish Age," and the last century in particular, the twentieth century, was "the Jewish Century." He writes that in "the age of capital, [the Jews] are the most creative entrepreneurs; in the age of alienation, they are the most experienced exiles; and in the age of expertise, they are the most proficient professionals." [34]

Start-Up Nation

Gilder further asserts that "the leading entrepreneurial talent of the world is disproportionately Jewish." He adds that, "Even though Jews are a tiny minority of less than a tenth of 1 percent of the world's population," at the same time they also "comprise perhaps a quarter of the world's paramount capitalists and entrepreneurs." [35] According to Dan Senor and Saul Singer's remarkable book, *Start-Up Nation: The Story of Israel's Economic Miracle*, "key economic metrics demonstrate that Israel represents the greatest concentration of innovation and entrepreneurship in the world today." [36]

A 1998 article commemorating Israel's fiftieth anniversary stated that "high tech industrial parks are springing up like wildflowers in the desert." [37] Semyon Litsin, a Russian Jewish immigrant to Israel, is considered the father of flash technology. In a recent interview, he noted that "the percentage of successful Israeli companies is three times higher than what it is in Silicon Valley." [38] The authors of *Start-Up Nation* note that "Israel specializes in high-growth entrepreneurship – startups that wind up transforming entire global industries." Beyond having "the highest density of startups in the world...more Israeli companies are listed on the NASDAQ exchange than all companies from the entire European continent." [39]

"A high-tech light unto the nations?"

Along the lines of Gilder's thinking that Israeli high-tech innovation could change the world, Todd L. Pittinsky, a senior lecturer at the Harvard Business School, believes that "Silicon Wadi," as the Israeli high-tech sector is often called, could "put its wizardry to a higher good, becoming a light unto an increasingly wired world in which so many still suffer from poverty, oppression, illness, and loneliness..."[40]

Resented by many

But this success and future promise are deeply resented by many. With respect to Israel itself, as Gilder points out, the fact that Israel has emerged as "a spearhead for the global economy and vanguard of human achievement" is not welcome news to those who envy or resent everything that Israel stands for. They seek retribution against the nation and a redistribution of wealth: For the haters, "Israel's wealth stems not from Jewish creativity and genius but from cadging aid from the United States or seizing valuable land and other resources from Arabs."[41]

CHAPTER SEVEN

Jewish 'Drivenness' and Generosity

Overview

In his book, *The Jewish Phenomenon*, author Steven Silbiger asserts that one of the 'keys' to Jewish success in the modern world is being "psychologically driven to prove something."[1]

Where does *drivenness* come from? Why do the Jewish people – corporately at least – seem to have it in abundance? Whom are they trying to prove something to? The first two questions remain more or less a mystery but not the third: the Jews are trying to "prove" themselves to the larger Jewish collective, but mostly to the Gentile world at large. This seems to be a given. Eric Weiner says that this attitude, which he attributes to Scots as well as Jews, stems "from a deeply felt tribal insecurity, a need to prove something to the world."[2] Authors Amy Chua and Jed Rubenfeld in their book, *The Triple Package*, describe this as a "chip on the shoulder...'I'll show them' mentality," but they also ascribe this attitude to some other highly successful groups in America that they've studied, including Chinese Americans, Indian Americans, Nigerian Americans, and others.[3]

Silbiger acknowledges that "Jews have always been trying to gain acceptance, while at the same time maintaining their cultural identity." This can lead to internal conflict – a striving for success and acceptance in order to show that, "if they wish, they are worthy to sit down at a table with anybody." Silbiger adds that "Jews are motivated to achieve and succeed" largely "to prove their individuality and mastery of their own destiny."[4] Jews are not alone in this, of course. Other groups strive for acceptance in every society if they are (or are perceived to be) a minority in that culture.

It is no accident that so many Jewish parents and relatives place great expectations upon the Jewish child from the child's earliest moments of consciousness. It is, rather, a collective Jewish way of expressing, 'We are here; we have a purpose; we must live out that purpose, whatever it is, to the utmost of our strength, talent and ability, and you, child, are the most recent person in a long line of those who came before you who also strove to live out that purpose.' As such, every Jewish child in one way or another when they come into the world is a faint representation of messianic hopes for the Jewish people as a whole: 'perhaps *this* child will fulfill a great destiny for both the Jewish people and for the world' is the hope. So, there is a distinct striving for *excellence* that is imprinted almost from birth on many Jewish children by their parents and the community. In many ways, this feeling or burden or whatever it is, is inescapable and haunts many Jews throughout their lives. Many are seeking all their lives to fulfill some great unseen duty or requirement that has been laid upon them – one that can never be fully satisfied (or so it seems): 'Am I good enough?'; 'Have I achieved enough?'

Besides succeeding personally and for their families, they feel they must strive to achieve whatever that great unknown purpose or destiny is of trying to make the world a better place. This is the Jewish 'burden,' so to speak – a burden carried by both the ultra-Orthodox on the one hand and even among many of the most secular atheistic Jews on the other hand. *Tikkun olam* – repairing a broken world by all means necessary, whether striving to become the world's best Talmudic scholar ever or perhaps the smartest theoretical physicist the world has ever seen – these are both examples of trying to fulfill that destiny.

It All Goes Back to Jacob

The striving itself – where does it originate? We do not know where it comes from, but we do know where it originated. That may sound like a complete contradiction, but it is not. The source of the striving is unknown but not the person it originated with. It originated with the patriarch Jacob (Israel) himself. Jacob is the one who 'strove with God' and prevailed (Genesis 32: 25-29). He is the 'striver with God' and the 'striver with men' – the one whose name was changed to *Isra-el* to reflect his new-found role.[5] Ever since, the Jewish people have been known as *Am Yisrael*, literally, "the people who have striven with God."

So, we have an entire people whose very name and purpose is 'to strive.' This is the Biblical origin of 'drivenness.' Is this not amazing?

Drivenness and 'Davka'

Ioan James states: "In those areas where originality is valued, the greater intensity of the Jewish mind is reflected in an incessant striving for greater originality."[6] Even the title of James' book, *Driven to Innovate*, reflects this: many segments of the Jewish community are indeed highly driven to achieve and to excel. One of the most driven Jewish population segments is the Russian Jewish community, with which I am very familiar. Natan Sharansky, one of the world's most famous Russian Jews - who spent years in a Soviet prison for agitating to emigrate to Israel - put it this way: because of anti-Semitism, Russian Jews in the then Soviet Union at the time "had to be exceptional in [their] profession, whether it was chess, music, mathematics, medicine or ballet... That was the only way to build some kind of protection for yourself, because you would always be starting from behind."[7]

This attitude has manifested itself in various ways, including, in some cases, a type of drivenness which is *never* satisfied. Any achievement – however substantial or extraordinary – is never enough. Why? Because someone else *might* do better, or some unforeseen circumstance might swoop down to steal away what has been achieved. These feelings are usually derived from a deep insecurity, one which finds it next to impossible *to rest*, to simply accept and celebrate achievement and success on their own terms without pushing for more. Sergey Brin, co-founder of Google, captured this feeling in describing his father's likely reaction to the news that a particular high school in Israel that Sergey was visiting had "received seven out of the top ten places in a math competition throughout all Israel." This was mostly a Russian Jewish high school that specialized in math and science. Brin said that his father would probably respond not with praise but rather with a challenge: *"What about the other three [spots]?"*[8] In other words, having 7 out of the top 10 spots in the whole country would not be good enough. Young people like Sergey must have felt enormous pressure to excel in such an environment. As author Alfred Kazin described attitudes in his Jewish immigrant neighborhood more than a half century ago: if a child received B grades on exams or papers, "the whole house went into mourning."[9]

I am reminded of the Jewish joke: "What is a Jewish student with a master's degree? *Answer:* A dropout." (because he or she hasn't already gone on to get a PhD).

In a broader sense, the fear of potentially falling behind and putting one's career at risk by *not* excelling is complemented by the protection offered (almost as a type of career insurance) in the larger Gentile world of trying to be the very best in one's field. Anti-Semitism against Jews *in general* can perhaps be overcome – at least one might think - by a Jewish individual's *specific* worth as a highly-valued professional. Thus, the Jewish drive to excel can be linked, at least in part, as a reaction to anti-Semitism – both as a protection from it, as well as an effort to prove anti-Semites wrong. But while these explanations are insightful, they are still incomplete.

Another means of proving anti-Semites wrong is captured by the Hebrew word *davka*. This has special meaning in Israel – a nation surrounded by enemies. Israelis seek to persevere and to succeed *in spite of* adversity and the opposition of those who hate them. One assessment describes it this way: 'The more they attack us, the more we will succeed.'[10]

A Spiritual Side to Drivenness

There is also a spiritual side to Jewish drivenness, although it may not be obvious. Many Jewish children are driven to try to succeed in order to bring *naches* (Yiddish for "joy") to their parents. The phrase, *shep naches*, to "experience joy, especially from children,"[11] is one of the highest forms of joy expressed in a Jewish household. That joy may equate to "bragging rights."[12] Another Yiddish word, to *k'vel* (or 'kvell"), is to take great pride in the achievements of one's children. In the past, in the Pale of Settlement, the *kvelling* might have been, 'Our son (or son-in-law), *the rabbi!*' Or later in America: 'Our son *the doctor!*' Or perhaps today: 'Our son (or daughter) *the scientist!*'

James Gleick, author of *Genius*, a biography about Jewish physicist Richard Feynman, attempted to capture this attribute. Gleick argued that the "parents' motives are selfish – for nothing can magnify parents in the eyes of their neighbors as much as the child's success." There is some truth in that, but I think that, standing alone, it remains an incomplete explanation. Gleick cited Richard's father, Melville Feynman, who once wrote to Richard on this very theme. The elder Feynman told his son that, when a Jewish child is very successful, "the neighbors help the ego of the parent along by acclaiming the wonders of the child and by admiring the parent for *his* success..."[13]

Silbiger writes that this characteristic in the Jewish community "is a very powerful motivator" for those children trying to please their parents, but "it is also a heavy burden."[14]

From the standpoint of both the parent and the child, there can be great *naches* in special achievement and success, but **there can never be *enough* of it**. In other words, there can be a lot of 'kvelling' among both parent and child, but never full contentment. Whatever success is achieved, financial or otherwise, this can never fully satisfy.

In that sense, Jewish drivenness can become a factor that becomes stronger and stronger, never leading to real contentment despite whatever success is achieved. Instead, the quest for success may not lead to happiness but may drive the person to despair or to the therapist's couch – perhaps to the rabbi; but the rabbi, as a key member of the community, may also be viewed as part of the problem in some cases. So, great success may be achieved but not necessarily with happiness or contentment. A PBS television program called "Hava Nagila (The Movie)" has an exchange where a young man named Josh Kun (a so-called "expert" on the song "Hava Nagila") is talking to a rabbi in a Jewish delicatessen. They are discussing life, Jews and happiness. Josh says, "We Jews aren't known for being happy." The rabbi, clutching his chest with faux hurt, says: 'Josh, you've wounded me!' But in mock exasperation, Josh delivers the ultimate response: "But we invented *therapy*!"[15]

Though funny on the surface, there was a lot of truth behind this good-natured exchange. Many Jewish comedians are known as being among the funniest people in the world but not for being happy and content themselves.

Happiness is often equated with contentment. Semyon Litsin, the famed Russian Jewish Israeli entrepreneur who is considered the father of flash drive technology, was quoted as saying that "a Jew who is content with everything simply does not exist."[16]

The reality of life is that lasting satisfaction and true contentment can never be achieved in this way; this is the spiritual heart of the matter.

God has given the Jewish people corporately great gifts, but individual Jewish achievers can never find true contentment in their accomplishments alone. That is because neither they nor any other human being was designed that way. If anything, God would like to use the emptiness of worldly success to drive people to Himself, both Jew and Gentile.

Success and the drive to achieve success are certainly not wrong – what is wrong (and this is true for everyone, Jew or Gentile at any station of life) is using them as a crutch to define one's very self-worth and choking God out of the process.

Drivenness comes in part from a desire to excel, which is a laudable and necessary attribute for almost anyone who wants to achieve something worthwhile in life. There are various types of *drivenness*. I, for example, have felt *driven* to write this book. That feeling has come from a sense of obligation deep within. Being driven is something that is important for most superior athletes or serious innovators. In the Western world at least, we celebrate drivenness. But at what point does *drivenness* take over one's life? At what point does it reflect a certain restlessness about life and the purpose of life?

Some drivenness can lead to restlessness. This is the opposite of what God means for us as human beings. God's intent for us is found in the Aaronic blessing, where the Lord lifts up His countenance upon us, and give us peace (Numbers 6: 24-26)

Part of the restlessness that many Jewish people experience is, I believe, imparted to them by God as a means of trying to draw them to Himself....

Jewish Generosity

Jewish giftedness and drivenness are often tied to another phenomenon that is also a key part of *tikkun olam* – Jewish generosity and philanthropy. Jewish philanthropy is especially striking – substantial gifts or endowments by Jewish donors are intended to lift the culture or well-being of an entire community or society, whether one is considering a new hospital, gifts to a university, an art museum, or underwriting the concerts of a great musician. As Silbiger writes: "...Jews happen to be the most philanthropic ethnic group in the country...Jews are among the largest contributors to universities, libraries, hospitals, museums, symphonies and opera companies."[17]

In this we see examples of *tikkun olam* in one of its purest and most direct forms. If one is very successful in business, for example, it is a way of giving back. While none of this is confined to Jews alone – throughout history there have been great donors and 'givers' from across the social and ethnic spectrum, Jews *excel* at the extent of their giving to improve society as they see it.

One of the best-known Jewish philanthropists from the past was Julius Rosenwald of the Sears, Roebuck empire. He helped finance thousands of so-called "Rosenwald Schools," working with the Tuskegee Institute and black parents in communities across the South to improve the educational opportunities of African Americans. He gave away the equivalent of $750 million in today's dollars to those schools and many other needy causes.[18]

Often this level of incredible generosity and philanthropy is individually-driven or family-driven, as in the case of David Rubenstein mentioned earlier.[19] At other times, it flows from various groups or organizations , such as the "the Mega Group," or the "Study Group," founded in 1991, which the *Wall Street Journal* in 1998 described in part as a "loosely organized club of twenty of the wealthiest and most influential Jewish businessmen in America...." The group's members "seek partnerships for their individual causes and learn from one another about their successes and challenges" through the group.[20]

Like Rubenstein, Russian-Jewish billionaire and particle physicist Yuri Milner, who lives in Moscow and who made a fortune through investments in Facebook and other technology ventures, is also a very special case. His generosity extends to spending huge amounts of money through his Fundamental Physics Prize program, described by *The New York Times* as "the most lucrative academic prize in the world."[21] In July 2015, he also announced a $100 million plan, called "Breakthrough Initiatives," which is described as "the most powerful, comprehensive and intensive scientific search ever undertaken for signs of intelligent life beyond earth."[22] While I think that Milner is wasting his money in this latter effort, his gesture is certainly a grand one.

Billionaire businessman Carl Icahn is listed as "one of the top fifty generous people in the United States." Besides many philanthropic ventures, he recently gave $200 million in one year to the Mt. Sinai Medical School in New York City. His foundations include the Icahn Charitable Foundation, Foundation for a Greater Opportunity, and the Children's Rescue Fund. Icahn also "owns controlling interest in many major corporations, including Time Warner, Marvel and Nabisco."[23]

We will now take a brief detour from the thesis that the Jewish people are special to looking at the idea that America herself was providentially chosen by God to be a sanctuary nation for the Jewish people.

CHAPTER EIGHT

America: A Special 'Sanctuary Nation' for the Jewish People

"... those of us who live in America are more influential and more secure than Jews have ever been." [1]

ERIC H. YOFFIE

Coming to America

The first Jewish person to arrive in the Americas was a Spaniard named Luis de Torres, who joined Columbus in 1492 on his famous voyage. De Torres was an interpreter who could speak Hebrew, Aramaic, and Arabic and was "the first person of Jewish birth to settle in the New World." De Torres settled in present-day Cuba. [2]

After de Torres, the "first Jew to set foot on North American soil was probably Elias Legardo," who arrived in Virginia aboard the *Abigail* in 1621. [3]

In 1654, the first Jewish *community* of some twenty-three Jews arrived in the New World, coming to present-day New York (then known as 'New Amsterdam' under the Dutch). [4] Thus, a Jewish presence in America is older than the founding of the United States itself, while a Jewish impact on New York City itself – in one form or another - has existed for more than three and a half centuries.

This first small contingent and another that arrived in 1655 were not exactly welcomed with open arms by officials on the ground – far from it. One protesting official of the Dutch Reformed Church in New Amsterdam, Dominie Johannes Megapolensis, complained back to Dutch authorities in Holland about whether "the immovable and obstinate Jews" should stay in the Dutch settlement. At the same time, however, the church did donate funds toward the plight of those "Jews [who] have come weeping and bemoaning their misery." Megapolensis himself was not necessarily anti-Semitic - he apparently was upset with *nearly everyone* in New Amsterdam who didn't agree with his views. In that same letter back to Holland he denounced "Papists, Mennonites and Lutherans among the Dutch" in New Amsterdam, as well as "many Puritans or Independents, and many Atheists and various other servants of Baal among the English...who conceal themselves under the name of Christians..." To Megapolensis, it was just an unworkable religious hodge-podge. He thought that also allowing Jews to settle permanently in New Amsterdam would create "still greater confusion."[5] New Amsterdam's despotic colonial governor Peter Stuyvesant, who, unfortunately, *was* anti-Semitic in his language and much harsher in his words than Megapolensis, referred to the Jewish people as a "deceitful race," "hateful enemies and blasphemers of the name of Christ." He did not want this small new group to "further infect and trouble this new colony."[6]

As it turned out, Megapolensis and Stuyvesant did not have their way. They were overruled. The Jewish community in New Amsterdam was able to stay for a number of years.[7]

Howard M. Sachar tells the tale of the ups and downs of this first Jewish community in his magisterial work, *A History of Jews in America.* Eventually, because of the impending takeover of New Amsterdam by the British, all the Jews from this original community decided to leave by 1663, except for one enterprising and dedicated pioneer settler by the name of Asser Levy.[8]

Within a few decades after the British takeover, Jews began immigrating back again to what was now called 'New York' (named for England's Duke of York). New York then became "the logical first port of call" for Jews arriving in North America. Under the terms of the 1667 Treaty of Breda, Britain "guaranteed full rights of worship, trade, individual property, and inheritance to all inhabitants of the former New Netherlands," which included the Jewish residents of the colony. By the end of the 1600s, there were about 250 Jews in the American British colonies overall.

Initially, the colonies had different policies and attitudes: Pennsylvania and New Jersey were welcoming to Jews, as were South Carolina and Georgia, but Jews were not welcome in Maryland or in New England - with the exception of Roger Williams' Rhode Island, which honored freedom of conscience.[9]

By the time of the American Revolution, the situation for Jews in America had continued to improve. Jews in England and the Netherlands were by then enjoying a high degree of religious and political freedom. But regardless of this, as Howard Sachar notes, Jews "were much better off in the New World than in the Old." They could live and engage in any trade anywhere in British North America without fear or discrimination. As Sachar concludes: "By 1776, the two thousand Jews of colonial America unquestionably were the freest Jews on earth."[10] On August 1, 1776, Francis Salvador, a Jewish representative of the South Carolina provisional congress, was one of the first Americans to be killed in the Revolution, while some 100 Jews served in the Continental Army.[11] By the time the Constitution was ratified, a newspaper account of a celebratory parade in Philadelphia described a "rabbi of the Jews walking arm and arm" with clergy of various Christian denominations. It was a scene, author Charles Silberman wrote, in *A Certain People: American Jews and Their Lives Today*, that one could not even have imagined "in any European city of that (or a considerably later) era."[12]

Opening Its Doors

This was America's early history. The fact is that America has nearly always opened its doors to the Jewish people, put out the welcome mat out and facilitated their integration into American life and culture. Yes, discrimination and anti-Semitism were sometimes part of the story, but, on balance, the New World was exactly that – a *New* World quite different from anything the Jewish people had experienced in Europe or throughout most of their history. In this respect, it is truly appropriate that the woman who wrote the famous poem, "The New Colossus": "Give me your tired, your poor, your huddled masses yearning to be free..." – Emma Lazarus (1849-1887), was Jewish, a descendant of "a group of predominantly Spanish-Portuguese Jews who began to arrive on the shores of America in the 1650s…"[13] One scholar notes that "The New Colossus" is "perhaps the most famous poem an American Jew ever wrote…"[14]

America, I believe, has been blessed in part because of its protection and support of the Jewish people. In his book titled, *Has God Finished with Israel?* author Rob Richards states, "Historically, the United States has welcomed Jewish people to its shores and, more consistently than any other nation, affirmed the homeland for Jews. Has God blessed that nation in part for that reason?"[15] Anita Libman Lebeson, writing in 1931, said: "Here then is the simple story of the men and women who looked upon America, and saw that it was good, and made it their home – the record of *Jewish Pioneers in America.[16]*

Although there have been some stains on America's past treatment of Jews – pockets of anti-Semitism,[17] past discrimination by setting Jewish quotas at some universities, the denial of entry into the United States of the ship MS *St. Louis* in 1939, which was full of German Jewish refugees trying to escape Nazi Germany,[18] it has generally been the United States – except for the State of Israel – which has served as the greatest and most welcoming 'sanctuary' for the Jewish people in the history of the world. Millions of Jewish refugees and freedom-seekers have been welcomed to America's shores and flourished in American society. That is an indisputable fact.

In his 2014 book, *Violins of the Holocaust*, James Grymes also makes the 'sanctuary' analogy with respect to Jewish immigrant musicians during World War Two: "All in all, the United States served as the sanctuary for approximately half of all Jewish immigrants from Germany and Austria, including 465 musicians."[19] This general policy of welcome to the Jewish people extended back to George Washington himself and his famous 1790 "Letter to the Jews of Newport [Rhode Island]." In that letter, America's Founding Father promised liberty and safety to the nation's Jewish residents. He cited Micah 4:4: "every one shall sit in safety under his own vine and fig tree, and there shall be none to make him afraid."[20] Other than the prejudice of some and the historical stains previously noted, that general welcome has continued to the present day.

But there are those historians who persist in the view that somehow America itself is at fault for not doing what it needed to do in saving more Jewish refugees from the Holocaust. Like many, I, of course, believe that the United States should have opened its doors to millions of Jewish refugees from Hitler's Europe, not the paltry 132,000 who were received from the countries of the Third Reich from the period 1933 to 1945. But the implication (whether verbalized or not) that America closed its doors to Jews because of a passive Christian anti-Semitism or that the majority of the people of the United States did not care what was happening to the Jews of Europe – is not supported by the facts.

David Hollinger, for example, tells us that "it cannot be repeated often enough that American authorities rejected multiple opportunities to receive or otherwise save Jews who looked to the United States for help," and he specifically cites the period from 1933-1945.[21] Fair enough, but who exactly were those "American authorities" who rejected these multiple requests? *It was the administration of Franklin Delano Roosevelt, liberal icon and ideological champion of progressive causes.*

Roosevelt is still strongly admired by an overwhelming majority of American Jews to this day. That's actually putting it mildly. Roosevelt was re-elected four times with massive majorities of the Jewish vote. Nevertheless, Roosevelt Administration State Department official R. Borden Reams opposed allowing more Jewish refugees from Europe into the United States – despite the fact that Jewish representatives from the Emergency Committee to Save the Jewish People of Europe were lobbying the U.S. government to do so much more. Another Roosevelt Administration official, Assistant Secretary of State Breckinridge Long, writing in his diary in January 1944, quietly praised Roosevelt's callous political shrewdness in creating the War Refugee Board and letting New York Jews *think* that he was really trying to help: "This will encourage them to think the persecuted may be saved and possibly satisfy them – politically,"[22] when in reality Roosevelt was doing next to nothing to save Jewish lives.

It was important for the Roosevelt Administration *to appear* concerned, especially after the Republican National Convention in June 1944 "adopted a first-ever plank endorsing rescue and Jewish statehood." According to Dr. Rafael Medoff, founding director of The David S. Wyman Institute for Holocaust Studies, "American Jewish Congress leader Rabbi Stephen S. Wise warned a Roosevelt aide [at that time] that if the Democrats failed to adopt a similar plank, 'it will lose the President 400,000 or 500,000 votes.'"[23] Medoff concludes: "in actuality, the State Department," and, by implication, Roosevelt himself, "never lifted a finger for [the] rescue" of Jews during the Holocaust.[24]

Liberals – including those liberal Jews today who condemn America's closing its doors to more Jewish refugees during the Second World War - need to seriously re-evaluate the Roosevelt era. Their parents' and grandparents' generations overwhelmingly supported and idolized politicians whose policies of inaction and indifference were directly responsible for the outcome that occurred. Many continue to idolize Roosevelt to this day, apparently completely oblivious to the fact that he bears the lion's share of blame for the door of rescue from Nazi Europe slamming shut to greater numbers of Jewish refugees under his direct watch.

An attitude of indifference toward the Jewish people did not bubble up from the core of America's heartland. It was the indifference of the Roosevelt Administration itself that was mostly to blame for America closing its doors to Jewish refugees, not something amiss in the heart and soul of America. On the contrary, after the horrors of the Holocaust became known, the American people responded overwhelmingly in welcoming new waves of Jewish people to our shores and in supporting the establishment of the State of Israel.

America, I believe, has been blessed in part, because of her support of the Jewish people. I believe that a strong case can be made that America's freedom and safety have fostered a flowering of Jewish creativity and brilliance on these shores. Indeed, while looking for an explanation of Jewish pre-eminence, Raphael Patai himself observed in *The Jewish Mind* that "one is forced…to speak only of Jewish talents as manifested within a definite Gentile cultural environment."[25] In other words – developing Patai's thoughts somewhat further: *provide the Jewish people in a given Gentile environment (or nation) the freedom, safety, and dignity that they deserve and crave, and they may flourish in ways that bring enormous benefit to that society.* In her book, *First Facts in American Jewish History*, author Tina Levitan wrote of Jewish "geniuses whose mental attitudes and intellectual viewpoints introduced new elements, new temperaments, and new tones in art, music, and literature in the superabundant energy and talent that America's openness released in them."[26]

Irving Berlin

One of the most quintessential patriotic songs of love and gratitude for the United States, "God Bless America," was written by a very grateful Jewish immigrant composer, Irving Berlin, who also wrote the American classic "White Christmas." One of Berlin's earliest memories as a very young child was hiding in a ditch in Russia with his relatives as anti-Semitic Cossacks burned down his family's village.[27] Coming to America, his songs became as 'American as apple pie,' becoming fully integrated into America's own story. Can the idea of America as a 'sanctuary nation' for the Jewish people be expressed any more clearly than the picture of a young Jewish boy who might have been slaughtered in a ditch in Russia by anti-Semites but who lived to write the song 'God Bless America'?

Or, consider Aaron Copland, son of Lithuanian Jewish parents, dubbed the "Dean of American Composers." Copland composed *Appalachian Spring* and iconic American music of all kinds, such as *Fanfare for the Common Man* (1942). His talents covered "a full plenum of twentieth-century American musical genres – neoclassical, folk, jazz, ballet, and film."[28]

Jewish Integration into Academia: "Unique in the History of the Diaspora"

On the academic scene, Jewish integration into American academic life is extremely significant; ironically, though, it has been so successful as to go almost unnoticed. That amazing development is the fact that Jews in America have been transformed "from victimized outsiders" in the past to "leaders of the American intellectual establishment" today. David Hollinger believes that this phenomenon "is unique in the history of the Diaspora."

Nevertheless, "surprisingly little attention has been paid" to what he says is "this remarkable case of over-representation." Not only did this group – the Jews - which "had been the victim of systematic and legal discrimination...suddenly become astonishingly over-represented" in academia, it "even more suddenly ceased to be counted as a group relevant to the whole calculus of group representation."[29] Jewish representation became so commonplace and rather routine that no one paid any attention to it anymore.

The case of Dartmouth College is especially striking. In 1945, the then president of Dartmouth, Ernest Hopkins, strongly defended his college's quota system concerning Jews. But just forty years later, in 1985, the situation had changed so dramatically that Dartmouth had installed its first Jewish president, James O. Freeman.[30]

A significant 1969 study "found that while Jews constituted only about 3 percent of the American population [at that time], they accounted for 17 percent of the combined faculties of the seventeen most highly ranked universities."[31] As this process went forward, Jews became so much a part of the American academic establishment that their presence came to be viewed as part of the norm. This is an even more remarkable achievement, given the fact that, according to one statistic, as recently as 1940 "only 2 percent of American professors were Jewish."[32]

The same phenomenon occurred in pre-war Europe but not on this scale.[33] It is an amazing success story - whether or not those involved in that story in the present generation understand or appreciate its ramifications.

Quotas and 'Genteel Anti-Semitism'

It did not begin that way. As has already been discussed, there used to be Jewish quotas at the nation's leading universities because 'too many Jews' were getting in, according to those who ran those institutions, such as President Lowell at Harvard. There was also a form of 'genteel anti-Semitism,' an anti-Semitism that was "ensconced in corporate boardrooms, country clubs, and literary salons since the end of the nineteenth century..." But after the end of the Second World War, all that changed. After Hitler, 'genteel anti-Semitism' was no longer fashionable or acceptable in elite circles of the American Establishment. Instead, as Leonard Silk and Mark Silk put it in their book, *The American Establishment*, "Genteel anti-Semitism slowly faded until, like the Cheshire cat, there was nothing left but its smile – and the memory of its claws."[34]

Beyond academia, a similar process of eventual acceptance took place in other areas of American culture. It did not happen immediately, but it did happen: "Many have claimed that in the late twentieth century, Jews became mainstream American culture, that in the literary world, in theater, in film, Jews *were* American pop culture...No longer were they outsiders looking in, but they were now insiders working on the inside. And that's a huge shift."[35]

'Special Seeds' and 'Special Soil'

Why are so many Nobel Prize winners and so many other brilliant and successful people both Jewish and Americans? Once again we might consider the role of providential history and the welcoming of the Jews. Anti-Semitism did indeed rear its ugly head at various times in American history, but at the same time, America must be applauded for the millions of Jewish people whom it has taken in and given full rights and freedom to pursue their dreams any way they see fit. Avraham Burg, a senior member of the Israeli Labor Party, writing for the essay series *I am Jewish*, has noted: "No nation in the world stands for the values of personal freedom and equality like the United States does."[36]

One might also compare Jewish giftedness to 'special seeds'. Those seeds were planted in the rich soil of American freedom and independence. As with any plantings of seeds, not all of them took root, but many sprouted and became incredibly beautiful plants that have enriched the whole world. With respect to the special role of New York City in that process, author James Gleick has observed that "around greater New York City...These hundred odd-square miles of the planet's surface were disproportionately fertile in the spawning of Nobel laureates. Many families, were embedded in a culture that prized learning and discourse..." He added: "They shared a sense that science, as a profession, rewarded merit."[37] That Jewish culture, combined with freedom in a welcoming atmosphere of great expectations in America, made this greatness possible.

Celebrating Jewish Achievement in America

In *The Israel Test*, George Gilder asserts that the "success or failure of Jews in a given country is the best index of its freedoms." There is a lot of meaning and history packed into that statement.

According to Gilder, the United States should be celebratory of Jewish achievement: "Americans should not conceal the triumphs of Jews on our shores but celebrate them as evidence of the superior freedoms of the U.S. economy and culture."[38]

But What of the Future?: The 'End of Days'

Will America always be a sanctuary nation for the Jewish people? The prophet Zechariah foretold a day when "all the nations of the earth will be gathered together" against Jerusalem and against the Jewish people (Zechariah 12:3). America must be included among "all the nations of the earth." Jerusalem shall become "a burdensome stone for all the peoples." (12:3) Does this mean that the tens of thousands of ultra-Orthodox Satmar Jews who live in Williamsburg, Brooklyn, New York, for example, and who view present-day Israel as an illegitimate state because it was not founded by the Messiah, shall eventually make *aliyah* to Israel? Yes it does, but how or when that will occur, of course, I have no idea.

In any event, when the Satmars return to Israel, *it will be the beginning of the end of America's long tradition of being a sanctuary nation for the Jewish people.* The Satmars, in that sense, are 'the canaries in the mine.'

This is because, to follow the Biblical prophecies to their logical conclusion, there must come a day when Israel stands all alone, and the peoples of the earth see that there is no one left to defend Israel. I realized this reality while listening to a presentation by best-selling author Joel Rosenberg. Joel was speaking at a conference in Jerusalem in 2015.

That is when God will deliver Israel.

I wish I were wrong, but the Biblical reasoning behind this conclusion is strong. It is also in God's nature. God does not need America to defend and support Israel! But I also believe that as long as evangelical believers stand with the Jewish people, God will bless those who bless the seed of Abraham, Isaac and Jacob. This does *not* mean that Christians who love Israel should by any means support all of the policies of the state of Israel, or equate those policies with justice or righteousness. We should be strongly critical of Israel when those policies do not measure up to what they should be. In that sense, caring for the Jewish people and standing by Israel is a little like defending and standing with a close relative. Despite their faults, that person is always still 'family' and we will stand with them to the end! Making that distinction makes all the difference.

When we speak about eschatology or what the Hebrew prophets called the "End of Days," Messianic believers in Yeshua have various views. In this book I have specifically refrained from expressing a particular eschatological viewpoint except to say that I and most Messianic believers believe that Scripture clearly teaches two points: first, that at some point during the End of Days, the Lord's "feet shall stand on the Mount of Olives" (Zechariah 14:4) – this speaks of Yeshua's return to the earth; and, the second point being that the Jewish people play a key role in the End of Days in a way that impacts the entire world.

"Judaica Americana"

I will close this chapter on America and the Jewish people by relating an experience I had while doing research in Widener Library at Harvard University in the fall of 2015. Widener Library is one of the great academic libraries in the world. While looking for something else, I stumbled across a two-volume set of a work titled, *Judaica Americana.*[39] These two volumes contain thousands of entries of America-related Judaica and similar topics. The *very first entry* in that two-volume set was a book by the Rev. William Hubbard (1621-1704), an early colonial

Puritan in America. Its title was, *The Happiness of a People in the Wisdom of their Rulers Directing and in the Obedience of their Brethren Attending Unto What Israel Ought to Do*, and it was published in Boston in 1676.

This quest soon led me to another library at Harvard, Houghton Library, the university's rare book repository. Soon an original copy of Hubbard's 1676 book was placed in a rare book 'cradle' before me by the library staff. What a thrill to see and touch this original book!

But more was to come. What did I find in this very first example of "Judaica Americana"? – a reference to Romans 11 in the Brit Chadashah! On page 59 of the Hubbard text from 1676 I found the following statement: "*God tells his people of old that he will move them to jealousie by them that are not a people...*"[40] The Jewish people will be moved to jealousy – spiritual jealousy - by Gentiles who have come to faith in the Messiah.

May America always be a beacon of light and a sanctuary for the Jewish people! But if and when that day comes to an end, may Gentile believers provide their own physical sanctuary to Jews in need, as the Ten Boom family and others did during World War II. There may come a time again when our very lives are on the line, such as occurred during the Nazi era, when some Gentile families hid Jewish children in secret rooms in homes, in barns, and wherever they could under sentence of death, simply because it was the right thing to do. Some of these are remembered in the Avenue of the Righteous Gentiles at the Yad Vashem Holocaust memorial in Jerusalem. Others remain unsung and unknown.

We should thank God that He providentially raised up America to be a sanctuary nation for the Jewish people. God bless America. *Am Yisrael Chai.*

Conclusion to Part I

"No productiveness of the highest level, no remarkable discovery, no great thought that bears fruits and has results, is in the power of anyone; such things are above earthly control. Man must consider them an unexpected gift from above."[1]

GOETHE

We close Part I acknowledging that there is an empirical reality that the Jewish people have been endowed with special gifts of intellectual pre-eminence, artistry, and communication. This by no means equates to every Jewish person having such gifts, but I believe that it does signify that the Jewish people taken as a whole have corporately been given these gifts by God.

There is a spiritual dimension to this that we shall examine next. Daniel Juster writes in *The Irrevocable Calling: Israel's Role as a Light to the Nations* that the Jewish people are "called to live as intercessory representatives before God for the sake of the nations of the world." They are supposed to serve as "a corporate nation to represent corporate humanity."[2]

Does saying that the Jewish people have special gifts from God in any way take away from the value or hard work of the individuals so gifted? In no way. These gifts represent, I believe, *a predisposition to greatness or uniqueness* but no guarantee of them.[3] In the same way that many African-Americans are predisposed to having great athletic ability, we are not surprised to see many African-Americans in leading positions in professional sports. It is certainly not racist to acknowledge that reality. But those African-Americans who excel in sports did not just have that status granted to them. They earned it through hard work, dedication and training. And we certainly are not speaking of *all* African-Americans here when we say that some are endowed with extraordinary athletic ability. Many are not.

It is the similar with the Jewish people but on a different plane. Stating that the Jewish people corporately have a natural giftedness in certain fields is not to steal any credit from those individuals who have made those achievements in their fields. They have earned their success and rewards through hard work.

So, does this thesis mean that all Jews will be pre-eminent? Far from it! So, while one might speak of a *corporate* blessing upon the Jewish people, there is also another principle at work when we consider success and achievement: 'What you sow, you shall also reap.'

That principle holds true regardless of whatever one wants to think about the question of Jewish giftedness. It also cannot be said that any Gentile is held back from being successful simply because he or she *not* Jewish! That certainly is not the case, and I also believe that God will bless those who bless the Jews.

There is a *calling* of God (*kleisis* in Koine Greek) upon the Jewish people to be a light to the nations. This is a *corporate calling* that transcends particular individuals. Corporate giftedness reflects this corporate calling.

I believe that this truth is substantively and empirically demonstrated in many areas of the arts and sciences and other fields of endeavor – a singularity that is so stunning as to defy rational explanation. *There is no other sociological or scientific explanation that comes close to explaining it.* As I have shown here in Part I, many observers have tried to explain it, and some have captured portions of its essence. But in the end, all their explanations fall short.

Jewish giftedness and calling indeed have the stamp of God upon them. They are a mystery, I believe, wrapped up in God's special covenant with the Jewish people:

> "And who is like your people Israel – the one nation on earth that God went out to redeem as a people for himself, and to make a name for himself...You have established your people Israel as your very own forever, and you, O Lord, have become their God." (2 Samuel 7: 23-24, *NIV*)

The sad reality, though, is that, for the most part, Jewish giftedness is not being used as intended. I believe it was intended to help equip the Jewish people to share with the world the story of redemption.

That leads us to Part II...

PART II:

THE JEWISH PEOPLE AND WORLD REDEMPTION

CHAPTER NINE

Jewish Redemption and 'Repairing the World'

Introduction

Tikkun olam – the desire to 'mend the world' - permeates Jewish consciousness today. It has almost completely supplanted any external missionary impulse within Judaism that may have existed in the distant past. In one sense, the desire for *tikkun olam* is a pale imitation of what the Bible predicts will someday occur – the "restoration of the Jewish kingdom."[1]

Yeshua's disciples asked Him: "Lord, are you at this time going to restore the Kingdom to Israel?" (Acts 1:6). Jesus answered that it was not for them to know when this would occur, but He did *not* deny that it *would occur* someday. In that day the nations of the world will look to Zion, because Israel will then be the "head" of the nations, the "chief" of the nations, and "all nations shall flow unto it." (Isaiah 2:2; Jeremiah 31:7; Zechariah 14:16). But more on that in a moment.

Tikkun olam is also associated with the Jewish concept of *mitzvot*. *Mitzvot* has two meanings in Judaism – technically, it means "the commandments," but it also carries a secondary meaning: doing "good deeds." The secondary meaning of *mitzvot* is more closely related to *tikkun olam* among the non-religious especially.

Doing Good Deeds

Doing good deeds (*mitzvot*) to 'repair the world' is not limited to Judaism. Evangelical Christians believe in doing good deeds and are commanded to do so in the New Testament Scriptures (James 2: 14), *but they have entirely different reasons and motivations for doing so*. This is because, as already noted, *tikkun olam* is a manmade concept; it is *not* based on Scripture. Evangelical Christians do good works (if their faith and actions are authentic) because the Holy Spirit has motivated them to do so, and because they are so thankful to God for their salvation. In fact, they are *compelled* in their spirits and conscience to do some good works if their faith is genuine, because "faith without works is dead." (James 2: 17)

But these good works are not necessarily oriented toward improving the world, although that is often a by-product in some cases, such as developing soup kitchens and shelters for the homeless or setting up health clinics for the poor in the Third World. These are wonderful ways of making the world a better place, but for true Christians, they are secondary. What comes first is being concerned about the state of souls for eternity. Doing "good works" is a way of showing God's love toward others and expressing our thankfulness to Him for our own salvation. That is the motivator, not 'changing the world' for its own sake. Such "good works," if done in the right spirit, are also done 'in His Name' – not in order to impress others or oneself.

At its heart, this is a very different approach than what is generally embodied in the Jewish concept of *tikkun olam* – although there is a bit of overlap on some levels.

The crucial element missing in most Jewish views of *tikkun olam* is a concern for souls and for eternal salvation, whereas this is the *very essence* of a New Testament view of 'doing good deeds.' The ultimate goal of the latter is not just to feed the poor and clothe the naked but to share the love of God with others so that some may come to a saving faith in Messiah.

Giftedness Can Be Both a Blessing and a Curse

That concern for salvation begins – or should begin – with their own souls. But, sadly, the blessing and giftedness that we have been describing throughout this book can be a hindrance to that. In this respect, one aspect of Jewish corporate giftedness must be seen as a tragedy on an individual level. Jewish giftedness can be used to bring great blessing to the world, but it can also bring immense pride, spiritual blindness and spiritual death to those individuals who possess such gifts if they use them completely in isolation from the purposes of God. The

Scripture poses the question this way: "What does it profit a man to gain the whole world but lose his own soul?" (Matthew 16:26)

The greatest gift of all is *salvation.* There is nothing more important than that. One might have fame and riches, Nobel Prizes and billions of dollars, one might hold the global media in the palm of one's hand, but if he or she does not have the Messiah in their hearts and *know* that they have eternal life, in the end it has profited them *nothing.*

This view is contrary to most Jews' understanding of reality today and their place in it. Many brush aside the very idea of salvation as a quaint anachronism; they don't see that it has anything to do with them – instead, *repairing the world* is their purpose and goal, not salvation! Repairing the world is in the here and now. *Salvation* is something that 'religious' people bother about, not those who have their feet firmly planted on the ground (or so they think) - those who are trying to better this world!

But the real truth is just the opposite. This is the tragic side of Jewish giftedness. The Jewish people have been gifted, in part, in order to better equip them in proclaiming salvation, *then* trying to change the world. Their priority is wrong.

The Jewish people were supposed to have a concern not only for their own souls and for the salvation of others – *they were also supposed to be the leaders of a global movement of preaching the message of salvation to the nations!* (That *still* is part of God's plan). They were to be a "royal priesthood," testifying to the nations of God's faithfulness and telling them that salvation is in the God of Abraham, Isaac and Jacob alone and in His Messiah, Yeshua. Instead, that "royal priesthood" has for the time being passed to Gentile believers in Jesus and to those Jewish believers who have come to faith (1 Peter 2:9; Luke 13:28-30). But, despite this, God's "irrevocable calling" upon Israel has never been revoked. It is still there, in the background, awaiting the day of its fulfillment: "But Israel will be saved by the Lord with an everlasting salvation…" (Isaiah 45:17) And they "will be called the priests of the Lord…ministers of our God…Instead of your shame you will have a double portion…" (Isaiah 61:7). Isaiah foresaw this incredible day that is coming: "For Zion's sake I will not keep silent, and for Jerusalem's sake I will not keep quiet, until her righteousness goes forth like brightness, and her salvation like a torch that is burning. And the nations will see your righteousness, and all kings your glory." (Isaiah 62:1-2, NASB). This is specifically referring to redeemed Israel in a time yet to come: "And they will call them, 'The holy people, the redeemed of the Lord." (Isaiah 62:12)

(Now I must ask my Jewish atheist friends and other skeptical readers who reject the essence of all this to skip over this next section and move on to "A Key Prediction," since what I will say next will probably make no sense to them and could confuse them.

The "Lost Gospel of Jerusalem"; When a Jew Rules the World

Combined with the promise mentioned in Isaiah above is another insight – one that my good friend Jim Sibley presented at our Lausanne Consultation on Jewish Evangelism tenth international conference in Jerusalem in August 2015. Jim calls it the "'Lost Gospel' of Jerusalem." As the conference organizer, I immediately embraced this provocative title when Jim first presented the idea to me. For what he was saying is something I deeply believe – that there is indeed a 'lost Gospel'! We are not speaking about some long-lost apocryphal manuscript that has just been discovered, but, rather, it is that the one, true Gospel that we already have in the Scriptures, that that Gospel that is Jewish-centered in its essence but that this aspect has been essentially lost to the Church for centuries, is only now, very slowly, being 'found' or, if you will, 're-discovered'. *That* Gospel and that view of the Scriptures centers on *Jewish salvation* and on missions to the Jewish people in order to bring them this message. Sibley states: "My thesis is a simple one: it is that Scripture teaches that the Jewish people should not only be a continuing priority in evangelism and missions, *but that this priority is intrinsic to the gospel itself.*"[2] (emphasis added) This is an extremely profound assertion, one with tremendous implications for the Church (the Body of Messiah) and the world at large if understood correctly.

Author Joel Richardson asserts something very similar in his 2015 book, *When a Jew Rules the World*. Richardson has written about the Jewish context of the Gospel. He laments how much the historic Church has wrongly minimized and sanitized "any Jewish dimensions of the

Gospel message." As the title of his book proclaims, "if the Gospel that one preaches does not culminate with a Jewish man ruling the world, then it is not the Gospel of the New Testament." Richardson's hope is that his book "will help Christians to better understand the Gospel in its actual Jewish context."[3] My hope is much the same for *this* book.

A Key Prediction

Scientists love predictions. For years, groups of physicists from around the world predicted that they would detect something that is called the "Higgs boson" within a certain energy range. (For those not familiar with particle physics, I will not try to explain what the Higgs boson is but rather the importance of the prediction behind it. For my scientifically-minded readers, please forgive this very incomplete explanation of the Higgs boson and the Standard Model).

The Higgs boson has been euphemistically referred to by some reporters as "the God particle"[4] – a moniker that many scientists deride, since, if we are to believe the statistics, sadly, a majority of leading scientists today say they do not believe in God.[5] But that is another issue.

Large-scale experiments with thousands of collaborators at the Large Hadron Collider (LHC) at CERN in Switzerland strongly indicate that the Higgs has been found. These indicators point to the Higgs' existence at an energy level of around 125 billion electron volts (GeV).[6] The significance of this would take a while to explain, but the simple fact is this: scientists *expected* to probably find the Higgs boson because its existence was predicted by theory, which seemed to be borne out by other experiments and predictions. They knew what to look for and where to look for it.

Our approach to predicting the role of the Jewish people in God's plan for the world, while not as scientifically-sounding as the search for the Higgs boson, is not entirely dissimilar, either.

The same type of approach can be taken to what the Bible says about the Jewish people. Is Jewish giftedness just a fluke, something "mysterious" but more or less just an anomaly that defies explanation but has no significance? Or is it linked into other indicators? Is it part of a larger prediction?

Knowing What to Look for

Scientists knew where to try look for the Higgs boson because of other evidence and theories that seemed to point to its existence. Their efforts paid off. In a similar way, a number of expositors successfully predicted the return of the Jewish people to the Land of Israel many decades or centuries before even Theodor Herzl or the Zionist movement were born. These predictions were based solely on the prophecies of the Bible itself. One of those was Sir Isaac Newton himself, who accurately foretold "a future restoration of the Jewish people to their land some two hundred fifty years before it happened."[7] This subject held great attention for Newton.[8] Newton wrote of a "final return of the Jews" to the Land of Israel.

While Jewish giftedness is not specifically predicted in the Bible, the enormous blessings that God has poured out upon the Jewish people infers the possibility of such giftedness. But, sadly, one can also look at the dispersion of the Jewish people to the ends of the earth and the sufferings that they have endured at the hands of Gentiles to have been predicted by the Scriptures, although this in no way excuses those who perpetrated such suffering upon them.

But looking beyond all of this, the Scriptures promise a glorious future! We will begin the discussion of this great prediction by looking at the words of Jonathan Edwards, one of the most famous ministers in American history. Edwards is "arguably the most significant and influential Christian in the history of the United States."[9]

Here is Edwards' prediction: *"Nothing is more certainly foretold than this national conversion of the Jews in Romans 11."*[10] Now the tables have turned, and I must ask my Bible-believing readers to be patient for a moment while I explain what "Romans 11" means to our secular readers. First of all, we must get past this very upsetting and incorrectly understood word, *conversion.* The Jewish people have suffered unspeakable loss and harm at the hands of so-called Christians who wanted to 'convert' them (make them to change their religion) by force. This part of Jewish history is so full of pain and grief that it is difficult to even know where to start, but start we must. What Jonathan

Edwards is referring to in his prediction has nothing whatsoever to do with forcing anyone to believe anything. Whatever one thinks of the word *conversion* and all of the negative connotations that go with it, *what Edwards is talking about does not relate to human action at all – it relates to what the Spirit of God will do. **That** is the prediction.

"Romans 11" refers to a passage in the *Brit Chadashah*. It was written by the Apostle Paul, once a persecutor of early Jewish believers in Jesus as the Messiah before he himself came to faith on the Damascus road. Paul's "Epistle to the Romans" in the *Brit Chadashah* is one of the theological cornerstones of the Christian faith. Whether you as the reader accept what Paul said or not as authoritative, the prediction remains and was repeated centuries later by Edwards: "*Nothing is more certainly foretold than this national conversion of the Jews in Romans 11.*" Isaac Newton also "believed that Romans 11…spoke of a latter-day Restoration."[11]

What does this mean?

It means that the Jewish people have a destiny that will change the world.

This destiny is something that mankind can neither control nor alter. God Himself will bring this to pass. If you are Jewish, reading such a claim may infuriate you or it may bemuse you. You may in the bottom of your heart also believe that the Jewish people have a destiny that is yet to be fully understood, even if you reject that that destiny has anything whatsoever to do with what many evangelical Christians believe.

Whatever your initial reaction to this idea, if I could ask you to lay aside your apprehension about this for a moment, I would like to fill in more of the 'canvas' related to what this prediction really means.

A Culmination Point

Let me begin with the bottom line first – **history is moving toward a culmination point, and that culmination point centers around the Jewish people**. Why? *Because the Jewish people remain the covenant people of God.* The Jews' rejection of Jesus, the destruction of the Temple in 70 AD, the Diaspora, the hatred of the Jewish people seen in the pogroms, the Inquisition, forced 'conversions', and, worst of all, the Holocaust, along with Jewish giftedness today, the strong desire deep in Jewish hearts to see *tikkun olam* (the repairing of the world), the quest or even drivenness for excellence, the re-establishment of a Jewish homeland in Eretz Yisrael – all of these aspects of history and of reality today are moving toward a culmination, a finality.

I believe that this culmination point will see the Jewish people as the head of the nations of the world – the head and not the tail. (Zechariah 12-14)

The Puritan Hope

Many Puritans and other believers earnestly prayed to God for the salvation of the Jewish people. In 1649, John Owen spoke before the British House of Commons, expressing his desire to see the Jewish people brought into "one fold with the fullness of the Gentiles...in answer to millions of prayers put up at the throne of grace, for this very glory, in all generations."[12]

In writing of the Puritans' faith, author Kelvin Crombie says that "these early Puritans saw the promises in the Hebrew prophets concerning the restoration of a scattered Israel to their own land." They believed what the Scriptures said in Romans 9-11 regarding "God's faithfulness towards the house of Israel and the promise of their eventual acceptance of Jesus as the Jewish Messiah."[13]

In 1669, Increase Mather, one of the past presidents of Harvard, published a book titled, *The Mystery of Israel's Salvation Explained and Applied.* He wrote: "One of those great and glorious things which the world, especially the people of God in the world, are in expectation of at this day, is *The general conversion of the Israelitish Nation."[14]*

Messianic musician Joel Chernoff sings a beautifully moving song called, "The Restoration of Israel." It is a cry to God to give the petitioner the same kind of love for the Jewish people that He Himself has: "Help me, Lord, to feel the love you feel....break my heart, so more Your burdens share, for the restoration of Yisrael...Make my heart like Yours, for Israel."[15]

The prediction of the Jewish people coming to faith cannot be proven until it actually occurs. But, as with any multi-level test of any major prediction, just as with the Higgs boson, there are *indicators* that can point to the ultimate truthfulness or validity of that prediction.

In the same way, with respect to the prophecy concerning the Jewish people coming to faith, there are *indicators* pointing to this future event.

1. *Destroyers Cannot Succeed.* The first indicator is that, try as they might, anti-Semites, diabolical regimes, and haters of all kinds from Haman to Hitler have dealt grievous blows against the Jewish people but have never destroyed them, try as they will.

2. *Flourishing during Peace and Security.* The second indicator is that, whenever the Jewish people have relative peace and security, they usually begin to flourish. This is evidence of God's blessing upon them despite the hatred of portions of the populations in so many of the places where they have lived in the Diaspora throughout the centuries.

   - Outside of Israel, the nation that has given the Jews the greatest peace and security has been the United States, and, I believe a strong case can be made for the fact that America has been blessed, in part, for how it has treated the Jews.

3. *Soviet Jewish emigration.* At a time when most Soviet Jews were completely secularized, had no desire or interest in being considered Jewish (with some exceptions) and where they could have been completely assimilated into Soviet atheistic society and disappeared as a recognizable people group, historical events, which I believe were guided by the hand of God, preserved them as a people. In this case, Soviet anti-Semitism was responsible in a perverse way for helping preserve the Jewish people in the former Soviet Union.[16] Soviet Jews then made an enormous contribution to Israeli society in terms of numbers and the talents and skills they brought with them.

4. *The Establishment of the State of Israel.* The Jewish people have returned to the Land. This was the age-old dream of Zionism. This was the hoped-for dream of centuries, not only of countless

Jews but also of many Christian Zionists and others. While some ignore or vehemently deny it, others see Israel's re-establishment as the fulfillment of prophecy.[17]

In his book, The Restoration of the Jews, The Crisis of All Nations, author James Bicheno wrote in 1807:

> "…although no one can say how near, or how distant, the time may be, when God will fulfill his promises to the Jewish nation; yet it is certain there never were so many reasons for concluding it not to be very far off, as at present. **We live in awful times.**"[18] (emphasis added)

Indeed, we still live in "awful times," but the awfulness of the current day is far different than what Bicheno had in mind in his day – or is it?

In his book, *Has God Finished with Israel?*, author Rob Richards wrote that God in Genesis 12 gave Abraham four things: a *People* (the Jewish people), a *Place* (the Land of Israel), a *Purpose* (to be a blessing to the nations), and that these gifts or promises would be in *Perpetuity*.[19]

This is "because the interests of the Gentiles themselves are bound up with God's design towards Israel."[20]

Daniel C. Juster writes that, "although the state of Israel is prominently visible on the world stage, few say anything on how God is currently at work in the life of the Jewish people and how he has gifted them to bless the present generation."[21]

There have been other Gentile believers throughout history who have had a profound love for the Jewish people, even if they did not completely understand the depth of that love and find it hard to describe why they have it. For me, as I've shared, it began with an appreciation of Jewish greatness in music. Later, after I became a believer and grew to love the Scriptures, I saw the extraordinary debt that was owed to the Jewish people. Books such as Edith Schaeffer's *Christianity is Jewish* helped confirm that debt and understanding. It is a journey that many Gentile believers have yet to make. But if they are open to God's leading, He will confirm that depth of love for the Jewish people.

John Charles Ryle gave an address in 1858 in which he said he believed that it was "a duty incumbent on all Gentile Christians to take a special interest in the spiritual condition of the Jewish nation…I speak…of our duty to Jewish souls. I say that we owe them a special debt, and that this debt ought to be carefully paid." It is also our duty to "be specially careful" that we "take up [any] stumbling-blocks out of the way of Israel…" The Church has largely failed on that score! In terms of how to reach Jewish people with the Gospel, Ryle concluded that "The Jews are a peculiar people, and must be approached in a peculiar way."[22] This is a great calling, but the Church has (mostly) failed at it. As Douglas Kittredge has aptly written, "rather than provoking the Jews to jealousy, the Gentile church simply provoked the Jews."[23]

Those who truly love the Jewish people will continue to work to try to find a better way.

CHAPTER TEN

The Unfulfilled Role of the Jewish People: 'A Light to the Nations'

W e now move the discussion to the next level and look at the unfulfilled role that the Jewish people are supposed to fulfill, the role that will not let them go.

A 'Light to the Nations': What Does It Mean?

Adolph Saphir
(Source: John Dunlop, *Memories of Gospel Triumphs
Among the Jews during the Victorian Era* (London, 1894, p. 457)

In the nineteenth century, Jewish believer in Jesus (Yeshua) Adolph Saphir wrote of "the mystery of Israel, the everlasting nation, chosen of God to be the centre of the earth… to show forth His power and goodness to all nations."[1] He added: "While the nations were in darkness, the bright light of God's favour visited Israel." The favor of God was visited upon Israel first so that it would eventually touch the whole world: "The great joy of David and all the prophets was that all ends of the earth shall be blessed and enjoy the knowledge and peace of God. Theirs was a worldwide hope."[2]

And that calling was and remains unique in history: "...no other nation was taught from the very commencement of its existence that its object was to benefit all the world, that its mission was to be a light-bearer to all people that on earth do dwell, to be a blessing to the isles afar off."[3]

My friend and Jewish believer in Jesus, Avi Snyder, has spoken many times of the special call of Messianic Jewish believers "to be a light to the nations." He has stated: "The Scriptures clearly show, from Genesis to Revelation, that Israel as a people have only received one call and that call is to be a nation of missionaries to the rest of the world. God chose the Jews because of His love for the nations. He chose us to take the Gospel to the nations."[4]

While some Jews apprehend that they have some special role to play,[5] others "have despised their own covenant role in being a 'light to the nations'."[6]

A "light to the world"; "A nation of missionaries to the world"

To non-believers, such assertions must sound like nonsense. What does it mean that the Jewish people should be "a nation of missionaries to the world"? The word 'missionary' itself usually carries very negative connotations in the Jewish community as a result of the terrible history of past forced conversion and persecution. The idea of being missionaries to the world is certainly not one that most Jews would embrace. 'Jews aren't missionaries!' many would respond. 'Just leave us Jews alone!' others would answer. 'We don't send missionaries to you, so why do you bother us?'

But that is not exactly true. Strange as it seems now, there was a time when Jewish 'missionizing' was a part of Judaism, although the extent of that 'missionizing' has been a point of sharp debate.[7] Nevertheless, since the destruction of the Temple in 70 AD and the council at Yavneh,

Judaism has largely been in a defensive mode. The Jewish people were eventually scattered to the four corners of the world in the Diaspora. Nevertheless, the global dispersion of the Jewish people with all its ramifications did not change their calling. Put simply: they were given a job to do, and they have not done it: "Israel, chosen to be the light to the nations, has not fulfilled its mission."[8]

The Calling Has Not Changed

That 'job' or role, if you will, even pre-dates the coming of Jesus. It received greater definition and specificity with the coming of Messiah, but the essential role itself has remained unchanged. As Snyder has noted: the Jewish people "have only received one call," and that call has not changed. Douglas Kittredge asks, will the Jewish people "take their leadership role before the nations?"[9]

Some Jews – like Jonah - will do everything possible to run away from that calling and from that role. Some even *recoil* from the very notion. For centuries, some "have wondered why they cannot be accepted just as other people."[10] Some are just tired of the implications of being 'chosen' or 'set apart.' Some, like Tevya in "Fiddler on the Roof," just ask: "Why don't You choose someone else for a while?"

Some plainly reject the calling; others just want to get as far away from it as possible. They immerse themselves instead in false imitations of it. This is one of the key unconscious reasons, I believe, why so many Jews are attracted to radical causes – they want to change the world, but they also want to submerge themselves in causes that *do not* focus on their proper spiritual calling. It is a paradox. Nevertheless, they often still rise to the top of whatever movements they commit themselves to. As George Gilder writes, "Around the globe, wherever freedom opens up, however briefly in historical terms, Jews quickly tend to rise up and prevail."[11] But that is not the same thing as answering or obeying the call.

Ignoring that call, obstructing or inhibiting it or lying about it – all are efforts preventing the world from being reached with the Gospel as it should. As Avi Snyder avers: "If you love Israel and the Jewish people, then understand we were chosen to be a light to the nations." When it comes to world evangelization, he adds: "The best way for the Church to interfere with the process of world evangelization is to keep the Gospel away from us Jews and not pray for the salvation of Israel and not pray for those who bring the Gospel to the Jewish people…"[12]

'A City Upon a Hill'

Perhaps the best-known encapsulation of American exceptionalism – the view that God ordained America for a special role in the world – came from Massachusetts Bay Governor John Winthrop's famous phrase in his sermon, "A Model of Christian Charity," delivered in 1630 to his fellow Puritans during their voyage to America prior to reaching their destination. Winthrop said: "For we must consider that we shall be as a city upon a hill. The eyes of all people are upon us." The 'city upon a hill' phrase was taken directly from Jesus' Sermon on the Mount.[13]

"The eyes of all people are upon us." The Puritans were distinctly aware of God's calling upon their lives. They made many errors, but, as David Aikman points out, they were "conscious that they were exceptional people, not in the sense of being superior to others but in the sense of being called by God to a unique purpose…"[14] The Puritans saw themselves as a 'New Israel, but many also believed the promises of Romans 11 with respect to a future Jewish spiritual restoration.

Adolph Saphir explained the ultimate purpose of the Jewish people being "a light to the nations" in a May 1868 sermon when he referred to "the special influence which they [the Jewish people] are to exert on the whole world." He believed that "through the restoration of Israel the golden era of the world will be ushered in."[15]

The Choicest Vine

God invested Himself in His Creation. This world does not exist on a whim, nor was it an accident. *It was planned for a purpose. That purpose was for God to have a relationship with mankind.*

God next decided to choose a particular group and to invest Himself specifically in that group. He did that for two reasons – the first reason was to take special delight in them, but the second reason was to cultivate that group to reach out to the rest of the world.

There once was a special vineyard on a fertile hill. According to the Prophet Isaiah, the Lord Himself planted this vineyard with "the choicest vine." It was "His delightful plant." The vineyard is "the house of Israel." (Isaiah 5:7)

Wedded to Israel

The Book of Hosea speaks of God's special relationship with Israel. He says that He is wedded to Israel: "...you will call me 'my husband'..." (Hosea 2:19) Though Israel is unfaithful to Him, and an adulterous nation, yet the Lord is faithful to her. Someday the children of Israel "shall return and seek the Lord their God, and David their king, and shall come with trembling to the Lord and to His blessings in the last days." (Hosea 3:5). Meanwhile, "My people are destroyed for want of knowledge." (Hosea 4:6)

To Whom Much Is Given, Much Also Shall Be Required

"...To whomever much is given, of him will much be required; and to whom much is entrusted, of him will more be asked."

LUKE 12:48

"...because salvation comes from the Jews."

JOHN 4:22

God has indeed blessed the Jewish people. He did so *for the sake of the fathers* – irrespective of their response: *"For the gifts and the calling of God are irrevocable."* (Romans 11: 28-29)

Christianity is Jewish.

Is it really *radical* to acknowledge the Jewish roots of Christianity? I think not. A 1989 book by Marvin R. Wilson titled, *Our Father Abraham: Jewish Roots of the Christian Faith*, states: "A profound and abiding Christian appreciation for Jewish culture and the Jewish people comes from sensing inwardly that one's deepest spiritual identity is with a Jewish Lord, and that "salvation is from the Jews." (John 4:22). He adds: "This personal perception is particularly fed by a consciousness that one owes an enormous debt of appreciation to the Jewish people."[16]

Horatius Bonar exclaimed more than a hundred and fifty years ago: "How great, then, are our obligations to a nation, from whose history we learn so much of God, and so much of ourselves!...God in a measure casts it upon us, and calls upon us to care for their souls..."[17]

Some Jews are put off by such statements. They are suspicious of Christians who employ the Jewish people in their theology in a reductionist way, that is, such Christians are perceived to only care about the Jews because of the latter's role in the fulfillment of Biblical prophecies. Jewish puzzlement and curiosity turn to suspicion when they think that they are just seen as pawns in a greater Christian agenda. Jewish atheist Sam Harris is representative of this attitude taken to an extreme. In *The End of Faith*, he makes the following bald assertion: "Fundamentalist Christians support Israel," he writes, "because they believe that the final consolidation of Jewish power in the Holy Land... will usher in both the Second Coming of Christ *and the final destruction of the Jews*."[18] (emphasis added)

Harris is wrong, of course. Such Christians do not believe that the Second Coming results in "the final destruction of the Jews" – quite the contrary. At the same time, putting the New Testament aside for a moment, there are many passages in the Hebrew Scriptures that portend great suffering and destruction in a regathered Israel before final redemption comes. These prophetic passages were written by Jewish prophets long before there was anything called 'Christianity'.

Nevertheless, many Jews remain baffled or suspicious of the love that many evangelicals say that they have for the Jewish people. They are not sure that it is genuine. Or, if they believe that it is genuine, some think it must be misguided or shallow – that it is based on a set of feelings that might turn on a dime if political and economic conditions changed. These "feelings" about the Jews, or so it is reasoned, could easily turn to bitter disappointment on the part of such Christians. Then they, the Jews, would be made the scapegoat again, blamed for something that didn't work out according to preconceived Christian expectations. 'Scratch a

Gentile and find a Nazi' is a deeply hurtful phrase that I have heard more than once. Yet it is something that many Jews still believe deep down. This is tragic, but we can all understand why some Jews feel this way.

To the Jew First

The Good News (or, "the Gospel") of salvation is *to the Jew first.* (Romans 1:16). There is also "glory, honor and peace" for "every man who works good, *to the Jew first*, and also to the Greek."[19] (Romans 2: 9-10)

At the same time, the Scripture says there will be "oppression and anguish on every soul of man who works evil, *to the Jew first...*" (Romans 2:9)

So, the Gospel of life and salvation is *to the Jew first - but so is the judgment of God.* This is a very sobering statement. This alone should propel us into Jewish outreach, *because the New Testament clearly teaches that the Jewish people will bear the first brunt of God's judgment, followed by the Gentiles.* Therefore, it is *a priority* that they hear the message of salvation, that those of us who are believers who love the Jewish people do everything we can by God's grace to reach them. Why does judgment begin with the Jewish people? In an 1839 sermon, after returning to Scotland from a mission to the Jews in Palestine, the Rev. Robert Murray M'Cheyne answered the question this way: "Because they have had more light than any other people. God chose them out of the world to be His witnesses." He trembled at the thought: "It is an awful thought," he said, "that the Jewish people will be the first to stand forward at the bar of God to be judged."[20]

At the same time, "glory, honor and peace go to every man who works good, *to the Jew first*, and also to the Gentile." (Romans 2:10) So, *God's rewards are also supposed to go to the Jews first.*

So, judgment is upon the Jew first but also God's rewards.

What does all of this mean? Clearly it shows that God is not done with the Jewish people. The plain meaning of the text shows that He is intimately concerned with their future.

We have seen plenty of judgment upon the Jewish people throughout history. But woe to those who thought that they were 'helping God along' by bringing their own judgments against them! God is the One who judges, not mankind. As I've said earlier, I believe that the nations of the world will be judged by God according to how they have treated the Jewish people.

"Rewards" versus "Blessing"

With respect to Jewish people being the first to receive *rewards,* I believe this is referring to the spiritual rewards that believers receive once they come to faith, as opposed to the *general* blessing upon Jacob and his descendants that is the major theme of this book regarding *giftedness*. In my view, we are talking about two different things, and yet they are also somehow mysteriously related.

A number of evangelical Christians in our day want to 'love' the Jewish people but without offending them by bringing the Gospel to them. As my late friend Jh'an Moskowitz of Jews for Jesus once said: "The greatest form of anti-Semitism is the withholding of the gospel from the Jewish people."

We understand the difficulties and historical baggage associated with trying to bring this message to the Jewish people. If anything, the 'baggage' that we must deal with today, because of all of the sins of the Church and the actions of anti-Semites throughout history,[21] have in some ways made it even more difficult to share the Gospel with Jewish people. But we can and we *must*.

Romans 9:33 says: "They stumbled over the stumbling stone," speaking of the Jewish people, and cites Isaiah, combining two passages: "Behold I lay in Zion a stone of stumbling and a rock of offense, and he who believes in Him will not be disappointed." (Isaiah 28:16 and 8:14). But "Blessed is he who keeps from stumbling over Me," or who is not offended by Me. (Matthew 11:6). Though some believed, the Jewish people *as a whole* did stumble over Him and continue to stumble over Him to this day – over "J" or "That Man," as He is sometimes referred to in some Jewish publications. Many cannot even bear to pronounce His name.

Nevertheless, "a true child of God will have a distinctive, persistent (though often anguished) love for the Jewish people notwithstanding their unbelief."[22]

An Unloved People?

Ephraim Sevela, the famous Russian Jewish writer and screenwriter, wrote in his 1977 book, *Farewell, Israel!* that the Jewish people are an unloved people. I once met Sevela briefly many years ago in Brighton Beach, Brooklyn, New York, when he was in the U.S. It was a wonderful but sad moment for me. He accepted me with warmth, but, try as I might I might to explain God's love for the Jewish people and the truth of the Gospel, he more or less brushed that thought aside.

Sevela dedicated *Farewell, Israel!* "to the memory of those who died for Israel." The closing pages of the book discuss his prediction that the nation of Israel will be destroyed because of the hatred of the world against the Jewish people. Writing more than 35 years later, Frederic Raphael has expressed much the same hopelessness about the world's hatred of Israel and the Jewish people, writing that now, having been "reupholstered as Zionists, Jews constitute the sole political 'other' whose extinction would bring harmony to mankind…"[23]

Sevela ended *Farewell, Israel* by painting a very poignant word-picture of Jesus, describing Him as "our last kinsman, the Son of God," gazing down "with sad Jewish eyes" from the walls of the churches "upon the men and women of the earth…," the One "Who came forth from the belly of a nation loved by none."[24]

I say with tears that Sevela was wrong. Yes, the Jewish people are hated by some, but they are deeply loved by others. And for those who love, it is a true, deep, and abiding love – a love that the New Covenant calls in Koine Greek '*agape*' love – a love, for those who will receive it, that will not let you go.

How should Gentiles respond to giftedness or success among Jewish non-believers? We should rejoice in Jewish giftedness inasmuch as we realize that it is a *corporate blessing* from God upon the Jewish people and use this understanding as an opportunity for testimony. Of course, this must be done sensitively, as there will be great resistance to this notion from many quarters. But it is nevertheless the truth, just like the truth that men and women *in general* have different types of abilities and roles, despite some of the confusion today in society about gender.

For those who are believers, God's plan was and is that Jews and Gentiles should help and support each other in both their unity and their distinctiveness. As Matthew Wilson states: "...we must understand that God's plan was to use Israel for the sake of the Gentiles and the Gentiles for the sake of Israel."[25] Each should be thankful for the gifts and blessing of the other.

Dan Gruber in his book, *The Church and the Jews*, cited the examples of Ruth the Gentile Moabitess and Cornelius the Roman officer. Both Ruth and Cornelius saw the truth of the God of Israel and both "embraced the Jewish people, and God blessed [both of them] eternally."[26] This is God's plan.

The 'Chosenness' of Israel

"I am a passionate Jewish agnostic who has always believed that we are the chosen people. So, go figure..."[27]

RICHARD DREYFUSS, ACTOR

"The point is not whether we feel or do not feel that we are chosen. The point is that our role in history is actually unique."[28]

MARTIN BUBER, PHILOSOPHER

"For God has chosen Jacob for himself, Israel for His own possession."

PSALM 135: 4

"The people I formed for Myself, so that they would proclaim My praise"

ISAIAH 43: 21

"It is for the sake of Ya'akov [Jacob] My servant, yes, for Israel my elect, that I call you by your name and give you a title, although you don't know Me."

ISAIAH 45: 4

The Blessings Upon "Jacob – Israel"

But what about the 'fairness' or 'unfairness' of the blessing itself? To that, I have no answer. God gives His blessings to whom He will. The blessing upon the Jewish people extends first back to Abraham: "In him all the nations of the earth will be blessed." (Genesis 18:18) And then again: "Indeed I will greatly bless you. and your seed shall possess the gate of their enemies." (Genesis 22:17) Sarah and Ishmael were also blessed (Genesis 17: 16, 20), "but My covenant I will establish with Isaac..." (17: 21). And then "It happened after Abraham's death that God blessed Isaac..." (Genesis 25:11) The next blessing was an earthly one, given to Jacob from his father Isaac. Through deception and the connivance of Rebekah his mother, Jacob received Isaac's fatherly blessing in place of his brother Esau, the first-born. (Genesis 27: 27-30)

Then Isaac called Jacob to himself and blessed him again: "So Isaac called Jacob and blessed him and charged him, and said to him, 'You shall not take a wife from the daughters of Canaan'." (Genesis 28:1)

In the final blessing, Jacob received blessing directly from God Himself:

> Next, when Jacob wrestled with the angel of the Lord, the angel said: "Your name shall no longer be Jacob, but Israel; for you have striven with God and with men and have prevailed... **And he blessed him there**." (Genesis 32: 28-29)

So we see a multitude of blessings upon Jacob – now Israel – both as an individual himself and also as the embodiment of the Jewish people for all generations to come.

The blessing of God is not limited to the Jewish people themselves. It also extends to those who *bless* the Jewish people! Therefore, all who seek to bless the Jewish people may at one level be said to come under the provision of blessing from God upon Israel. This also is a mystery but is part of God's plan for mutual blessing of the world.

Why Were the Jewish People Chosen?

They were the chosen instrument by God as a people to bring His Word to the rest of the world, the people from whom came the prophets, and, finally, the people group from whom came the Messiah, Yeshua, the King of the Jews

The Jewish people were chosen out of all of the people groups of the world for **special blessing**

They also were chosen for **suffering** and to be an example to the world

In what remains a mystery, God chose the Jewish people for both blessing and suffering, in order that their blessedness as well as their travails should be a witness and testimony to the world of God's faithfulness and an example of what He requires

He also chose them to be a **kingdom of priests** to the rest of the world of the knowledge of the One True God. But they must first come to faith before these promises come into their full fulfillment

CHAPTER ELEVEN

The Jews and the Calling of the Nations: The Greater Vision

"No greater evidence for the truth of Scripture can be given than the existence and history of the Jews. Here is a book of many pages, held up for the reading and instruction of all nations."

ADOLPH SAPHIR, CHRIST AND ISRAEL (1868, P. 110)

How can a people be so special, so successful (as a people group), be able to continue to rise up even in the midst of the worst persecution, violence and hatred through the centuries, flee and to re-settle and eventually thrive once again, yet never be fully victorious and never fully at rest?

This is the great mystery and the great paradox of the Jewish people. It is the bane and frustration of the anti-Semites and the haters of the Jews throughout the generations, from Haman to Hitler and beyond.

The salvation that God first extended primarily to the Jewish people, He then extended to the nations of the world. This is for His greater glory:

> *"He has said, 'It is not enough that you are merely My servant to raise up the tribes of Ya'akov [Jacob] and restore the offspring of Israel. I will also make you a light to the nations, so that My salvation can spread to the ends of the earth."*

ISAIAH 49: 6

Relating to Individual Gentiles and the Nations

Almost since the time of Abraham, there have been two competing and often contradictory attitudes by Jews toward Gentiles. On the one hand, there are examples of tenderness and love toward some Gentiles (such as the relationship between Naomi and her daughter-in-law Ruth) and an understanding that faith in the God of Israel and His commandments should be shared with the nations. On the other hand, there is an equally strong, some would say, even much stronger sense that Israel (the Jewish people) must remain set apart from the nations (the Gentiles) in order not to be polluted or stained by them.

One sees these two conflicting attitudes played out again and again in Jewish life and practice throughout the centuries. Much of the struggle between these two views for the heart of Judaism were playing themselves out in Jesus' day between the disciples of the two schools exemplified by the Beit Hillel (House of Hillel, School of Hillel) and Beit Shammai (House of Shammai, School of Shammai). Hillel and Shammai were both major teachers among the Pharisees. Each had many disciples. Both sat on the Sanhedrin, but they often represented very different interpretations of the Scriptures. In areas of Biblical interpretation and practice, where Shammai was usually very strict and unyielding, Hillel would often be more flexible and understanding.[1] One of the key differences between the two men was over how Jews should relate to Gentiles. Shammai was very concerned about Jewish assimilation with the Greek and Roman cultures. He sought to build up greater walls between Jews and the nations in how he and his disciples interpreted the Law, while Hillel and his followers wanted to find ways to reach out to the Gentiles while still maintaining the purity of Jewish faith and practice. Hundreds of clashes were recorded between the followers of these two different schools of Jewish thought.

"Will he go to the Dispersion...?"

Understanding this dichotomy is important for comprehending a key verse in the New Testament. The scene (as recorded in John 7) is as follows: Jesus is telling a multitude of people in Jerusalem: "I will be with you a little while longer, then I go to Him who sent Me." He is speaking of His impending death. He says: "You will seek Me, and won't find Me…" His hearers, though, completely miss the point. They ask themselves: "Where will this man go that we won't find him? Will he go to the Dispersion among the Greeks, and teach the Greeks?" (John 7:35)

Several important points are implicit in how these Jews responded to Jesus. First was the idea that there were at least some Jews in Israel at the time who felt the need to leave Israel in order to bring the truth of the God of Israel to the nations. These were part of Jewish communities scattered throughout the Greek-speaking world, who, along with other Jews because of their background, family ties or trade, together constituted the Dispersion. On the other side were primarily Judean Jews, some of whom would never even conceive of leaving Eretz Yisrael (the Land of Israel). Many of these also would have little dealings with Gentiles within Israel if they could avoid them.

In this sense, there were different kinds of Jews and different kinds of Judaisms. They might be held together by the Torah and the rest of the Scriptures, but they had very different backgrounds and attitudes.

Jesus was looked upon by the Jews of Jerusalem as a 'Galilean Jew' who already would have been more prone (in their minds) to have dealings with Gentiles than, say, most Judean Jews, simply because of where He was from. The Jews in Jerusalem – in misinterpreting what Jesus was trying to tell them – simply assumed that Jesus might be taking the next step: that of leaving Israel to go 'abroad' to teach the Gentiles.

This response showed that the Jewish crowd in Jerusalem *expected some Jews to go abroad to the Dispersion* and that some of these would teach the Gentiles. Even if other Jews wanted nothing to do with Gentiles, there were other Jews who did.

Thus, the dichotomy now makes sense. Despite this differentiation, in Biblical times there was Jewish concern for Gentiles. While the Temple stood, there was a Court for the Gentiles. This concern was manifested within Biblical Judaism for the fate of the Gentiles. The Scriptures themselves are filled with this concern.

Even in exile in Babylon, Jews were commanded by God to live their lives, have babies, and to "*seek the welfare of the city where I have sent you into exile and pray to the Lord on its behalf; for in its welfare you will have welfare.*" (Jeremiah 7) Here we see two very important spiritual principles from God's perspective: Jewish people were to pray for those Gentiles around them and to seek their welfare. By doing so, Jewish welfare would also be enhanced. While this command had some specific application to the Babylonian exile, in a broader sense, these same principles could apply to the Jewish Diaspora over the centuries. But how many religious Jews today pray for the welfare of the Gentiles in the places in which they live? I do not know, and I may be wrong, but I suspect that the number is not very large. Meanwhile, most secular Jews around the world, if they are truly secular, are not praying at all, certainly not on behalf of the Gentile cities in which they live! Instead, many of those secular Jews are busy trying to 'make the world a better place' along the lines of *tikkun olam*, not praying to God for the welfare of Gentiles. So, this principle has been largely lost in Judaism.

Proselytes in Biblical Times

> *"Woe to you, scribes and Pharisees, hypocrites! For you travel by sea and land to make one proselyte, and when he becomes one, you make him twice as much of a son of Gehenna as yourselves."*

> MATTHEW 23:15

Although the context is negative, what Jesus says in this passage shows us the Jews' commitment at that time to making converts to Judaism. Jesus was not condemning the act of bringing Gentiles to faith in the God of Israel; instead, He was condemning the perversion of that process.

The Jews' reputation at that time for making proselytes was so well known that there was even a Roman proverb about it, as we shall discuss in a moment.

The Greek word for a Gentile proselyte was *proselutos*. This is the term used generally in the Septuagint for the Hebrew word *ger*. The "pious Gentile" was known as a *ger shaar.*

Proselytes were Gentiles who either converted to Judaism from heathenism or who became identified with the children of Israel by seeking refuge with Israel's God. Proselytes were Gentile *strangers* or *foreigners* who became part of the people of Israel. We see the reference to *strangers* and *foreigners* that God makes in Exodus 12 with respect to keeping the Passover. According to various Bible commentaries, there were two types of Gentile proselytes. They included *proselytes of the gate* and those who were called *proselytes of righteousness* ("ger ha-zedek" or "ger ha-berit").[2] The latter embraced Judaism and were circumcised. According to Thomas Coke's commentary on Matthew, "[t]he zeal of the Jews making proselytes was so remarkable, that it was taken notice of by the heathen, and turned into a proverb."[3] The reputation of the Jews for making proselytes in the Roman world was reportedly at one time legendary.[4] This proverb (in Latin) appeared in one of the satires of the famous Roman poet Horace (Quintus Horatius Flaccus), who lived from 65 BC to 8 BC, long before the birth of Christ or the start of Christianity. It stated:

"Ac veluti te Judeaei, cogamus in hanc concedere turbam."[5]
"Like the Jews, we will compel you to yield to our throng."

Some paraphrases have also appeared: "We'll force you, like the proselytizing Jews, to be like us," or: "... just as the Jews do in Rome, we'll force you to join our congregation."[6]

And then there is Seneca, who complained that "the customs of this accursed race" – referring to the Jews – "have gained such influence that they are now received throughout all the world. The vanquished have given their laws to the victors."[7] Other Roman sources we see that the Jews were expelled from Rome around 19 AD "because 'they were converting many of the natives to their customs.'"[8]

Jewish influence had by this time extended to most of the Roman world. Philo extolled Mosaic teachings as applicable to the nations at large, while Moses was viewed as "a unique teacher of true wisdom and righteousness."[9]

The "God-fearers"

Beyond proselytes, numbers of Gentile men and women from among the nations (the *goyim*) had enormous respect for the God of Israel. These came to be known as the *God-fearers.* According to the *Encyclopedia Judaica*, in the Diaspora there was "an increasing number, perhaps millions by the first century, of *sebomenoi* (...God-fearers), gentiles who had not gone the whole route toward conversion."[10] According to scholar Michael Avi-Yonah, the God-fearers made up a "numerous class" of Gentiles. While "they sympathized with Judaism," most "did not feel able to shoulder the whole burden of the Law..."[11] They were not homogeneous, and within their ranks, "they included a wide range of Gentiles who adhered to Judaism in different ways."[12] Many embraced Jewish monotheism and "the Jewish moral law without however accepting circumcision."[13]

One example immortalized in the New Testament was the Roman centurion who came to Jesus asking him to heal his servant. This soldier recognized that Jesus had authority from God. Jesus replied, "Most certainly I tell you, not even in Israel have I found such faith." (Matthew 8:5-10)

Proselytes to Judaism Later Seen as "a Scab"

By the time of the compilation of the Talmud (which occurred centuries after the destruction of the Second Temple in Jerusalem in 70 AD), Gentile proselytes to Judaism were being considered by some as more of a nuisance than anything else. In the Tractate Yevamot (Chapter 4) in the *Gemara*, a Rabbi Chelmo said, "Proselytes are as bad for Israel as a scab, as it is written, 'And strangers shall join them and shall cleave to the House of Jacob.' (Isaiah 14:1)." This notion seems to be as far as possible from the Gentile view that Jews should be reaching out to the nations in order to bring them to the knowledge of the one true God.

A further departure from concern for the Gentiles can be seen in how a passage in the Babylonian Talmud altered what was expressed in the Mishnah. The Mishnah passage expressed concern for every individual soul created in the image of God – whether Jew or Gentile. The Talmud inserted "of Israel" to completely change and restrict the meaning of the passage to apply only to Jews, dropping any concern for the *goyim*. This was too much for Maimonides (Rambam), who stuck with the more expansive Mishnaic version, which showed concern for *all* souls, whether Jewish or Gentile. The Jewish atheist father-daughter team of Amoz Oz and Fania Oz-Salzberger saluted the Rambam for this effort, praising him by saying, "Well done, Maimonides." They understand, of course, that every soul has value (although as atheists, their view of the soul does not extend to an afterlife, but that is another story): "Each and every soul," they write, is a full world, be it of Israel or not."[14]

God's Concern for the Gentiles: The Greater Meaning of Sukkot

Many rabbis and other Jews kept themselves very set apart from Gentiles because of their deep concern over any hint of supporting idolaters or idolatry. But this sometimes also led to a deep antipathy.[15] But God Himself had concern for the Gentiles. He commanded the Children of Israel to sacrifice 70 bullocks each year during the seven-day Feast of Tabernacles (Sukkot) on behalf of the nations of the world. Each day over the seven days a given number of bulls were sacrificed, ending with seven bulls on the seventh day (Numbers 29: 12-32). These bulls represented the 70 'root' nations of the world (Genesis 10), the main nations from which all the tribes and peoples of the earth have sprung.

The sacrifices of the seventy bulls "offered for all the nations of the earth" was "a further example of Israel's life of intercessory mediation and activity for the sake of the nations of the world."[16]

There is a further gem about this hidden away in the Talmud, which, rather than seeing Gentiles as "a scab" or a nuisance if they want to convert to Judaism, expressed deep concern for the nations of the world and their spiritual well-being. In Sukkah 55b of the Babylonian Talmud we read: "Rabbi Johanan observed, 'Woe to the idolaters, for they had a loss and do not know what they have lost. When the Temple was in existence the altar atoned for them, but now who shall atone for them?"[17] Who indeed? Those of us who believe in the atoning ministry of Yeshua the Messiah know who has atoned for us.

Although Rabbi Johanan saw most of the non-Jewish world as idolaters, at least he had a concern for their souls and their standing before God.

In other words, by the time the Talmud was compiled and completed - centuries after Yeshua's death and resurrection had provided the way for salvation for both Jews and Gentiles, Judaism had by then lost most of its spiritual concern for Gentiles. Rabbi Johanan's expression in Tractate Sukkah appears as probably the last authoritative vestige of that concern within Orthodox Judaism. Bereft of the Temple and of Jerusalem, an anchor-less Judaism was by now mostly insular and inward-focused, seeking to survive in a sea of hostility and uncertainty, just trying to hold the Jewish people themselves together. The nations would have to wait.

The Book of Jonah as a Template for God's Call Upon the Jewish People to Be a Light to the Nations

The entire Book of Jonah shows God's concern for the lost people of Nineveh – a people for whom Jonah himself had no personal concern, since they were his enemies. Jonah had great faith in God but had no great love for the people of Nineveh. From his attitude, it appears that he would just as soon have enjoyed watching their destruction at God's hand as not. Indeed, the Book of Jonah records that Jonah himself was *annoyed* that God had compassion upon the people of Nineveh and spared them from destruction after they repented.

We don't know if Jonah ever came to love the people of Nineveh. The Book of Jonah ends before we know how Jonah responded (or not) to God's admonition to him about his attitude.

The call to Jonah to go to the people of Nineveh is a *template* for God's call upon the Jewish people as a whole to go to the nations, even those whom they despise, to bring the Good News of salvation.

But this sense of a Jewish calling to the nations – so clearly reflected in the Book of Jonah – seems largely lost in Judaism today. It can only be restored by a return to true Biblical faith on the part of the people of Israel. This is part of God's plan.

The Calling of the Gentile Nations

Israeli Messianic pastor and friend Eitan Shishkoff has written a wonderful book titled, *What About Us? The End-Time Calling of Gentiles in Israel's Revival.* He has stated: "The clear teaching of Scripture is that Israel will be used to bring the nations... to the saving knowledge of the God of Abraham." He adds: "I am convinced that the partnership of Yeshua's Gentile and Jewish followers is essential for the salvation of Israel, and thus for the Second Coming of Messiah."[18] Dan Juster has written about "the call to be a part of the nation of Israel in its distinctive task of witness."[19]

CHAPTER TWELVE

The Calling of the Jews

"...and in Israel the light and the power of God shall be made manifest unto all the nations."

ADOLPH SAPHIR

A Central and Unique Role

The calling upon the Jewish people is tied to God's plan not only for Israel but also for the nations. In a May 1868 sermon, Jewish believer Adolph Saphir proclaimed that the Jewish "nation has a position, central and unique, according to the divine purpose." This is because of "the decisive love," he added, "with which God regards them, and by the special influence which they are to exert on the whole world."[1]

There is an incredible richness and a depth of theology regarding the future of the nations of the world and how this is tied to the calling of the Jewish people. We see this in what is sometimes called 'the Puritan Hope' and other examples throughout history.[2]

Daniel Juster expresses this is in *The Irrevocable Calling*, where he considers the passage in Matthew 23: 37-39. Jesus is crying out to Jerusalem: "O Jerusalem, Jerusalem! You will not see me again until you say, 'Blessed is He who comes in the name of the Lord!" Juster extends the meaning of this passage to Israel's "priestly representative" role on behalf of all the nations of the world. Israel "has been specifically instructed that it must call out to Yeshua to come and rule." Israel as a nation has a "redemptive purpose...to call upon Yeshua and invite him to rule Israel and the nations."[3] This, of course, cannot occur until the Jewish people repent, mourn, and recognize that Yeshua – That Man - was and is the Messiah. We see this recognition take place in Zechariah 12:10: "*I will pour out on the house of David, and on the inhabitants of Jerusalem, the spirit of grace and of supplication; and they will look*

to me whom they have pierced; and they shall mourn for him, as one
mourns for his only son…"

It is *this calling* that will determine the future of the world. Only the
Jewish people can fulfill it. Everything else is building up to it.

Building Up to It

And what builds up to it? There are unique roles for both
redeemed Israel and the Church. Juster continues: "Israel and the
Church are interdependent and fulfill different but complementary
priestly roles…. The Jews are dependent on God's work through the
Gentiles for their salvation and the Gentiles are dependent on God's
work through the Jews."[4]

In 2011, I had the privilege of reviewing several books at the British
Library in London, finding some of the following passages.

In 1621 in London, William Gouge published the book, *The World's
Great Restauration [Restoration] or Calling of the Jews* by Sir Henry
Finch (1558-1625). Finch, a well-known lawyer at the time, wrote
that wherever "Israel, Judah, Zion, Jerusalem, etc. are named" in these
Scriptures, the Lord is not referring to "the spiritual Israel, or Church
of God collected of the Gentiles… but Israel properly descended out
of Jacob's loins. The same judgment is to be made of their returning to
their land and ancient seats, the conquest of their foes, the fruitfulness of
their soil, the glorious Church they shall erect in the land itself…. These
and such like are not Allegories…but meant really and literally of the
Jews."[5] These words were written more than three hundred years before
the establishment of the State of Israel in 1948! So, here we see a key
prediction fulfilled (the return to the land) and others yet to be fulfilled.

At the time, both Finch and his publisher Gouge [also "Goudge"]
were promptly arrested by English authorities for expressing such views.
Although Finch was quickly released "because of his great distinction as
a jurist…., he was sharply censured by speakers in Parliament."[6]

A similar book was published the year before, also in London. It was
titled, *A Plain Exposition* by Elnathan Parr. Parr wrote: "Again, here we
are to be put in mind, to pray for the calling of the Jews [Iewes], which
shall bring so much good to the world: as the sisters sent to Christ in the

behalf of their brother Lazarus, so let us Gentiles, importune the Lord for our brethren the Jews." And then this: "The end of this world shall not be til the Jews are called, and how long after that none yet can tell."[7]

Almost two hundred years later, James Bicheno, writing in 1807 in his book, *The Restoration of the Jews, The Crisis of All Nations*, would remark:

> *"A time must, therefore, come,* **when the Messiah shall reign for the good of the Jews,** *and when the Gentiles shall see their righteousness, and all kings their glory; for, if they perish in their present miseries, the prophecies prove nothing, and our faith is vain."[8] (emphasis added)*

These were men who earnestly believed, based on the Scriptures, that God's promises to the Jewish people would be fulfilled. That fulfillment, in turn, would someday impact the entire world.

My dear friend, Anna Portnov, a former Soviet Jewish atheist who later came to faith in Yeshua, expressed this in a note to me before she died. "Israel," she wrote, "won't be blessed" by God until this repentance takes place. What Anna meant is what I have tried to express throughout this book. Yes, there is a *general blessing* upon Israel because of God's promises to the Jewish people. But there is also a *general judgment.* That judgment is upon all people because of mankind's sin, but the Bible teaches that the Jews are first in line. This judgment cannot be lifted, nor the full blessing come, until their sins are atoned for by faith in the Messiah.

The Greater Glory

> *"I am one of those who believe in Israel's restoration and conversion; who receive it as a future certainty, that all Israel shall be gathered, and that all Israel shall be saved...I believe that it is not possible to enter God's mind regarding the destiny of man, without taking as our key...His mind regarding the ancient nation – that nation whose history, so far from being ended, or nearly ended, is only about to begin."[9]*

HORATIUS BONAR (1808-1889)

The Greater Glory is yet to come! Daniel C. Juster closes *The Irrevocable Calling* with the following stirring words, calling on all true believers to pray for "the restoration of the Church, the restoration of Israel, and the saved remnant of Israel." As this occurs, the Church will fulfill her own "call and destiny,...helping to restore Israel's irrevocable call, which is key to world redemption."[10]

Isaiah 49 so incredibly expresses this "Greater Glory." The LORD and His Messiah are speaking: "And now says the Lord, who formed Me from the womb to be His Servant, to bring Jacob back to Him, in order that Israel might be gathered to Him." (49:5) This was and is God's priority in mission and world evangelization – *to bring Jacob back to Him.* And yet, He then says: "It is too small a thing" (or "too light a thing") "that thou shouldest be My servant to raise up the tribes of Jacob and to restore the offspring of Israel." Further, He proclaims, *"I will also give You for a light to the nations that My salvation may be unto the end of the earth."* (49:6)

Salvation began with the Jewish people, and it was then extended to the nations of the world. It shall come to the Jewish people again: "Israel shall be saved with an everlasting salvation." (Isaiah 45:7)

Has God forgotten or turned His back on Israel? Isaiah writes: "But Zion said, 'The Lord has forsaken me...the Lord has forgotten me'."

Does that not sound like the plaintive cry of the Jewish people throughout much of the Diaspora and also today in this post-Holocaust world? That cry shall be answered.

Yet God says, "Can a woman forget her sucking child?... Behold, I have graven thee upon the palms of My hands; thy walls are continually before Me." (verses 15-16). The Lord GOD has promised *never* to forget or forsake Israel – Israel remains forever upon His heart.

Thanks and Acknowledgements

Blessing and honor and glory and power,
Wisdom and riches and strength evermore
Give ye to Him Who our battle hath won
Whose are the kingdom, the crown, and the throne

HORATIUS BONAR, 1866

M any people helped to make this book possible – and some didn't even know it! I especially want to thank readers of early drafts and sections of the book for their comments, insights and suggestions. Whatever faults remain are my own, and all views expressed in this book are my own and not necessarily the views of anyone else. Friends and colleagues in the spiritual vineyard of Jewish ministry who were early readers included: Howard Bass, Michael Brown, Jeff Ludwig, Jeannie Goldstein, and Jeff Swank, and, of course, my publisher at Messianic Jewish Publishers, Rabbi Barry Rubin and his assistant Mark Rantz. All provided important advice and assistance at various stages of this book's development for which I am very thankful.

Whether they all realized it or not (and whether they agreed with my all presuppositions or not), Mitch Glaser, James Miller Peck, Larry Plating, Jim Sibley, and Michael Zinn all helped me refine some of the concepts expressed in this book as I tried to explain my thesis to them and others at various points along the way, whether at Life in Messiah's Immanuel House in Brooklyn, at a past Jewish evangelism conference in Kiev, Ukraine, at a men's Bible study retreat deep in the West Virginia mountains, or in a small café in Jerusalem tucked away off Ben Yehuda Street. This book has been a global effort in many ways.

I want to especially thank Wes and Lori Taber and the entire Life in Messiah family for all of their support and encouragement over the years in Jewish ministry, along with my LCJE network 'family.' This *mishpochah* of close friends and 'fellow-travelers' nurtured and sustained the kind of environment needed for a book like this to emerge. My dear friend, Avi Snyder, of Jews for Jesus, as he has for so many things, plowed this field ahead of me with his understanding, boldly expressed, that God's *calling* upon the Jewish people has never changed, even with the coming of Messiah. That simple but startling insight started me on the path of writing this book. I urge readers to consult Avi's writings on this subject listed in the bibliography.

I want to thank my good friend and retired art professor, Joseph DiBella, for his insights on Jewish contributions to the arts, as well as to our care group of special friends from New Life in Christ for the blessing they are in my life and my wife Karen's life. Our pastor, Dr. Douglas Kittredge, has been my very dear friend and a special encouragement and inspiration over the years on what the Scriptures teach about the role of the Jewish people in God's plan for the world. I don't think that this book would ever have been possible without him.

The loving support of my wife, Karen, and my children is very precious to me and has made it possible for me to complete the task of writing this book. I am so thankful for all that God has given me, the people that He has brought into my life, and the opportunities He has given me to serve Him. I pray that I have faithfully reflected here the Truth from His Word. In the end, however, what I have expressed in this book is only my opinion, and all our opinions in this life are fallible.

Besides extensive use of Google Books and other online resources, the following libraries were useful to me in my research in preparation of this book: the Library of Congress in Washington, D.C., the British Library (London), the National Library of Israel (Jerusalem) the Life in Messiah International Library (Brooklyn, New York), the Vancouver Public Library (Vancouver, British Columbia), the England Run and Porter public libraries (Stafford County, Virginia), the Simpson Library (University of Mary Washington, Fredericksburg, Virginia), the Buhl Library (Grove City College, Pennsylvania), the Klau Library (Hebrew

Union College, Cincinnati), the Maag Library at Youngstown State University (Youngstown, Ohio), and, finally, the Widener and Houghton libraries at Harvard University.

Oftentimes, though, in developing my thesis on God's plan for the Jewish people, I made some discoveries where I didn't expect to find them - in previously untapped books right on my own bookshelves! These were books that, in many cases, I had bought years ago intending to read *someday* but had had very little time in the intervening years (until "retirement") to look at before commencing this book. However, when I finally did have time to consult them while doing research for this book, they yielded special treasures. One was Howard Sachar's delightful tome, *The Jews in America*. Another was John Murray Cuddihy's *The Ordeal of Civility: Freud, Marx, Levi-Strauss, and the Jewish Struggle with Modernity*, which I had not looked at since graduate school days when I had the privilege of taking a class at Harvard under Daniel Patrick Moynihan, and he used that book as a text for the class. But now I had the opportunity to look at this book in a whole new light. Another was Barry Horner's very important book, *Future Israel: Why Christian Anti-Judaism Must Be Challenged.*

All of this yielded another realization – sometimes we can scour the world looking for things that have been sitting right at Home all along. That principle applies to more than just books on our bookshelves...

On behalf of my fellow bibliophiles who buy some books with the best of intentions to read 'some day,' but as the years go by and such volumes gather dust on their shelves, let me say that *sometimes* 'some day' really does arrive - those books do eventually get read and become cherished parts of one's intellectual and spiritual makeup, providing a little further light to outshine the darkness.

I can only hope that some readers will 'some day' feel the same about this book.

Soli Deo Gloriam

Endnotes

Preface

1. Daniel C. Juster, The Irrevocable Calling: Israel's Role as a Light to the Nations (1996, 2007 edition), 9.
2. Eitan Shishkoff, "What About Us?" – The end-time calling of Gentiles in Israel's revival (2013), 28-29.
3. David Suissa, cited in the book of essays titled, I Am Jewish (2004, 2015 Paperback edition), 86.
4. Isaac Deutscher, The Non-Jewish Jew and Other Essays (1968), 86.
5. Raphael answered his own question in this way: "The primary, by no means obsolete, answer is that, in Christian scripture and mythology (if they can be distinguished), the so-called 'Chosen Race' were responsible for the death of the Son of God and deemed to be ejected forever from divine favour." (Frederic Raphael, Anti-Semitism (2015), 3). This is indeed what some Christians throughout history have believed and have acted upon, but such a view is not what the New Testament teaches – in fact, it teaches just the opposite, that the Jewish people are not "ejected forever from divine favour" but remain "beloved of God." (Romans 11:28) And, as far as the death of Jesus (Yeshua) is concerned, every true Christian knows that all of our sin put Him on the cross, since all men and women are sinners. He lay down His own life for our sakes; it wasn't taken from Him (1 John 3:16; John 15:3).
6. Murray Tilles, "The Chosen People – Chosen for a Purpose," Devoted to Israel (2011), 35-36.
7. E. Shishkoff, op. cit. (2013), 30.

Introduction

1. Although my paternal grandfather Arseny Melnick, who emigrated first to Canada and then to the United States prior to World War One, came from a small village in Ukraine that was settled by ex-Cossacks and Jews, and I know that there was at least one Jewish 'Mel'nik' (which means "miller" in Russian) from that village who died during the Second World War. Short of genetic testing, which as of this writing my family has not yet done, whether we ever had any Jewish background or not is obscured in the distant past.
2. This book originally began as an assessment of Jewish secularization in our society and the growing trend of 'Jewish atheism.'- what some might consider an oxymoron. Unfortunately, it is not. For data on Jewish secularization trends in America, see the Pew Research Report titled, "A Portrait of Jewish Americans" (2013) http://www.pewforum.org/files/2013/10/jewish-american-full-report-for-web.pdf. But trying to describe the 'why' of Jewish atheism turned out to be too difficult a task without first examining two characteristics that ironically are often intertwined with it - 'Jewish giftedness' and 'Jewish drivenness.' How these two factors connect would take some time to 'unpack' for the reader. I ultimately realized that I had to put the atheism book aside in order to first develop this book.
3. Foreword by Geoffrey Wigoder, Dictionary of Jewish Biography (1991), 7.
4. Daniel Juster, Jewish Roots: Understanding Your Jewish Faith (Shippensburg, PA: Destiny Image Publishers, Inc., 2013, Revised Fourth Edition), 246.
5. Rabbi Sherwin T. Wine, in the book of essays, I Am Jewish (2004, 2015 ed.), 64.
6. George Soros, Soros on Soros: Staying Ahead of the Curve (1995), 242, cited in Steven Silbiger, The Jewish Phenomenon, 165.
7. According to a December 20, 1998 interview broadcast on the television news program "60 Minutes," Soros said that he did not believe in God. Cited on the atheist website: www.celebatheists.com/wiki/George_Soros.

8.   Isaac Disraeli, *The Works of Isaac Disraeli: The Literary Character of Men of Genius Drawn from Their Own Feelings and Confessions.* (London: Routledge, Warnes, and Routledge, 1818, 1859), 24.
9.   Eric Weiner, *The Geography of Genius: A Search for the World's Most Creative Places, from Ancient Athens to Silicon Valley* (2016), 2, citing researcher Margaret Boden. Weiner states that Boden's definition also represent "the criteria the U.S. Patent Office uses when deciding whether an invention deserves a patent."
10.   Darrin M. McMahon, *Divine Fury: A History of Genius* (2013), 186.
11.   D. McMahon, op. cit., 98, citing Edmond Halley, found in Patricia Fara, *Newton: The Making of a Genius* (New York: Columbia University Press, 2002), 163.
12.   D. McMahon, *Divine Fury*, 56.
13.   Weiner, op. cit., 207.
14.   James Gleick, *Genius: The Life and Science of Richard Feynman* (1992), 312.
15.   Two studies, published in 1985 and 1999 respectively, and dealing with two different sample sets of Einstein's brain, each claimed some irregularity. The first asserted that "Einstein's brain exhibited a higher-than-average concentration of 'glial' cells that aid neurons on the processes of neurotransmission." The second claimed that "Einstein's parietal lobe...was 15 percent wider than normal." But as Darrin M. McMahon concluded in *Divine Fury: The Making of Genius*: "These studies generated a great deal of publicity, although their scientific value is questionable." (D. McMahon, *Divine Fury*, 230-231).
16.   The measuring of skull size and morphology and weighing the brains of geniuses and other great men after their deaths in an effort to discover the source of greatness or genius was a wildly popular practice in the nineteenth century. While there are some who still believe that certain aspects of phrenology are scientific, it is broadly discredited today. For a history of phrenology as related to genius, see D. McMahon, Chapter V, "Geniology," *Divine Fury* (2013), 151-188.
17.   D. McMahon, *Divine Fury: A History of Genius*, "Introduction: The Problem of Genius," xiv.
18.   Michelangelo: the "divine one"; da Vinci: "...through celestial influences": found in Giorgio Vasari, *Lives of the Artists,* cited by D. McMahon in *Divine Fury: A History of Genius*, 62-65, Chapter 2 footnote 48, p. 261; "a creature set apart, elected and chosen..." (D. McMahon, op. cit., 65).
19.   "...was the deciding factor..." (D. McMahon, op. cit., 82);
20.   Steven L. Pease, *The Debate Over Jewish Achievement* (2015), 40.
21.   Richard Lynn, *A Study of Jewish Intelligence and Achievement* (2011), 3. Lynn adds: "...it is curious that the high Jewish IQ has almost invariably been ignored by historians, sociologists, and economists who have written on the high achievements of the Jews..." (p. 5)
22.   Amy Chua and Jed Rubenfeld, *The Triple Package: How Three Unlikely Traits Explain the Rise and Fall of Cultural Groups in America* (2015 ed.), 194-195.
23.   "An odd but brilliant man": Eric Weiner, *The Geography of Genius: A Search for the World's Most Creative Places, from Ancient Athens to Silicon Valley* (2016), 3. Weiner writes that Galton had an IQ of "nearly 200." (p. 4) "Measure the gradations of greatness": Charles Murray, *Human Accomplishment*, 72-73.
24.   Darrin M. McMahon, *Divine Fury: A History of Genius* (2013), 178-185.
25.   Steven Pease notes in *The Debate Over Jewish Achievement* that, for many multiculturalists, "race is simply a fabrication of no real usefulness, except as a rationalization for discrimination.... Multiculturalists generally," Pease continues, "believe that race is a 'social construct,' racial differences do not exist, and anyone who seriously studies them or espouses them must be academically and publicly ostracized." (Pease, *The Debate,* 269).
26.   I say this based both on his name and some of the comments Weiner makes in the book, such as an oblique comment about Jewish geography and "tribal insecurity". (Weiner, op. cit., 169)
27.   Eric Weiner, *The Geography of Genius*, 5. Weiner cites no reference for this statistic, only unnamed "psychologists." His view is also completely contrary to Charles Murray: "Hence my view that something in the genes explains elevated Jewish IQ..." (Charles Murray, "Jewish Genius," *Commentary*, April 1, 2007. http://www.commentarymagazine.com/articles/jewish-genius/)
28.   E. Weiner, *The Geography of Genius*, 277.
29.   Steven L. Pease, *The Golden Age of Jewish Achievement* (2009), 15. With regard to the second-generation immigrant argument for Jewish achievement, Pease avers that, while it may be a contributing factor in many cases, it suffers from a logical flaw as a full explanation. He also gives numerous counter examples of where it fails (Pease, op. cit., 381-383). See also the section, "A Second-Generation Jewish Immigrant Phenomenon" in his second book, *The Debate Over Jewish Achievement* (2015), 56-59.

30.   Pease, *The Debate Over Jewish Achievement,* 29. He adds: "I believe the strongest case squarely favors Jewish culture as the most important force behind [disproportionate] performance." (p. 90) Pease also discusses the significance of the relatively new area of *epigenetics*, which demonstrates that "environmental conditions…can cause genes to be turned on and off, or up and down without changing the underlying DNA or genes themselves." (p. 28). Epigenetics may thus turn out to be the missing link *between* 'nature' and 'nurture'.

31.   Adolph Hitler in *Mein Kampf,* cited in D. McMahon, *Divine Fury: A History of Genius* (2013), "Introduction: The Problem of Genius," xvi.

32.   Adams used this description of genius in a letter to Benjamin Waterhouse dated May 21, 1821, but he was probably quoting an 1803 poem by Wentworth Apthorp Morton that used the phrase. See wikiquote.org/wiki/John_Adams.

33.   E. Weiner, *The Geography of Genius,* 55, 58, 22, 87-88.

34.   Letter from John Adams to Francois Adriaan van der Kemp dated February 16, 1809. Cited in wikiquote.org/wiki/John_Adams

35.   Dennis Prager and Joseph Telushkin, *Why the Jews? The Reason for Anti-semitism,* 30.

36.   Prager and Telushkin, op. cit.

37.   George Gilder, *The Israel Test* (2009), 32.

38.   George Gilder, op. cit., 32.

39.   See Joseph Jacobs, *Jewish Contributions to Civilization: An Estimate.* Modern 2009 reprint of the 1919 edition, 3.

40.   Darrin M. McMahon, *Divine Fury: A History of Genius* (2013), 215.

41.   Pease, *The Debate Over Jewish Achievement,* 121-122, citing Dr. Mendel Silber, *Jewish Achievement* (St. Louis Missouri: Modern View Publishing Co., 1910).

42.   Joseph Jacobs, *Jewish Contributions to Civilization: An Estimate* (2009 reprint of 1919 edition), 323.

43.   C. Murray, op. cit., 87.

44.   Found in Charles Murray, *Human* Accomplishment, 93, citing Francis Galton, *Hereditary Genius: An Inquiry into Its Laws and Consequences* (London: Macmillan, 1869), 78.

45.   C. Murray, op. cit., 90-91. While a 2003 article in the *New Yorker* mocked Murray's use of the "Lotka Curve," it produced no evidence to show that it was wrong or misguided (see Rebecca Mead, "The All-time Greats," *New Yorker,* November 10, 2003. www.newyorker.com/magazine/2003/11/10/the-all-time-greats

46.   C. Murray, op. cit., Chapter 6, "The Lotka Curve," *Human Accomplishment,* 87-106. The mathematical formula and relationship that Lotka discovered to create his hyperbolic curve is found in Murray's book on page 595, footnote 4.

47.   Eric Weiner, *The Geography of Genius: A Search for the World's Most Creative Places, from Ancient Athens to Silicon Valley* (2016), 8-9. Although Simonton has done interesting work, he is a thoroughgoing Darwinist, even dedicating his 1999 work, *Origins of Genius* "To All Darwinists." This obviously colors his presuppositions and conclusions through a Darwinian prism, even as I view reality through a Biblical one.

48.   E. Weiner, *The Geography of Genius* (2016), 252.

49.   The "geography of genius" view is also at odds with "the theory of natural genius, according to which the power [of genius] had little to do with place." (McMahon, *Divine Fury,* 2013, 149).

50.   Steven Beller, cited in E. Weiner, *The Geography of Genius,* 277.

51.   Charles Murray, *Human Accomplishment,* 280.

52.   E. Weiner, op. cit., 120, 124-126, 141.

53.   Margaret A. Boden, *The Creative Mind: Myths and Mechanisms,* 3-5.

54.   Arthur Koestler, *The Act of Creation* (London, 1975 ed.), 211.

55.   M. Boden, op. cit., 5.

56.   E. Weiner, *The Geography of Genius* (2016), 279-281.

57.   Prager and Telushkin, op. cit., 26.

58.   Prager and Telushkin, op. cit.

59.   Frederic Raphael, *Anti-Semitism* (2015), 18-19. Raphael's book is definitely worth reading as a modern-day plaintive cry against the despicable hatred of some who call themselves "Christians" against the Jewish people, witnessed so often throughout history. Raphael's anger for what has been done to the Jewish people in Christianity's name is palpable – and understandable. It breaks one's heart to realize that his view reflects the views of many Jews today – but what else do they have to go on? However, while important, Raphael's book also has some serious shortcomings. One is

the notion that "Christianity was the first religion to demand universal obedience to dogma and to require subservience, on pain of death, to those who preached it." (page 46) This is simply false. As one example, those early Christian believers – many of them *Jewish-Christian* believers – who were thrown to the lions in the Coliseum in Rome or set alight as human torches because they would not worship the Roman emperor under the religion of Rome – was that not the demand of "universal obedience to dogma...[requiring] subservience on pain of death"? Of course it was! Next, on page 48, Raphael claims that Jesus never said that he was the Son of God. Of course he did! This is contradicted in several places in the New Testament but most clearly in Mark 14:61-62, when Jesus was being interrogated by the High Priest. When asked, "Are you the Messiah, the Son of the Blessed One?" Jesus answered, "I Am," and quoted Daniel 7:13. At this, the High Priest tore his robes and cried out, "What further need do we have of witnesses? You have heard the blasphemy." It was *because* Jesus claimed to be the Son of God and *because He said so out of His own mouth* that He was condemned to death for blasphemy by the Sanhedrin.

60.   F. Raphael, *Anti-Semitism* (2015), 54.

61.   Frederic Raphael says: "We are never quite out of earshot of the loud whisper that if Israel did not exist, all would be nice and orderly again." Raphael realizes that anti-Zionism, no matter what its adherents say, is really at its heart, anti-Semitism: "This claim [of anti-Zionism] carries a rider that the wish to destroy 'the Zionists' has nothing whatsoever in common with the old-fashioned anti-Semitism." (F. Raphael, *Anti-Semitism*, 104). But of course it does! With respect to anti-Zionists who are *not* anti-Semites, I know that there are many nuances, including numbers of sincere Hasidic Jews, such as the Satmars, who are anti-Zionistic (because modern-day Israel was not founded by the Messiah) who are obviously not anti-Semitic (!), as well as some well-meaning Christians who have no particular animus against Jewish people but are indifferent to them and Israel per se. Such people would certainly not support Israel's destruction or any discrimination against the Jewish people, but they might fall into the category of those people who question whether Israel has any modern-day right to the Land. These might classify themselves as 'anti-Zionistic' without necessarily being anti-Semitic.

62.   Prager and Telushkin, op. cit., 3.

63.   Ephraim Kishon, cited in the book of essays, *I Am Jewish* (2004, 2015), 93.

64.   Richard Feynman and Murray Gell-Mann had an unusual relationship as colleagues and sometime friends but later became somewhat estranged. One biographer describes Feynman's connection to Gell-Mann as "his sometime friend, collaborator, office neighbor, foil, competitor, and antagonist..." (James Gleick, Chapter: Prologue, *Genius: The Life and Science of Richard Feynman*, 11).

65.   James Gleick, Chapter: Prologue, *Genius: The Life and Science of Richard Feynman*, 8.

66.   J. Gleick, op. cit., 323.

67.   Fritzsch (2010), op. cit., p. 26.

68.   William H. Cropper, *Great Physicists: The Life and Times of Leading Physicists from Galileo to Hawking,* Ch. 26: "Telling the Tale of the Quarks: Murray Gell-Mann" (New York: Oxford University Press, 2001), p.404.

69.   George Johnson, *Strange Beauty: Murray Gell-Mann and the Revolution in Twentieth-Century Physics* (1999), 44, 8.

70.   G. Johnson, *Strange Beauty*, 213-214. Other famous Hungarian Jewish physicists include John von Neumann, Theodor von Karman and Georg von Hevesy (Richard Lynn, *The Chosen People: A Study of Jewish Intelligence and Achievement*, Ch. 4, "Austria and Hungary," 52). Additional Hungarian Jews who have made enormous contributions to science include Dennis Gabor, "the Nobel laureate who invented holography," and Michael Polyani, "the eminent chemist-philosopher who inspired a school of followers around the globe." (George Gilder, *The Israel Test*, 73). Regarding Jewish inventors generally, the "second most prolific" inventor in American history (after Thomas Alva Edison, who was not Jewish), was Edwin Land, who held some 535 patents (Steven L. Pease, *The Golden Age of Jewish Achievement*, 43).

71.   Einstein is said to have responded (about the possibility of an atomic bomb): "I never thought of that!" Found in James Gleick, *Genius: The Life and Science of Richard Feynman,* 136, citing Richard Rhodes, *The Making of the Atomic Bomb* (1987), 305, 308. On a more amusing note, just as Hungarian Jews dominated the earlier understanding of the atomic bomb, other Hungarian Jews also emerged around the same time frame as the world's best table tennis players! ("Victor Barna," *Dictionary of Jewish Biography*, 47)

72.   Max Born, *My Life: Recollections of a Nobel* Laureate (New York: Charles Scribner's Sons,

1975), 236-237.

73.   Biographer James Gleick describes Feynman as "a New York Jew distinctly uninterested in either the faith or the sociology of Judaism." (J. Gleick, *Genius*, 85).

74.   This was the case even though Feynman faced discrimination because of his Jewishness. He was reportedly turned down at Columbia University because of the Jewish quota at that time (J.J. O'Connor and E.F. Robertson, "Richard Phillips Feynman," August 2002, University of St. Andrews; http://turnbull.mcs.st-and.ac.uk/~history/Biographies/Feynman.html. Accessed Sept. 24, 2015). He attended MIT as an undergraduate.

In his book, *Quantum Man*, Lawrence Krauss notes: "The head of the physics department at Princeton had written to Philip Morse about Feynman, asking about his religious affiliation: 'We have no definite rule against Jews but have to keep their proportion in our department reasonably small because of the difficulty of place them'." Krauss states that, in the end, "it was decided that Feynman was not sufficiently Jewish 'in manner' to get in the way. The fact that Feynman, like many scientists, was essentially uninterested in religion never arose as part of the discussion." (L. Krauss, *Quantum Man,* 2011, 22-23). Feynman was eventually accepted at Princeton.

75.   Feynman commented to Wouk: "Talk more about the Talmud," but then later added, "I don't believe any of it, that's all…" Wouk told him straight: "forgive me, friend Nobel genius, you're as ignorant of religion as I am of calculus, because you shut out religion for good when you were only ten." (Wouk (2010), op. cit., 156, 166).

76.   M. John Harrison, "Physics, bongos and the art of the nude," *The Telegraph.* (www.telegraph.co.uk/culture/books/3643596/Physics-bongos-and-the-art-of-the-nude.html Accessed September 24, 2015)

77.   Daniel Gill, cited in the *I Am Jewish* book of essays (2004, 2015 paperback ed.), 86. Gill was a childhood friend of famed journalist Daniel Pearl.

78.   Noah J. Efron, *A Chosen Calling* (2014), 6, 10.

79.   Anne Frank quote from *Anne Frank's Tales from the Secret Annex.*

80.   One example of a world-renowned collector was the late Shlomo Moussaieff, who, until his death, had the world's largest private collection of Near Eastern Antiquities (Hershel Shanks, "Renowned Collector Shlomo Moussaieff Dies at 92," *Biblical Archaeology Review* (November/December 2015), Vol. 41 (6), 62.

81.   Morley Safer profile of David Rubenstein, "All-American," on the CBS "60 Minutes" television program, May 3, 2015. www.cbsnews.com/news/patriotic-philanthropist-david-rubenstein-morley-safer-60-minutes/

82.   Steven L. Pease, *The Golden Age of Jewish Achievement* (2009), 13.

83.   Miles D. Storfer (1990), 322.

84.   Storfer, op cit., footnote 19, 333.

85.   See the comment in Stephen J. Whitfield, *Jewish Voices of Jacob, Hands of Esau: Jews in American Life and Thought* (1984), 76.

86.   S.J. Whitfield, op. cit., 82-83.

87.   George Soros, *Soros on Soros: Staying Ahead of the Curve* (1995), 242, cited in Steven Silbiger, *The Jewish Phenomenon*, 165.

88.   Isaac Deutscher, *The Non-Jewish Jew* (1968), 60.

89.   F. Raphael, op. cit., 116. Along with millions of other victims, Stalin decided to destroy a number of Jewish literary figures.

90.   Isaac Deutscher, *The Non-Jewish Jew* (1968), 59. It should be added, though, as another author has observed, that "Jews who are the most radical are often the most ignorant of their religion, including the concept of *tikkun olam.*" (Stephen J. Whitfield, *Jewish Voices of Jacob, Hands of Esau: Jews in American Life and Thought,* 1984, p. 86).

91.   Isaac Deutscher, *The Non-Jewish Jew and Other Essays* (1968), vii-x, 5-12; 91-93.

92.   See Mitch Glaser and Alan Shore, *Remnant and Renewal: The New Russian Messianic Movement* (New York: Chosen People Ministries, 2006).

93.   Ruth R. Wisse, *Jews and Power* (2007), x-xi.

94.   A good example of that type of thinking can be found in the views of Isaac Deutscher himself, who, as noted, was raised in Hasidic Judaism but later rejected it for atheism and Communism. In his 1968 book, *The Non-Jewish Jew*, Deutscher wrote: "The Jewish heretic who transcends Jewry belongs to a Jewish tradition…" Deutscher believed that many of his revolutionary heroes – and he included Spinoza, Heine, Marx, Rosa Luxemburg, Trotsky and Freud in that list - could be placed within a Jewish tradition: "They all went beyond the boundaries of Jewry…They all looked for

ideals and fulfillment beyond it, and they represent the sum and substance of much that is greatest in modern thought…" (Isaac Deutscher, *The Non-Jewish Jew*, 26) This shows Deutscher's frame of mind, which is shared by many Jewish radicals who are dedicated to 'changing the world'.

95.   George Gilder, *The Israel Test* (2014), 40-41.
96.   Jim Holt, *Why Does the World Exist? An Existential Detective Story* (2012), 120. See also my review of Deutsch's *The Beginning of Infinity* in A.J. Melnick, "David Deutsch's strange reality," *Journal of Creation* 28(1) 2014: 39-44.
97.   David Deutsch, *The Beginning of Infinity* (2011), 64, 221.
98.   George Gilder, *The Israel Test* (2014), 42.
99.   Frederic Raphael, *Anti-Semitism* (2015), 3.
100.   Encyclopedia entry for "Tikkun" in *Encyclopedia Judaica*, Second Edition, Vol. 19, 722.
101.   "Tikkun Olam: The Spiritual Purpose of Life." http://www.innerfrontier.org/Practices/ TikkunOlam.htm. Accessed October 15, 2015.
102.   S. Herzig, op. cit., 167.
103.   S. Herzig, op. cit., 165-167.
104.   Paul Johnson, *A History of the Jews*, 2.
105.   Nikolai Berdyaev, *Smysl' istorii: Opyt filosofii chelovecheskoi sud'by* ("The Meaning of History: The Experience of Philosophy of Human Destiny"), based on a series of lectures originally given in Moscow in 1920-21 prior to Berdyaev's expulsion from the Soviet Union under Stalin. This work was published in Paris by the YMCA Press (1969, 2nd Edition). The key chapter in this work is Chapter V ("Sud'ba evreistva" – "The Destiny of Jewry"). The Russian online version can be found at: www.odinblago.ru/smisl_istorii. The modern English version of *The Meaning of History* was published in 2006 (with a 2009 update) by Transaction Publishers, New Brunswick, New Jersey, based on a 1963 London edition by Geoffrey Bles. Berdyaev himself generally viewed genius as a religious phenomenon (see D. McMahon, *Divine Fury: A History of Genius*, 203). The first part of this quote was translated from the Russian original by the author. The latter part of the quote is from the Transaction version, with this section found at pages 86-87.
106.   See "Mathematician-Apologist Leonhard Euler," www.christianity.com/church/church-history/timeline/1701-1800/mathematician-apologist-leonhard-euler-11630191.html. Updated May 2007. This view is certainly confirmed in multiple sources. See also Charles Murray, *Human Accomplishment: The Pursuit of Excellence in the Arts and Sciences, 800 B.C. to 1950* (2003), "Mathematics" chart and accompanying text, 127; Neil Turok, *The Universe Within: From Quantum to Cosmos* (2012),75.
107.   "Mathematician-Apologist Leonhard Euler," www.christianity.com/church/church-history/ timeline/1701-1800/mathematician-apologist-leonhard-euler-11630191.html. Updated May 2007
108.   I have seen at least three different names proposed in various published accounts of who purportedly gave this response to Frederick the Great: from a General Ziethen, to a royal physician named Zimmerman of Brugg-in-Aargau, to the Marquis d'Argens (Jean-Baptiste de Boyer). See one online version of this story at JRBenjamin, "Do the Jews Prove God's Existence?" The Bully Pulpit, 23 April 2015 entry. www.jrbenjamin.com/2015/04/23/could-the-history-of-the-jews-prove-gods-existence/
109.   See, for example, Adolph Saphir, *Christ and Israel*, 110.
110.   Simon Schama, *The Story of the Jews: Finding the Words, 1000 BC – 1492 AD* (New York: HarperCollins, 2013), xvi.
111.   Amos Oz and Fania Oz-Salzberger, *Jews and Words* (2012), 107, 133.
112.   Max I. Dimont, *The Indestructible Jews* (New York: New American Library, Revised edition, Paperback, April 1973), 20. Dimont was also the author of *Jews, God and History* (1962).
113.   Thomas Cahill, "Introduction," *The Gifts of the Jews: How a Tribe of Desert Nomads Changed the Way Everyone Thinks and Feels* (New York: Nan A. Talese/Anchor Books, 1998), 3-4.
114.   In *Cultures of the Jews*, Stephen J. Whitfield writes that "…individualism does not fit snugly with *k'lal yisrael*, an ideal that subordinates the promotion of self-interest to communal claims." (S.J. Whitfield, Ch. 9: "Declarations of Independence: American Jewish Culture in the Twentieth Century," cited in David Biale, *Cultures of the Jews: A New History*, 1141-1142).
115.   Joel Richardson, *When a Jew Rules the World* (2015), 55. Richardson states, "Throughout the hundreds of times that God pledged Himself to the future salvation of Israel, His words were always directed to a corporate people." (op. cit., p. 56)
116.   S. Snobelen, "'The Mystery of This Restitution of All Things': Isaac Newton on the Return of the Jews," Chapter 7 in J.E. Force and R.H. Popkin (Eds.), *Millenarianism and Messianism in*

Early Modern European Culture: The Millenarian Turn, 103.

117. Joel Richardson, *When a Jew Rules the World* (2015), 35.

118. Quote from Hegel cited in Adolph Saphir, *Christ and Israel*, 17.

119. Rob Richards, *Has God Finished with Israel?* 69.

120. J.C. Ryle, *Coming Events and Present Duties* (DATE?), Chapter VII, "And So All Israel Will Be Saved," 109.

121. Steven Silbiger, *The Jewish Phenomenon* (2009), 9.

122. Adolph Saphir, *Christ and Israel*, 54.

123. A. Saphir, op. cit., 107, from a sermon given on May 18, 1868.

124. Douglas W. Kittredge, *God's Plan for Peace in the Middle East* (2006), 30.

125. Steven Silbiger, *The Jewish Phenomenon* (2009), 9.

126. Regarding the differences between the Ashkenazim and the Sephardim, Pease notes that, "In the Middle Ages, the gifted Jews were not the Ashkenazi, but the Sephardics, such as Maimonides. They were the high achievers of Jewry." (S.L. Pease, *The Golden Age of Jewish Achievement*, 385). Charles Murray takes this discussion even further. He writes that, "After being expelled from Spain at the end of the 15th century, Sephardi Jews rose to distinction in many of the countries where they settled." He cites Benjamin Disraeli and economist David Ricardo as two examples (Charles Murray, "Jewish Genius," *Commentary*, April 1, 2007. http://www.commentarymagazine.com/articles/jewish-genius/). Two others include Spinoza and Montefiore.

127. Yosef Tobi, Ch. 5 "Challenges to Tradition: Jewish Cultures in Yemen, Iraq, Iran, Afghanistan, and Bukhara," edited by David Biale, *Cultures of the Jews*, 933-934.

128. As Jewish Marxist Isaac Deutscher lamented at the time, although there were plenty of Marxist and socialist Jews, Jewish scholars in the West who were *anti*-Communist were also "most prominent": "…when we move to the departments of humanities we see among the hosts of historians, politicians, sociologists, etc., a great number of Jews furiously engaged in this cold war on behalf of this society of ours…" (Isaac Deutscher, *The Non-Jewish Jew*, 59).

129. George Gilder, *The Israel Test* (2009), 73.

130. Arthur Koestler, *The Thirteenth Tribe* (New York: Random House, 1976).

131. Koestler biographer Michael Scammell asserts that, with respect to his writing of *The Thirteenth Tribe*, Koestler "was convinced that if he could prove that the bulk of East European Jews (the ancestors of today's Ashkenazim) were descended from the Khazars, the racial basis for anti-Semitism would be removed and anti-Semitism itself would disappear." (Scammell, 546).

132. In the 1,150-page historical work on *Cultures of the Jews* (2002), edited by David Biale, the "Khazars" do not even merit a passing reference in the index. In a 2007 JewishPress.com article on the Khazars, author Steven Plaut noted: "…*The Encyclopedia of Judaism* (1989) emphatically states, 'The notion that Ashkenazi Jewry is descended from the Khazars has absolutely no basis in fact.'" (Steven Plaut, "The Khazar Myth and the New Anti-Semitism," JewishPress.com, May 9, 2007. www.jewishpress.com/indepth/front-page/the-khazar-myth-and-the-new-anti-semitism/2007/05/09/). A 2013 report on a genetics study on Ashkenazic Jewry in *Nature Communications* concluded that "The origins of Ashkenazi Jews remains highly controversial" and "enigmatic." With respect to the Khazar thesis, however, the analyses of the study "suggest that the first major wave of assimilation probably took place in Mediterranean Europe…with substantial further assimilation of minor founders in west/central Europe. There is less for assimilation in Eastern Europe, and almost none for a source in the north Caucasus/Chuvashia, as would be predicted by the Khazar hypothesis…" (Marta D. Costa, Joana B. Pereira, Maria Pala, et al. "A substantial prehistoric European ancestry amongst Ashkenazi maternal lineages," *Nature Communications* **4** No. 2543. www.nature.com/ncomms/2013/131008/ncomms3543/full/ncomms3543.html). 8 October 2013).

133. "The authors of this book, perhaps partially descended from those emblematic Khazars and Cossacks, have nothing to say about a presumed genetic, racial or ethnic continuity of the Jews." (Amos Oz and Fania Oz-Salzberger, *Jews and Words*, 52). In his 2015 book *Anti-Semitism*, Frederic Raphael refers to Koestler's *The Thirteenth Tribe* as a "wishful essay." (F. Raphael, *Anti-Semitism*, 17, fn. 10. Shlomo Sand, an Israeli, has been one of the latest to embrace the Khazar hypothesis (see Pease, *The Debate Over Jewish Achievement*, 185, 217).

134. See, for example, the interesting work of Kevin Alan Brook and his (2000-2013) article, "Are Russian Jews Descended from the Khazars?" (www.khazaria.com/khazar-diaspora.html). Brook takes a middle position. He believes that "Eastern European Jews descend both from Khazarian Jews AND from Israelite Jews." He is also the author of *The Jews of Khazaria*. However, he had the scholarly integrity to add the following note: "Although subsequent genetic evidence found no

trace of Khazarian-related ancestry in any modern Jewish population, I'm keeping this essay online for the time being so you can analyze different writers' arguments for and against this proposition."

135. Steven Plaut, "The Khazar Myth and the New Anti-Semitism," JewishPress.com, May 9, 2007. www.jewishpress.com/indepth/front-page/the-khazar-myth-and-the-new-anti-semitism/2007/05/09/

136. Letter to the author from Arthur Koestler, March 21, 1977 (London).

137. This scholar told me that the source Koestler referred to was not part of the original text that was cited (Discussion with leading scholar on Iran at Harvard University, 1977).

138. M. Scammell, op. cit., 548.

139. "Theodor Lessing: Jewish Self-Hatred (1930)," cited in Paul Mendes-Flohr and Jehuda Reinharz, *The Jew in the Modern World: A Documentary History* 272-274, fn. 1.

140. Sander Gilman, *Jewish Self-Hatred: Anti-Semitism and the Hidden Language of the Jews* (1986),1.

141. Paul Mendes-Flohr, Ch. 3, "The Throes of Assimilation: Self-Hatred and the Jewish Revolutionary," *Divided Passions: Jewish Intellectuals and the Experience of Modernity*, 67.

142. From Robert Wistrich, *Revolutionary Jews from Marx to Trotsky* (London, 1976), 6,8, cited in Paul Mendes-Flohr, *Divided Passions*, op cit., 68.

143. Charles E. Silberman, *A Certain People: American Jews and Their Lives Today* (New York: Summit, 1985), 36.

144. George Eliot, cited in Gilman, op. cit., 19-20.

145. Charles E. Silberman, op. cit., 37.

146. Frederic Raphael, *Anti-Semitism*, 130.

147. Cuddihy wrote that "secular Jewish intellectual ideologies," by which he means Marxism, Freudianism, Reform Judaism, and others, "are exercises in antidefamation, addresses in defense of Jewry to the cultured among its despisers." (John Murray Cuddihy, *The Ordeal of Civility: Freud, Marx, Levi-Strauss, and the Jewish Struggle for Modernity*, 4).

148. P. Mendes-Flohr, *Divided Passions*, 67. Norman Mailer is quoted as saying that "No anti-Semite can begin to comprehend the malicious analysis of his soul which every Jew indulges every day." ("Responses and Reactions VI," cited in Cuddihy, ix).

149. Eitan Shishkoff, *'What About Us?' – The end-time calling of Gentiles in Israel's revival* (2013), 39.

150. Steven L. Pease, "Afterword," *The Golden Age of Jewish Achievement* (2009), 407.

151. Joseph Jacobs, *Jewish Contributions to Civilization: An Estimate* (Philadelphia: The Conant Press, 1920), 49.

152. Sanford Pinsker, "Smart [Academic] Jews," *The Georgia Review* **51**(1), Spring 1997: 162.

153. David A. Hollinger, *Cosmopolitanism and Solidarity*, 163; also cited in Efron (2014), 6. For more references to the "booster-bigot trap" idea, see also D.A. Hollinger, *Science, Jews, and Secular Culture: Studies in Mid-Twentieth Century American Intellectual History* (1996), 11, as well as his *In the American Province: Studies in the History and Historiography of Ideas* (1985), 56. Hollinger adds this comment: "The best way to avoid both boosterism and bigotry was, and is, to avoid talking about Jews." (D.A. Hollinger, *Science, Jews, and Secular Culture: Studies in Mid-Twentieth Century American Intellectual History* (1996), 11).

154. D.A. Hollinger, *Science, Jews, and Secular Culture...* (1996), 12-13.

155. Amy Chua and Jed Rubenfeld, *The Triple Package: How Three Unlikely Traits Explain the Rise and Fall of Cultural Groups in America* (2015 ed.), 61. At the same time, they contend that "even as the notion of chosenness waned, Jews rarely gave up the idea of their exceptionality." (p. 62)

156. S. Pinsker, "Smart [Academic] Jews," 162.

157. Steven Silbiger, *The Jewish Phenomenon: 7 Keys to the Enduring Wealth of a People* (2009), 3.

158. George Gilder, *The Israel Test*, 245-249.

Chapter One

1.   Gordon Fraser, *The Quantum Exodus*, 6-8, citing Primo Levi.

2.   Charles Murray, *Human Accomplishment*, 282.

3.   George Gilder, *The Israel Test*, 246.

4.   Steven L. Pease, *The Golden Age of Jewish Achievement*, 405. See also Pease's chart, "Disproportionate Jewish Achievements – A Thumbnail" on page 13 of his second book, *The Debate Over Jewish Achievement* (2015). He shows at a glance the multiples at which Jews have achieved beyond what might ordinarily be expected in terms of their population size for numerous

categories; for Nobel Prizes, for example, it is a startling multiple of 101 times more than what should be expected.

5.   One example includes: Nir Gaist (Israeli) cyber-security, "Meet Mr. Gaist, cyber-security wunderkind," Abigail Klein Leichman, Israel21c, February 4, 2014 http://israel21c.org/people/meet-nir-gaist-cyber-security-wunderkind/; See also www.israel21c.org for more examples.

6.   Andrew Schlesinger, *Veritas: Harvard College and the American Experience* (Chicago: Ivan R. Dee, 2005), pp. 163-165; see also Leonard Silk and Mark Silk, *The American Establishment* (1980), 37-41. Intellectual historian David A. Hollinger claims that "Harvard's president emeritus Charles W. Eliot and some other liberals within the establishment opposed the quotas that capped Jewish enrollment in the early 1920s...," but then he blames a "stuffy and snobbish Protestantism that favored quotas for Jews at Harvard and Columbia." (David A. Hollinger, *Science, Jews, and Secular Culture: Studies in Mid-Twentieth-Century American Intellectual* History, 25, 51). In broadly blaming "Protestantism" for the quotas, Hollinger has set up an historical straw-man. He counterposes "Eliot and some other liberals" with a "stuffy and snobbish Protestantism," but leaves out the fact that Harvard by this time had been run by Unitarians and liberal Protestants for more than a century. Those at Harvard and elsewhere who at that time still clung to a "genteel tradition" (Hollinger, 58. fn. 49) and perpetuated Brahmin snobbishness and exclusivity had nothing to do with historic Biblical Christianity as defined in the Protestant Reformation, nor the beliefs of the original founders of Harvard College. "Snobbish Protestantism" of the variety described by Hollinger was perpetuated by a certain type of Gentile liberal who did not want to let too many Jews into 'the club.'

7.   Steven L. Pease, *The Golden Age of Jewish Achievement*, 46-47. Meanwhile, some Jewish families anglicized their names in order to hide their Jewish background. To try to get around this, Harvard even altered its application form to ask, "What change, if any, has been made since birth in your name or that of your father?" (R. Lynn, *The Chosen People*, 284).

8.   Howard M. Sachar, *A History of the Jews in America*, 754. For comparative purposes, Jews were not even allowed admitted to the University of Oxford and the University of Cambridge until 1871 (Richard Lynn, *The Chosen People*, 72).

9.   Steve Nadis and Shing-Tung Yau, *A History in Sum: 150 Years of Mathematics at Harvard, 1825-1975* (Cambridge, Massachusetts: Harvard University Press, 2013), 81. Famed astronomer Vera Rubin, as both a Jewess and a woman, had a double discriminatory strike against her: in the latter instance, when she sought information from Princeton about their graduate program in astronomy, the university even refused to send her a graduate school catalogue, since at that time "the astronomy department didn't accept female graduate students." (Sean Carroll, *The Particle at the End of the Universe*, 243). See also "Vera Rubin: biography" (www.fampeople.com/cat-vera-rubin, accessed May 2015).

10.   David A. Hollinger, *Science, Jews and Secular Culture: Studies in Mid-Twentieth Century American Intellectual History* (1996), 7.

11.   Hollinger, op. cit., 67.

12.   Steven L. Pease, *The Golden Age of Jewish Achievement* (2009), 56.

13.   According to a complaint filed in 2015 by a coalition of 64 organizations, "Many studies have indicated that Harvard University has been engaged in systemic and continuous discrimination against Asian-Americans during its very subjective 'Holistic' college admissions process." (Douglas Belkin, "Harvard Accused of Bias Against Asian-Americans ," Wall Street Journal, May 15, 2015 http://www.wsj.com/articles/asian-american-organizations-seek-federal-probe-of-harvard-admission-policies-1431719348).

14.   Amy Chua and Jed Rubenfeld, *The Triple Package: How Three Unlikely Traits Explain the Rise and Fall of Cultural Groups in America* (2015 ed.), 47-48. In 2011, Chua was named one of the 100 most influential people in the world by *Time* magazine.

15.   Julie R. Posselt recently published a book titled *Inside Graduate Admissions: Merit, Diversity and Faculty Gatekeeping*. In it, she carefully assessed internal faculty meetings where graduate school candidates were evaluated for admission. What she discovered behind closed doors was that there was one standard for Graduate Record Examination (GRE) scores for students from China or elsewhere in East Asia, and lower standards for everyone else. (see Julie R. Posselt, *Inside Graduate Admissions: Merit, Diversity and Faculty*, Harvard University Press, 2016).

16.   Mark Malseed, "The Story of Sergey Brin," Moment, February-March 2007. http://www.momentmag.com/the-story-of-sergey-brin/

17.   Tanya Khovanova and Alexey Radul, "Jewish Problems," arXiv.org, arXiv:1110.1556v2, Oct. 18, 2011 http://arxiv.org/pdf/1110.1556.pdf; see also Mark Malseed, "The Story of Sergey Brin,"

Moment, February-March 2007 http://www.momentmag.com/the-story-of-sergey-brin/. An 1861 imperial decree in Russia granted Jewish university graduates the same rights and privileges as their Russian Christian counterparts. Jewish university-level participation grew steadily until, by the 1880s, it was reaching levels that were upsetting to some Russian authorities, and "quotas were instituted to limit the number of Jews in universities and liberal professions." (N. Efron, 43)

18.   Mark Malseed, "The Story of Sergey Brin," Moment, February-March 2007 http://www. momentmag.com/the-story-of-sergey-brin/

19.   *"Zhdanovshchina"* takes its name from the campaign's patron, Andrei Zhdanov, who sat on the Soviet Politburo of the Communist Party of the Soviet Union (CPSU) at the time. See Paul Josephson, "Science, Ideology and the State," *The Cambridge History of* Science, Volume 5. *The Modern Physical and Mathematical Sciences*, p. 585. Edited by Mary Jo Nye. Cambridge University Press: 2003. Paul and I were master's degree students together at Harvard in the Soviet Union Program in the mid-1970s.

20.   Pedro G. Ferreira, *The Perfect Theory – A Century of Geniuses and the Battle Over General Relativity* (2014, 2015), 122-123.

21.   Noah Efron, *A Chosen Calling* (2014), 54.

22.   Charles Murray, "The sudden emergence of Jewish significant figures, 1800-1850," *Human Accomplishment: The Pursuit of Excellence in the Arts and Sciences, 800 B.C. to 1950* (2003), 276-277. Following the French Revolution, the National Assembly "voted a decree of complete emancipation for Jews (27 September 1791)." (Paul Johnson, *A History of the Jews,* 1988, 306). Steven Pease asserts that, "Practically speaking, it was Napoleon who launched the Jewish Emancipation, and thereby began to break down most of the barriers against Jews." Pease believes that Emancipation "was adopted, country by country, in Europe over the next 100 years." (S. Pease, *The Golden Age of Jewish Achievement*, 15 & 234).

23.   For example, Melville Feynman, father of one of the greatest physicists in world history, Richard Feynman, had "a fascination with science but, like other immigrating Jews of his era, no possible means to fulfill it." (James Gleick, *Genius: The Life and Science of Richard Feynman,* 24). Perhaps if his father had had the opportunity, he might also have become a world-class scientist.

24.   See, for example, Joel Richardson's sobering historical account titled, "Christian Jew-Hatred: From the Fourth Century to the Holocaust" (Ch. 10), *When a Jew Rules the World* (2015), 132-154.

25.   Charles Murray, *Human Accomplishment: The Pursuit of Excellence in the Arts and Sciences, 800 B.C. to 1950* (2003), 275.

26.   Murray (2003), op. cit., 276-277.

27.   Steven L. Pease, *The Golden Age of Jewish Achievement*, 392.

28.   In his 1999 book, *Origins of Genius*, Dean Keith Simonton wrote: "…Jews could rise above historical obscurity only in those nations where they enjoyed at least the basic freedoms." He then compared Switzerland and Russia. Jews in Switzerland, he noted, were "83 times more likely to pick up a Nobel Prize in science than" Jews in Russia on a per capita basis (p. 213).

29.   One example related to observing *kashrut* (keeping kosher) was the original command "not to boil the kid in its mother's milk" (Exodus 23:19), which was considered an abomination. But this evolved into not mixing dairy products with meat products during the same meal. Over time, the prohibition went even further, banning substances such as *coffee* with an evening meal where meat is also being served because the *tendency* of those who would drink coffee with their meal would be to add a creamer or milk to the coffee, thereby violating *kashrut.* This shows how far the practice of some rabbinical commands had expanded from the original prohibition laid down by God – not to "boil a kid in its mother's milk."

30.   Charles Murray provides an amazing quotation by Lord Ashley, the future seventh Earl of Shaftesbury, speaking to the British House of Commons in 1847 about the Jewish people, where it was noted that, "even in their days of dispersion…their literature [yet] embraced every subject of science and learning, of secular and religious knowledge….The Jews presented…in proportion to their numbers, a far larger list of men of genius and learning than could be exhibited by any Gentile country…" Cited in Murray (2003), 278 – from Lord Ashley speech to the British House of Commons, December 1847; see also Patai (1977), 318. As Murray adds, it is even more telling that "Lord Ashley's comments were made in 1847, when Jews had barely begun to reappear on the world stage as leading figures within the arts and sciences." (Murray, op. cit., 278)

31.   John Murray Cuddihy, *The Ordeal of Civility*, 9.

32.   Part of this "predicament," to use Cuddihy's word, facing newly emancipated Jews was to figure out how to relate to the broader Gentile cultures around them. As Cuddihy states: "Jewish Emancipation involved Jews in collisions with the differentiations of Western society." How should

they respond? Should they assimilate and how much of Jewish culture and identity should they retain? It took time to work through these issues – issues that have not gone away in Jewish-Gentile cultural interactions. At the time, though, "Jews were being asked, in effect, to become bourgeois, and to become bourgeois quickly." (Cuddihy, op. cit., 12-13)

33. The countries examined were: Austro-Hungary, Britain, France, Germany, Russia and the United States. "In each instance," the author tells us, "the hypothesis that Jewish accomplishment is explained by the activity of the countries where they worked fails." (Charles Murray, "Jewish Disproportional Representation Within Countries," *Human Accomplishment* (2003), 280.

34. Marie Curie, one of the most brilliant female scientists who ever lived and the recipient of *two* Nobel Prizes, one in Physics and the other in Chemistry, was once subjected in France to a smear campaign in which she was *accused* of being Jewish - which she was not - among the accusations that were held against her by anti-Semites and other enemies (Amir D. Aczel, *Uranium Wars: The Scientific Rivalry that Created the Nuclear Age*, New York: Palgrave Macmillan, 2009, p. 49).

35. C. Murray, op. cit., 281.

36. C. Murray, op. cit., 282.

37. Richard Feynman, *The Feynman Lectures on Physics* (Reading, MA: Addison-Wesley Publishing Co.; California Institute of Technology: 1963, 1977 edition), p. 3-1.

38. M. Gell-Mann, *The Quark and the Jaguar*, 107.

39. One author compares Einstein's output in 1905 with Newton's nearly two and a half centuries earlier, the so-called *annus mirabilis* ('year of miracles'): "In the annals of science only one other scientist and one other year bears comparison with Einstein and his achievements in 1905: Isaac Newton in 1666..." Found in Manjit Kumar, *Einstein, Bohr, and the Great Debate about the Nature of Reality* (New York: W.W. Norton, 2008), 32.

40. Darrin M. McMahon, *Divine Fury: A History of Genius* (2013), "Introduction: The Problem of Genius," xvi.

41. James Gleick, *Genius: The Life and Science of Richard Feynman*, 8.

42. Sheldon Glashow, a US particle physicist, shared the 1979 Nobel Prize with Steven Weinberg and Abdus Salam. Glashow was "the son of immigrant Jewish parents from Tsarist Russia." He received his PhD from Harvard in 1958 and also worked with Niels Bohr and Murray Gell-Mann, later becoming a professor of physics at Harvard (from *The Biographical Dictionary of Scientists,* Third Edition, Vol. I, New York: Oxford University Press, 2000, 419-420).

43. Jim Baggott, *The Quantum Story:* "Hava Nagila (The Movie)," PBS television program. 2012 by Katahdin Productions. *A History in 40 Moments* (2011), p. 55.

44. Max Born, *The Born-Einstein Letters 1916-1955: Friendship, Politics and Physics in Uncertain Times* (New York: Macmillan, 2005), 228. Cited in Manjit Kumar, *Quantum: Einstein, Bohr, and the Great Debate about the Nature of Reality* (New York: W.W. Norton, 2008), 157.

45. Manjit Kumar, *Quantum: Einstein, Bohr, and the Great Debate about the Nature of Reality*, 158. Max Born himself had "never felt particularly Jewish," according to Kumar, until Nazi persecution of the Jews began, but then became "extremely conscious of it" in the face of injustice and oppression." (Kumar, op. cit., 295, also citing Born letter to Einstein in Max Born, *The Born-Einstein Letters 1916-1955: Friendship, Politics and Physics in Uncertain Times* (New York: Macmillan, 2005), 114, 2 June 1933.

46. Einstein's letter to President Roosevelt was dated August 2, 1939.

47. James Gleick, "Los Alamos," *Genius: The Life and Science of Richard Feynman*, 159.

48. "J. Robert Oppenheimer" entry, *Encyclopedia Judaica*. Second Edition. Volume 15, 450.

49. 'Oppenheimer' entry in Geoffrey Wigoder, *Dictionary of Jewish Biography* (New York: Simon & Schuster, 1991; The Jerusalem Publishing House Ltd.), 382.

50. Gilder, op. cit., 92. See also a "list of emigrant scientists" – many of whom were Jewish refugees who fled Nazi Germany under "Appendix 1: A list of emigrant scientists," in Gordon Fraser, *The Quantum Exodus*, 241-249, as well as the site: http://www.rsl.ox.ac.uk/dept/scwmss/online/modern/spsl/spsl.html at the Bodleian Library, Oxford.

51. Jean Medawar and David Pyke, *Hitler's Gift: Scientists Who Fled Nazi Germany* (2000), "Sir Francis Simon", 80-85, 221.

52. George Johnson, *Strange Beauty*, 57.

53. James Gleick, *Genius: The Life and Science of Richard Feynman*, 165-167.

54. "About Hans Bethe," Personal and Historical Perspectives of Hans Bethe, http://bethe.cornell.edu/about.html

55. J. Gleick, *Genius*, op. cit., 212.

56.   M. Kumar, *Quantum*, op. cit., 93, 322-325.

57.   See *Dictionary of Jewish Biography* entry on 'Niels Bohr' at pages 78-79. A photo of Niels Bohr with Ben Gurion is found between pages 300-301 (Plate 28) in Abraham Pais, *Niels Bohr's Times: In Physics, Philosophy, and Polity* (Oxford: Clarendon Press, 1991); Bohr also lectured in Jerusalem in November 1953 (Plate 26).

58.   Medawar and Pyke, *Hitler's Gift*, 222-223.

59.   James Gleick, *Genius*, 185, citing James Tuck in Nuell Pharr Davis, *Lawrence and Oppenheimer* (1968), 184.

60.   Amir D. Aczel, Ch. 11, "The Nazi Nuclear Machine," *Uranium Wars: The Scientific Rivalry that Created the Nuclear Age* (2009), 131-137.

61.   Amir Aczel, *Uranium Wars* (2009), 179-181.

62.   Regarding the establishment of the State of Israel, Jewish Marxist scholar Isaac Deutscher (who actually grew up in Poland not far from Auschwitz) wrote that Zionism achieved its goal, but "one which it could neither wish nor expect: six million Jews had to perish in Hitler's gas chambers in order that Israel should come to life." He continued: "It would have been better had Israel remained unborn and the six million Jews stayed alive..." (Isaac Deutscher, *The Non-Jewish Jew and Other Essays*, 1968, 97)

63.   I.I. Rabi, *Science: The Center of Culture* (1970), 140-141. The video program dramatization series titled, "Heavy Water" depicts the Nazi effort under Werner Heisenberg to develop the atomic bomb.

64.   N. Efron (2014), 15.

65.   Ioan James, op. cit., Preface, 7.

66.   H. Sachar, op. cit., 748. In the development of the atomic bomb, Ulam helped develop "a new field of probability called branching-processes theory." (James Gleick, *Genius,* 168).

67.   Steven L. Pease, *The Golden Age of Jewish Achievement* (2009), 16.

68.   Amos Oz and Fania Oz-Salzberger, *Jews and Words*, 95-96.

69.   Oz and Oz-Salzberger, op. cit., 102-103.

70.   Amir D. Aczel, *Uranium Wars* (2009), 97, 104, 110-111.

71.   Alfred Einstein, cited in Ioan James, *Driven to Innovate*, 186-187; also cited in Neil Turok, *The Universe Within*, 180-181.

72.   Victor J. Stenger, *God and the Multiverse* (2014), 126.

73.   M. Kumar, *Quantum*, op. cit., 336.

74.   Roger Penrose, *Shadows of the Mind: A Search for the Missing Science of Consciousness* (1994), 317 (footnote); James Gleick, *Genius*, 181-182.

75.   George Gilder, *The Israel Test* (2009), 126-127.

76.   Ioan James, op. cit., 7, 100-104.

77.   Gordon Fraser, *A Quantum Exodus* (2012), 237.

78.   Steinberger has also been claimed as a "German-American-Swiss physicist".

79.   "Jewish Nobel Prize Winners" chart, *Encyclopedia Judaica*, Second Edition, Volume 15, p. 292; entry information source cited from: www.jinfo.org

80.   "Saul Perlmutter," The Jewish Virtual Library (undated) https://www.jewishvirtuallibrary. org/jsource/biography/saulperlmutter.htmlhttps://www.jewishvirtuallibrary.org/jsource/biography/ saulperlmutter.html

81.   Paul Josephson, *Red Atom* (2000), 13, 15; Noah Efron, *A Chosen Calling* (2014), 54.

82.   Nadis and Shing-Tung Yau (2013), p. 76. Abraham Flexner launched the Institute for Advanced Study (IAS) with a $5 million dollar donation. Flexner recruited Einstein for IAS while Einstein was visiting California in late 1931, prior to Hitler's election as German Chancellor. Einstein still held his post in Berlin at the time and initially agreed to "spend five months a year at the institute [in Princeton] and the remainder in Berlin." At the time, Einstein was also still connected to Caltech. (M. Kumar, *Quantum*, op. cit., 290); see also Howard M. Sacher, *A History of the Jews in America* (New York: Alfred A. Knopf, 1992): "Directed by Flexner and heavily funded by Jewish philanthropists, the Institute within a year became a lifesaver for refugee scholars." (p. 499). Flexner himself also had a profound impact on shaping medical education in the United States (Steven L. Pease, *The Golden Age of Jewish Achievement*, 54).

83.   "Edward Witten," Biography-Center, http://www.biography-center.com/biographies/3741-Witten_Edward.html

84.   "Jewish American physicist says he'll send part of $3 million prize to J Street," JTA, *Haaretz*, August 4, 2012. http://www.haaretz.com/jewish-world/jewish-world-news/jewish-american-

physicist-says-he'll-send-part-of-3-to-j-street-1.455893

85. Steven Silbiger, *The Jewish Phenomenon*, 59.

86. S. Silbiger, op. cit., 61.

87. James and Marti Hefley, Ch. 9, "Nobels and Nightmares," in *Where in the World Are the Jews Today?* (1974), 116. Funk was a Polish Jew who discovered the properties of what later came to be called 'vitamins' "while working at the Lister Institute in London in 1912…" (C. Roth, op. cit., 213).

88. Cecil Roth, Ch. IX "Medicine," *The Jewish Contribution to Civilisation* (London: Macmillan and Co. Ltd., 1938) 205-207.

89. Cecil Roth, op. cit., 207-208.

90. Sadly, though, the author of this tribute to Rita Levi Montalcini adds that "she abandoned religion and embraced atheism." (Costantino Ceoldo, "Homage to Rita Levi Montalcini," Dec. 31, 2012, Pravda.ru, http://english.pravda.ru/society/anomal/31-12-2012/123358-rita_montalcini-0/

91. Cecil Roth, op. cit., 210-211. Israeli biologist Aaron Ciechanover won the 2004 Nobel Prize in Chemistry (Efron, op. cit., 104)

92. Howard M. Sachar, Chapter XXI, "A Jewish Impact on American Culture," *A History of the Jews in America*, 748-749.

93. Having lived for a while on food stamps, Koum became an instant billionaire in February 2014 with the purchase of his What'sApp company by Facebook. "WhatsApp co-founder Jan Koum: New billionaire once lived on food stamps," NDTV.com, February 21, 2014. http://gadgets.ndtv.com/apps/features/whatsapp-co-founder-jan-koum-new-billionaire-once-lived-on-food-stamps-486290

94. Mark Malseed, "The Story of Sergey Brin," Moment, February-March 2007 http://www.momentmag.com/the-story-of-sergey-brin/

95. "Larry Ellison," www.isjewish.com. Accessed in August 2014.

96. Vauhini Vara, "Just How Much Do We Want to Share on Social Networks?" Wall Street Journal (Online), Updated Nov. 28, 2007, http://online.wsj.com/news/articles/SB119621309736406034. Interestingly, since Zuckerberg and Facebook bought WhatsApp from Koum for $19 billion, Iran has since denounced WhatsApp and banned its use. The head of Iran's Committee on Internet Crimes, Abdolsamad Khorramabadi, stated that this ban has gone into effect because Facebook was founded by "Mark Zuckerberg…an American Zionist," (Lisa Daftari, Iran bans WhatsApp because of link to 'American Zionist' Mark Zuckerberg," Fox News, May 4, 2014 (http://www.foxnews.com/world/2014/05/04/iran-bans-whatsapp-because-link-to-american-zionist-mark-zuckerberg/)

97. ForeignPolicy.com, April 29, 2013. http://www.foreignpolicy.com/articles/2013/04/29/the_500_most_powerful_people_in_the_world

98. "Jewish World Chess Champions," http://www.jinfo.org/Chess_Champions.html. Accessed August 2014. See also Steven L. Pease, *The Golden Age of Jewish Achievement*, 90-91. Pease notes that Kasparov and Spassky are "half-Jewish," while Kramnik "does not claim Jewish background," although some of his relatives have moved to Israel.

99. Vox Day, *The Irrational Atheist*, 200.

100. "Jewish Nobel Prize Winners," http://jinfo.org/Nobel_Prizes.html (between 1901-2012).

101. It goes without saying that many brilliant or genius-level physicists have *not* been Jewish. These include such individuals as: Max Planck (German), Werner Heisenberg (German), Erwin Schrodinger (Austrian), and Paul Adrien Maurice Dirac (born to a Swiss father and an English mother), among many others.

102. Hollinger, op. cit., 162. Merton's given name was 'Meyer R. Schkolnick'. Efron writes that Merton "did not speak publicly of his Judaism until his eighth decade…" (Efron, op. cit., 27)

103. Hollinger, op. cit., 162. As a brief historical aside regarding Jewish influence on sociology – the study of social interactions and society, besides Merton, Jews in Central Europe before World War II dominated the field. Prior to being driven out by the Nazis and coming to the U.S., they held some two-thirds of the professorial chairs. (Howard M. Sachar, Chapter XXI, "A Jewish Impact on American Culture," *A History of the Jews in America*, 750).

104. Steven Silbiger, *The Jewish Phenomenon: 7 Keys to the Enduring Wealth of a People* (2009), 2.

105. George Soros, *Soros on Soros: Staying Ahead of the Curve* (1995), 242, cited in Steven Silbiger, *The Jewish Phenomenon*, 165.

106. In contrast, Chinese Americans have won six Nobels. (Chua and Rubenfeld, *The Triple Package*, 48).

107. Peter Watson, *Ideas: A History of Thought and Invention, from Fire to Freud*, 2, citing the views of Cambridge historian of science Joseph Needham and his book, *The Great Titration* (1969).

108. "Developing countries headed by China are posing a threat to American dominance in science," SciElo in Perspective, blog.scielo.org, April 17, 2014, http://blog.scielo.org/en/2014/04/17/ developing-countries-headed-by-china-are-posing-a-threat-to-american-dominance-in-science/#. U8PGD0AvCN8. "A report produced by the National Science Board (NSB) and titled, "Science and Engineering Indicators 2014" shows that "…China recorded an impressive increase in scientific output, measured by the number of publications produced…. China, with a per capita income comparable with other developing countries, stands out as being the only nation to have a global presence in high-tech economic activity and R&D comparable with the developed countries… The number of publications from China in peer review journals had the largest increase among the developing countries during the [period covered], going from 3% to 11% of the world total." "Scientometrics" (as defined by the journal of the same name) "is concerned with the quantitative features and characteristics of science and scientific research. Emphasis is placed on investigations in which the development and mechanism of science are studied by statistical mathematical methods." http://link.springer.com/journal/11192. Accessed July 2014)

109. Eric Weiner, *The Geography of Genius* (2016), 83.

110. On a financial and entrepreneurial level, one exception has been the success of the more than 30 million overseas Chinese migrants who settled in places like Singapore and Indonesia. Steven Pease asserts that "In every locale where the Chinese have been a minority, they have been disproportionately successful." (Pease, *The Debate Over Jewish Achievement*, 58. They have sometimes been referred to as 'the Jews of Southeast Asia'. This has still not changed the current status quo, however, with respect to the frustrated Chinese quest to develop originality.

111. Amy Chua and Jed Rubenfeld, *The Triple Package*, 223.

112. Eric Weiner, *The Geography of Genius* (2016), 67, 77. The merit-based examination system was called the *jinshii* and centered around a mastery of Confucian classics (Weiner, 80) and a deep grasp of Chinese culture and history. An eleventh-century Chinese intellectual named Shen Kuo was considered a Chinese Leonardo da Vinci (Weiner, 77).

113. See Charles Murray, *Human Accomplishment*, 259.

114. P. Watson, Ibid, 2

115. James Gleick, *Genius* (1992), 314.

Chapter Two

1.   "Shmuel Yosef Agnon," *Dictionary of Jewish* Biography, 18-19.

2.   See S. Silbiger, *The Jewish Phenomenon*, 111, for a reference to this statistic.

3.   Steven Silbiger, *The Jewish Phenomenon*, 112; S.L. Pease, *The Golden Age of Jewish Achievement*, 18 & 111-112.

4.   Howard M. Sachar, *A History of the Jews in* America, 769-770.

5.   George Gilder, *The Israel Test* (2009), 253.

6.   Howard M. Sachar, *A History of the Jews in America,* 764.

7.   James A. Grymes, *Violins of Hope: Violins of the Holocaust – Instruments of Hope and Liberation in Mankind's Darkest Hour* (New York: HarperCollins, 2014), 58.

8.   See "The Story of the Jews" with Simon Schama television series from the program "A Leap of Faith." (Comments by Norman Lebrecht)

9.   J. A. Grymes, *Violins of Hope* (2014), 4, 10. Haendel describes her own connection to the Israel Philharmonic Orchestra in the book of essays, *I Am Jewish* (2004, 2015), 78-79.

10.   Brahms at first was highly skeptical that any 14 year-old could have the depth of feeling needed to perform his violin concerto as he wanted it to be played. In a wonderful 'completion of the circle' story concerning the Huberman Stradivarius and the Brahms Violin Concerto, Joshua Bell performed the concerto in Huberman's town of Czestochowa, Poland ("History of the Huberman," *The Strad* **124** No. 1483 (November 2013), 51. See also the moving video, "The Return of the Violin," at roymandel.co.il/video/86412100 (accessed May 2015).

11.   Josh Aronson, "Orchestra of Exiles: The Story of the Israel Philharmonic," 2011, www. seenandheard-international.com/2011/04/orchestra-of-exiles-the-story-of-the-israel-philharmonic

12.   "History of the Huberman," *The Strad* **124** No. 1483 (November 2013), 51.

13.   Isaac Deutscher, *The Non-Jewish Jew and Other Essays* (1968), 155.

14.   David Biale, "Preface: Toward a Cultural History of the Jews," *Cultures of the Jews* (2002), xix-xx. Ivan Marcus asserts in the same volume that "there is no blanket opposition in Jewish tradition to representational art." (Ivan G. Marcus, "A Jewish-Christian Symbiosis," *Cultures of the Jews,* 499).

15. Amoz Oz and Fania Oz-Salzberger, *Jews and Words*, 40.

16. I wish to thank my good friend and art professor, Joseph DiBella, for his insights and contribution to this section.

17. Richard Lynn, *The Chosen People: A Study of Jewish Intelligence and Achievement*, 210.

18. Steven L. Pease, *The Golden Age of Jewish Achievement*, 131-132.

19. Howard M. Sachar, "A Jewish Impact on American Culture," *A History of Jews in America*, 761-762.

20. See testimony of Dr. Bunjes, recorded in *Nuremberg Trials*, Vol. 9, 547-549, cited in Robert M. Edsel, *Rescuing Da Vinci*, 292. Bunjes testified to the "written order for the transfer to Germany of the confiscated Jewish art treasures."

21. Robert M. Edsel, op. cit., 179, citing the written report of Dr. Scholz at the Nuremberg Trials.

22. "Woman in Gold (2015)", History vs. Hollywood, http://www.historyvshollywood.com/reelfaces/woman-in-gold/

23. Steven Silbiger, *The Jewish Phenomenon*, 154.

24. "Woman in Gold (2015)", History vs. Hollywood, http://www.historyvshollywood.com/reelfaces/woman-in-gold/

25. George Gilder, *The Israel Test* (2009), 12.

26. In what must constitute one of the greatest ironies in world history, Auschwitz survivor and camp orchestra member Henry Meyer has related how Nazi SS-men in Auschwitz "were crazy" for the music of George Gershwin and Irving Berlin – both Jewish and both Americans – and as such, double enemies to the Nazi regime: "Who played [for them]? Jews. And who listened and sang along with these schmaltzy songs until tears rolled down their faces? The members of the SS, our tormentors…" (Henry Meyer, "Anscheinend ging nichts ohne Musik," 144, cited in James Grymes, *Violins of Hope: Violins of the Holocaust – Instruments of Hope and Liberation in Mankind's Darkest Hour* (2014), 134. Jazz was strictly forbidden in Nazi Germany, but this was Auschwitz, which, along with many other death camps, had its own demonic reality and played by different rules than the rest of the Third Reich. After surviving the Holocaust, Meyer "moved to the United States and became a founding member of the world-famous LaSalle Quartet." (J. Grymes, 146-147).

27. Simcha Jacobovici, "Pink, the Oscars and the…rebirth of Israel?" blogs.timesofisrael.com/pink-the-oscars-and-the-rebirth-of-israel/ (March 4, 2014). Accessed August 1, 2015.

28. James Pool and Suzanne Pool, *Who Financed Hitler* (1978), Chapter 3, "Ford and Hitler," 87. There are strong indications that Hitler copied portions of *Mein Kampf* from Henry Ford's virulently anti-Semitic book, *The International Jew* (Pool and Pool, op. cit., 91).

29. Howard M. Sachar, op. cit., 751-753.

30. From page 1 and the book jacket back cover of Anne C. Heller's biography of Rand, *Ayn Rand and the World She Made* (2009).

31. Anne C. Heller, *Ayn Rand and the World She Made* (2009), xii.

32. S. Silbiger, *The Jewish Phenomenon*, 102-103.

33. Howard M. Sachar, op. cit., 773.

34. Source on Matt Drudge: www.getnetworth.com/matt-drudge-net-worth/ (2013; Accessed September 2015)

35. H. Sachar, op. cit., 772.

36. Jackie Mason, quoted in *I Am Jewish* book of essays, 80.

37. Bill Maher, a self-proclaimed atheist, had a Jewish mother and an Irish Catholic father and was raised a Catholic until his rejection of religion. (see www.isjewish.com/bill_maher/. Accessed November 2015)

38. L. Brent Bozell and Tim Graham, "Cancel the Unethical Daily Show," CNSNews.com, Sept. 24, 2014 http://cnsnews.com/commentary/l-brent-bozell-iii/cancel-unethical-daily-show

39. "The Marx Brothers," http://www.jewishvirtuallibrary.org/jsource/biography/Marx_Brothers.html

40. For an extensive list of (primarily) American Jewish comedians, see Steven Silbiger, *The Jewish Phenomenon*, Tables 4.1 & 4.2, 91-92; see also James and Marti Hefley, Ch. 9, "Nobels and Nightmares," *Where in the World Are the Jews Today?* (1974), 116.

41. Howard M. Sachar, op. cit., 767.

42. "Analyzing Jewish Comics," *Time* magazine, October 2, 1978, 76, cited in S.J. Whitfield, Ch. 9: "Declarations of Independence: American Jewish Culture in the Twentieth Century," in David Biale, *Cultures of the Jews: A New History*, 1103.

43. Dagobert D. Runes, *The Hebrew Impact on Western Civilization* (New York: Philosophical Library, 1951), 594.
44. Steven Silbiger, *The Jewish Phenomenon*, 97.
45. D. D. Runes, *The Hebrew Impact on Western Civilization,* 605.
46. J. Hoberman and Jeffrey Shandler, *Entertaining America: Jews, Movies and Broadcasting* (2003), 35.
47. David Robinson, *Chaplin: His Life and Art* (New York: McGraw-Hill, 1985), 154. See also Hoberman and Shandler, op. cit., 35
48. "Broadway Musicals: A Jewish Legacy," 2012 documentary. Great Performances. Television Special. An Albert M. Tapper Production. (PBS premier in January 2013).
49. "The Jazz Singer" began as a short story by Samson Raphaelson and was titled, "Day of Atonement." (Steven L. Pease, *The Golden Age of Jewish Achievement*, 121-122; 137-139).
50. Steven Silbiger, *The Jewish Phenomenon,* 139.
51. Howard M. Sachar, op. cit., 767. See also Pease's list of Jewish playwrights and screenwriters at Steven L. Pease, *The Golden Age of Jewish Achievement*, 102.
52. S. Silbiger, op. cit., 32.
53. Pease, op. cit., 164.
54. S. Silbiger, op. cit., 98.
55. Pease, op. cit., 172-174.
56. As Steven Silbiger relates it, Samuel Goldwyn was born in Warsaw, Poland, as Schmuel Gelbfisz, came to New York and worked as a telegraph delivery boy, later becoming a successful salesman. He saw his first movie in New York and fell in love with the idea of making movies. (Silbiger, op. cit., 95).
57. S. Silbiger, *The Jewish Phenomenon*, 29.

Chapter Three

1. James Pool and Suzanne Pool, *Who Financed Hitler* (1978), 89, 93, citing Henry Ford, *The Independent Jew: The World's Foremost Problem* (Los Angeles, 1964 edition), 191-192.
2. R. Patai, *The Jewish Mind*, 343, 347.
3. Paul Buhle, op. cit., 1-2.
4. The film "Being There" was based on the novel of the same name by Polish-Jewish American Jerzy Kosinski (Jozef Lewinkopf, 1933-1991).
5. Noah J. Efron, *A Chosen Calling: Jews in Science in the Twentieth Century* (2014), 4.
6. Ioan James, *Driven to Innovate* (2009), Preface, 8.
7. David A. Hollinger, "Why Are Jews Preeminent in Science and Scholarship? The Veblen Thesis Reconsidered," *Aleph* 2 (2002), 145. Paper first presented at AAAS annual meeting in San Francisco, California, on February 18, 2001. Hollinger based these measurements on representation in academic departments in the U.S. during the second half of the twentieth century.
8. Lewis S. Feuer, "The Scientific Revolution Among the Jews," *The Scientific Intellectual: The Psychological and Sociological Origins of Modern Science* (New Brunswick, New Jersey: 1963, Transaction Publishers: 1992 edition), pp. 301, 303.
9. Thorstein Veblen, "The Intellectual Pre-Eminence of Jews in Modern Europe," *Political Science Quarterly,* Vol. 34, No. 1 (March 1919): 33-42.
10. David A. Hollinger, "Why Are Jews Preeminent in Science and Scholarship? The Veblen Thesis Reconsidered," *Aleph* 2 (2002), 146.
11. Hollinger (2002), op. cit., 147-148.
12. Benjamin Braude, review of Sander Gilman's book *Smart Jews* in *The Jewish Quarterly Review* **92**(1/2). July-October 2001: 180.
13. Feuer, op. cit., 306-307.
14. Hollinger, op. cit., 146.
15. Steven Silbiger, *The Jewish Phenomenon*, 153.
16. Eric Weiner, *The Geography of Genius* (2016), 266, 269-270.
17. Dean Keith Simonton, *Origins of Genius – Darwinian Perspectives on Creativity* (New York: Oxford University Press, 1999), 122.
18. Feuer, op. cit., 307. From the 1480s when many were expelled through the early nineteenth century, Jews in Italy were mostly heavily discriminated against. However, after 1859 they

experienced little anti-Semitism and enjoyed civil liberties throughout the country. "Not surprisingly, Jews flourished during this period." (Richard Lynn, *The Chosen People,* 181-182; 183).

19. Hollinger writes that Volkov conducted "the most careful empirical study to date of leading Jewish and non-Jewish physical and biological scientists in modern Germany." His conclusion was that "the most successful of the Jewish scientists were anything but [alienated] Veblenesque skeptics." Hollinger also viewed Volkov's work as "an extremely valuable corrective against the facile use of Jews and of science itself as instruments in the celebration of critical detachment." (Hollinger, op. cit., 156, 158).

20. Noah J. Efron, *A Chosen Calling: Jews in Science in the Twentieth Century* (2014), 10-11.

21. J. Hoberman and Jeffrey Shandler, *Entertaining America: Jews, Movies and Broadcasting* (2003), 11.

22. Richard Lynn, *The Chosen People: A Study of Jewish Intelligence and Achievement,* 4. See Thorstein Veblen, "The Intellectual Pre-Eminence of Jews in Modern Europe," *Political Science Quarterly,* Vol. 34, No. 1 (March 1919): 42. Veblen wrongly thought that once the Jewish people were re-established in their homeland, they would "turn inward on themselves" and "their prospective contribution to the world's intellectual output" would move instead in the direction of "Talmudic lore." (Veblen, op. cit., p. 42)

23. David A. Hollinger, "Why Are Jews Preeminent in Science and Scholarship? The Veblen Thesis Reconsidered," *Aleph* 2 (2002), 152.

24. Feuer, op. cit., 308. Raphael Patai adds in *The Jewish Mind* that Nobert Wiener and J.B.S. Haldane were two others besides Feuer who subscribed "to this hypothesis of a Jewish genetic selection for intelligence..." (R. Patai, *The Jewish Mind,* 306)

25. Charles Murray, *Human Accomplishment,* 291.

26. Charles Murray, "Jewish Genius," *Commentary,* April 1, 2007. http://www.commentarymagazine.com/articles/jewish-genius/

27. Amos Oz and Fania Oz-Salzberger, *Jews and Words* (2012), 7, 26-27, 29.

28. Arthur Herman, *How the Scots Invented the Modern World,* 26.

29. Steven Silbiger, *The Jewish Phenomenon,* 32-33.

30. Patai, 302-303; in 1969 British novelist Charles Percy Snow was also one who hypothesized that there was a "genetic" predisposition to scientific success within the Jewish community. (see Efron, 2014, 2-3)

31. Hollinger (2002 essay, 154). See also Steven Silbiger: "Forty percent of the top 40 of the Forbes 400 richest Americans are Jewish." (Silbiger, 4).

32. S.L. Gilman, 70-71, citing Mark Twain's comments in Mark Twain, *Concerning the Jews* (Philadelphia: Running, 1985), 12. Original in *Harper's* New Monthly Magazine, Vol. XCIX, June to November 1899.

33. Noah J. Efron cites British novelist Charles Percy Snow, who wrote that, with respect to Jewish contributions to world science, "the Jewish performance has been not only disproportionate, but *almost ridiculously disproportionate.*" (N. Efron, 3, citing *New York Times* article on C.P. Snow, footnote 11: Lawrence Van Gelder, "C.P. Snow Says Jews' Success Could Be Genetic Superiority," *New York Times,* April 1, 1969, 37.

34. Interestingly, author Paul Buhle has asserted that, "Perhaps only in organized sports have Jews been represented so sparsely as their numbers would suggest." See Paul Buhle, *From the Lower East Side to Hollywood: Jews in American Popular Culture* (2004), 18.

35. Hollinger (2002), op. cit., 154.

36. Ioan James states, for example, that "David Hollinger, in his interesting critique (2002) of Veblen's thesis... argues that Veblen's extravagant admiration for a sensibility of alienation and his almost fanatical antipathy for commercial pursuits blinded him to a number of facets of Jewish history that could help solve the puzzle." (Ioan James, *Driven to Innovate,* 17). On the other hand, Hollinger explains that one of the reasons for Veblen's silence with respect to Jewish economic activities and economic levels might have been "a refusal on [his] part to accommodate and reinforce anti-Jewish stereotypes." (Hollinger, op. cit., 153)

37. Ioan James, *Driven to Innovate* (2009), 12-14.

38. R. Patai, 352, also citing Joseph Jacobs.

39. Richard Lynn, *The Chosen People: A Study of Jewish Intelligence and Achievement,* 6.

40. R. Lynn, op. cit, 8, citing Colin Berry (1999), "Religious tradition as contexts of historical creativity: patterns of scientific and artistic achievement and their stability," *Personality and Individual Differences,* 26, 1125-1135.

41. R. Lynn, op. cit., 10.

42. R. Lynn, op. cit., 37.

43. R. Lynn, "Table 6.11 Jewish Fellow of the Royal Society," *The Chosen People: A Study of Jewish Intelligence and Achievement* (2011), 85.

44. Richard Lynn, *The Chosen People: A Study of Jewish Intelligence and Achievement,* "Italy", 189.

45. Amy Chua and Jed Rubenfeld, *The Tripe Package,* 51.

46. Steven L. Pease, *The Golden Age of Jewish Achievement,* 52, 69.

47. Chua and Rubenfeld, *The Triple Package,* 52.

48. Jewish Marxist and atheist Isaac Deutscher, in fact, saw the Holocaust in part as the Nazis' counter-offensive against Communism and socialism. He believed that "European Jewry…paid the price for the survival of capitalism…" (I. Deutscher, *The Non-Jewish Jew,* 49).

49. In Deutscher's view, the Nazis destroyed the Jews because they were seen as the agents of Bolshevism. But, in a complete contradiction, they were also destroyed because they were considered too successful at capitalism. (Deutscher, op. cit.)

50. "Henry Adams: The Jews Make Me Creep (1896. 1901, 1914)," cited in Paul Mendes-Flohr and Jehuda Reinharz, Ch. IX, "The American Experience," *The Jew in the Modern World: A Documentary History,* 467.

51. Steven Silbiger, *The Jewish Phenomenon: 7 Keys to the Enduring Wealth of a People* (2009), 133.

52. S. Silbiger, op. cit., 138.

53. S. Silbiger, op. cit., 138.

54. S. Silbiger, *The Jewish Phenomenon,* 1, 7.

55. See S. Silbiger, *The Jewish Phenomenon,* 7-8.

56. George Gilder, "Capitalism, Jewish Achievement, and the Israel Test," *The* American, July 27, 2009, http://www.discovery.org/a/11771

57. For a recent book on the birth of democracy in ancient Greece and ancient Greece's impact on the world, see Nicholas Kyriazis, *Why Ancient Greece? The birth and development of democracy* (Greece: Psichogios Publications S.A.). In the area of Greek art and sculpture, while we can marvel at what has been preserved, we don't even have the best samples from that time: "The Greek statuary that we still find so compelling today consists largely of what the ancient world considered its second-tier work." (Charles Murray, *Human Accomplishment,* 26). For David Deutsch's interpretation of and appreciation for periods of great intellectual achievement in human history, see his *The Beginning of Infinity* (216-219). Regarding the Golden Age of Athens, Deutsch writes: "The best-known mini-enlightenment was the intellectual and political tradition of criticism in ancient Greece which culminated in the so-called 'Golden Age' of the city-state of Athens in the fifth century B.C.E." (D. Deutsch, *The Beginning of Infinity,* 216).

58. Eric Weiner, *The Geography of Genius* (2016), 20.

59. Weiner, op. cit., 14, 142.

60. See Peter Watson's *Ideas: A History of Thought and Invention, from Fire to Freud,* 409-411. Watson adds: "Renaissance thinkers…believed that the entire universe was a model of the divine idea and that man was 'a creator after the divine creator.'" Artists and geniuses were believed to be especially able to apprehend the beauty and harmony of that creation, according to the thinking of the time (Watson, 409). See also Jacob Burckhardt's *The Civilization of the Renaissance in Italy.* Regarding the Golden Age of Florence, David Deutsch has written of the "short-lived enlightenment" that occurred there, a "time of the early Renaissance, a cultural movement that revived the literature, art and science of ancient Greece and Rome after more than a millennium of intellectual stagnation in Europe." (D. Deutsch, *The Beginning of Infinity,* 218).

61. See generally, Arthur Herman, *How the Scots Invented the Modern World.* Herman writes about what he terms *politeness* emerging in sophisticated cultures during various historical periods (which means much more than simply good manners). As an historian, Herman is identified with the 'Great Man' approach to history, which was originally developed by another Scot, Thomas Carlyle. The 'Great Man' approach, which looks at the impact of individual heroes in history and is further associated in the modern era with Jewish philosopher and historian Sidney Hook, author of the influential work, *The Hero in History.*

62. Neil Turok, *The Universe Within,* 213.

63. Arthur Herman, op. cit., 11.

64. I have been unable to confirm this, but it seems to be the case, given some of the Jewish publications where Herman's work has appeared, as well as the fact that the Tikvah Fund in New York City lists Herman as one of its visiting faculty or speakers. See Tikvahfund.org/faculty/Arthur-herman (Accessed October 7, 2015).

65. A. Herman, op. cit., 309-310.
66. A. Herman, op. cit., 25-26.
67. A. Herman, op. cit., 74-75.
68. Peter Watson, *Ideas: A History of Thought and Invention, From Fire to Freud* (2005), 2.
69. Plato, cited by Eric Weiner, *The Geography of Genius*, 61-62.
70. A. Chua and J. Rubenfeld, *The Triple Package*, 8-12. This chip on the shoulder is further described an 'I'll show them' mentality. (p. 12)
71. S.L. Gilman, 70-71, citing Mark Twain's comments in Mark Twain, *Concerning the Jews* (Philadelphia: Running, 1985), 12. Original citation from *Harper's* New Monthly Magazine, Vol. XCIX, June, 1899, to September, 1899.
72. Noah J. Efron, A *Chosen Calling: Jews in Science in the Twentieth Century* (2014): 5-6.
73. Efron, op. cit., 6. At the end of his book, Efron offers his own thesis about Jewish pre-eminence in science in the twentieth century – the fact that Jews, whether in America, the Soviet Union, or in Palestine (before and after Israel became a state) were all in new worlds with "new opportunities that could hardly have been imagined in prior generations." Facing these new opportunities in new worlds led to a "great shared experience" in Efron's view, "[a]nd it was this great shared experience that begins to explain the affinity and ardor these far-spread Jews shared for science." (pp. 99-100). While Efron's observation is true and in part explains Jewish *interest* and *attraction* to science, it doesn't really explain Jewish pre-eminence in scientific fields. Such an explanation, if it were comprehensive, should also explain Jewish pre-eminence in other fields as well, which it does not.
74. Paul Mendes-Flohr, *Divided Passions: Jewish Intellectuals and the Experience of Modernity* (1991), 23.
75. Steven L. Pease, *The Debate Over Jewish Achievement* (2015), 70-71.
76. Pease, op cit., 62.
77. Occupational choice is the factor cited in a 2006 article titled, "Natural History of Ashkenazi Intelligence," in the *Journal of Biosocial Science* by authors Gregory Cochran, Jason Hardy and Henry Harpending. Also cited in Charles Murray, "Jewish Genius," *Commentary*, http://www. commentarymagazine.com/articles/jewish-genius/ (April 1, 2007). Besides choosing certain occupations where they have excelled, Richard Lynn has presented what he calls the "Discrimination Hypothesis," as a result of which Jews, because of discrimination, were forced or channeled into certain types of occupations. (see Richard Lynn, "The Discrimination Hypothesis," *The Chosen People: A Study of Jewish Intelligence and Achievement* (2011), 331-333.
78. Dennis Prager is quoted as saying that "Jews are probably the most insecure group in the world." Cited in Chua and Rubenfeld, *The Triple Package*, 155. Original source: Dennis Prager, "Explaining Jews, Part 3: A Very Insecure People," WND Commentary, February 21, 2006. http://www.wnd.com/2006/02/34917
79. Chua and Rubenfeld, *The Triple Package*, 195. The authors say the following about the Jewish people: "In no other group has the coupling of a superiority complex and insecurity been so core to its historical identity." (p. 195)
80. David Brooks, "The Tel Aviv Cluster," *The New York Times*, January 12, 2010.
81. Steven L. Pease, "Threads of Part 2 – Chronology of the Debate," *The Debate Over Jewish Achievement* (2015), Ch. 8, 105-112.
82. Ioan James, op. cit., 17.

Chapter Four

1. Luke Harding, "Can Russia's oligarchs keep their billions – and their freedom?" *The Guardian*. 1 July 2007, www.theguardian.com/world/2007/jul/02/lukeharding1; see also R. Lynn, *The Chosen People*, 233.
2. In his 2008 book, *McMafia: A Journey through the Global Criminal Underground*, which looks at the rise of the Russian oligarchs and their enterprises, author Misha Glenny has noted that "[a] disproportionate number of the most influential Russian oligarchs and gangsters were Jewish." (Misha Glenny, *McMafia: A Journey through the Global Criminal Underground* (2008), 75, 112-114).
3. In post-Soviet Russia, some Russian Jews became extremely prominent financially not as "the result of some grand conspiracy," but as a result of previous cultural and economic ties and how events unfolded following the collapse of Communism. Previously, the Soviet Union had "restricted Jews' ability to assimilate and rise in society…. Jews who wanted to get ahead were forced into the black market economy. When communism collapsed and the black market was legalized as free

market capitalism, the Jewish entrepreneurs had a head start." (Luke Harding, *The Guardian*, op. cit.). These men also had a knack to excel at business or to thrive in this environment once the shackles of communism and state discrimination fell away. Interestingly, prior to the Russian Revolution, although most Jews who lived in the Russian Empire were forced to live in the Pale of Settlement, by the close of the nineteenth century, some Jewish businessmen thrived outside the Pale: "...the Jewish Gintsburg family controlled a large portion of the Siberian gold mining industry; the Jewish Gessen brothers ran the main shipping business between the Baltic and Caspian Seas; and Jews developed the Caucasus oil industry...." (R. Lynn, *The Chosen People,* 214).

4.   Jim Melnick, "The Underside of Russian Jewish Ministry in Israel and around the World Today," *Mishkan,* Issue 69 (2011), 67.

5.   This is very much along the lines of a 2011 paper that Steven Pease cites in his book that alleges "pro-Jewish bias in the selection of Nobel Laureates." (Pease, *The Debate Over Jewish Achievement,* 54). Pease himself doesn't believe this - in a sub-heading titled, "Anti-Semitism: They Cheat, Or the Deck is Stacked in Their Favor," he only repeats this as one of the absurd explanations some people give to try to explain away Jewish achievement and pre-eminence. He blames envy as the main cause: "Envy is the source of nearly every contemporary allegation that Jews have cheated or have benefitted unfairly from a bias in their favor." (p. 56) I don't fully agree with Pease, since I think that virulent hatred and angry bewilderment at Jewish achievement are also root causes for this type of pseudo-explanation among anti-Semites and other haters.

6.   By various accounts, Jews were reportedly on the lower end of the bell curve in the early measurements, which were started in 1914, and a number of explanations were offered to explain both that data and the very marked change in later measurements where Jews excelled (See Gilman 1996 (a), 64). However, Charles Murray makes clear that this may be an urban legend: "The widely repeated story that Jewish immigrants to this country in the early 20th century tested low on IQ is a canard." (Charles Murray, "Jewish Genius," *Commentary,* April 1, 2007. https://www.commentarymagazine.com/articles/jewish-genius/).

7.   Hernstein and Murray, 275 ("Jews, Latinos and Gender") and 717; Hernstein and Murray cite Storfer (1990), 314-321 for his review of the literature. In an April 1, 2007 article in *Commentary* (I wonder if the editors of *Commentary* timed this piece to be published on April 1?!), Charles Murray notes that his co-author of *The Bell Curve,* the late Richard Herrnstein, who was Jewish himself, "gently resisted the paragraphs on Jewish IQ that I insisted on putting in" the book. Interestingly, Murray also observed that *Commentary* "had never published a systematic discussion of one of the most obvious topics of all: the extravagant overrepresentation of Jews, relative to their numbers, in the top ranks of the arts, sciences, law, medicine, finance, entrepreneurship, and the media." (Charles Murray, "Jewish Genius," *Commentary,* April 1, 2007. http://www.commentarymagazine.com/articles/jewish-genius/).

8.   Charles Murray, *Human Accomplishment,* 292, citing P.M. Sheldon, "The families of highly gifted children," *Marriage and Family Living,* **16**: 59-61 (1954)

9.   Gilman (1996a), 64.

10.   Gilman, *Smart Jews* (1996b), 6.

11.   Gilman (1996b), 7.

12.   In *Start-Up Nation,* Senor and Singer make this comment regarding 'unitary Jewishness' with respect to Israel: "For starters, the idea of a unitary Jewishness – whether genetic or cultural – would seem to have little applicability to a nation that, though small, is among the most heterogeneous in the world. Israel's tiny population is made up of some seventy different nationalities." (Senor and Singer, *Start-Up Nation,* 17)

13.   Sander L. Gilman, *Smart Jews* (1996), Chapter 1. In recent years, Gilman has started to look at other cultural historical problems far afield from Jewish identity, such as the problem of obesity. He has published *Fat: A Cultural History of Obesity* (2008), *Diets and Dieting: A Cultural Encyclopedia* (2008), *Fat Boys* (2004), *Making the Body Beautiful* (1999). *Jewish Self-Hatred* came out in 1986, with *Smart Jews* appearing a decade later. Apparently, Gilman believes he has exhausted his earlier Jewish topics and has moved on to diets and obesity as being more relevant to his analysis.

14.   Sigmund Freud, cited by Joseph Wortis, *Fragments of an Analysis with Freud* (New York: Simon and Schuster, 1954), 145, in John Murray Cuddihy, *The Ordeal of Civility,* 7.

15.   Martin Peretz, cited in Gilman, op. cit., 64-65.

16.   In his book *Violins of Hope,* author James Grymes discusses the "music-loving environment"

in the Jewish community in Palestine before the establishment of the State of Israel. Bronislaw Huberman, who founded the Israeli Philharmonic Orchestra, organized numerous concerts in Palestine during this period. Grymes writes that "Huberman estimated that the percentage of concertgoers within the general public was *six to eight times higher within the Jewish community of Palestine* than it was in European cities." (Grymes, *Violins of Hope*, 34) (emphasis added). *Violins of Hope* further chronicles how some violins literally saved the lives of certain Jewish musicians during the Holocaust. I had the privilege of seeing some of these violins in person during a 2014 visit to the shop in Tel Aviv where they are kept when not on international display.

17. Thomas Sowell, "Achievement under attack" column, *The Vindicator* (Youngstown, Ohio), August 13, 2014, p. A10.
18. Efron (2014), 102.
19. George Gilder, "Capitalism, Jewish Achievement, and the Israel Test," *The American*, July 27, 2009. http://www.discovery.org/a/11771

Chapter Five

1. Alan Dershowitz, cited in the *I Am Jewish* book of essays (2004, 2015 ed.), 118.
2. Gotthard Deutsch, Richard Gottheil, J. Friedlander, "Belgium," *Jewish Encyclopedia* (1906 edition). http://www.jeiwshencyclopedia.com/articles/2803-belgium (Accessed November 2015), also cited in J. Richardson (2015), op. cit., 140.
3. Haya Benhayim with Menachem Benhayim, *Bound for the Promised Land* (San Francisco, CA: Purple Pomegranate Productions, 2004, 60.
4. J.C. Ryle, *Coming Events and Present Duties* (1867, 1879), Chapter V. "Scattered Israel to be Regathered."
5. Found in Barry E. Horner, op. cit., 297, citing Rev. John Charles Ryle, *Coming Events and Present Duties, being Miscellaneous Sermons on Prophetical Subjects Prophecy.* (London: William Hunt and Company). This book is available online via Google Books (accessed June 2015). Additional background on Ryle as well as individual sections of *Coming Events* can be found at: http://futureisraelministries.org/j_c_ryle.html; see *Coming Events*, Ch. VII, 111. When he wrote *Coming Events*, Ryle was at that time the vicar of Stradbroke, Suffolk. This work was later republished as *Are You Ready for the End of Time?* (Fearn, Scotland: Christian Focus, 2001). In his time, Charles Spurgeon called Ryle "the best man in the Church of England."
6. Adolph Saphir, Chapter VIII, *Christ and Israel*, 144-145, from a lecture given on April 26, 1864.
7. Amoz Oz and Fania Oz-Salzberger, *Jews and Words*, 38.

Chapter Six

1. George Gilder, *The Israel Test* (2014), 41, 234.
2. J. Grymes, *Violins of Hope* (2014), 18-19.
3. Saul Friedländer, *Nazi Germany and the Jews. Volume I: The Years of Persecution, 1933-1939* (1997), 52. Haber died on January 29, 1935. Though it was strongly forbidden by the authorities, Planck went ahead and held a memorial meeting at the Kaiser Wilhelm Society in Haber's memory at the Kaiser Wilhelm Society in defiance of the Nazis (Friedländer, op. cit., 130-131).
4. Max Tegmark, *Our Mathematical Universe* (2014), 175.
5. M. Kumar, op. cit., 293, citing Alan D. Beyerchen, *Scientists Under Hitler: Politics and the Physics Community in the Third Reich* (New Haven, CT: Yale University Press, 1977), 43. See also Edward Y. Hartshorne, Jr., *The German Universities and National Socialism* (Allen and Unwin, 1937), 112, and Brian VanDeMark, *Pandora's Keepers: Nine Men and the Atomic Bomb* (2003), 15.
6. D. McMahon, *Divine Fury: A History of Genius* (2013), 225, citing Alan D. Beyerchen, *Politics in the Physics Community in the Third Reich* (1977), 10.
7. Pedro G. Ferreira, *The Perfect Theory: A Century of Geniuses and the Battle Over General Relativity* (2014, 2015 paperback ed.), 69.
8. D. McMahon, op. cit., 214-215.
9. D. McMahon, op. cit., 217.
10. Brian VanDeMark, *Pandora's Secrets: Nine Men and the Atomic Bomb* (2003), 15.
11. Helmut Heiber, *Goebbels* (New York: Da Capo Press, 1972), 276.

12. "Adolf Hitler: A Prophecy of Jewry's Annihilation (January 30, 1939)," cited in Paul Mendes-Flohr and Jehuda Reinharz, Ch. XI, "The Holocaust," *The Jew in the Modern World: A Documentary History*, 656-658.

13. Gilder, op. cit., 147.

14. Darrin M. McMahon, *Divine Fury: A History of Genius* (2013), "Introduction: The Problem of Genius," xv.

15. D. McMahon, op. cit., 226.

16. George Gilder, *The Israel Test* (2009), 147.

17. G. Gilder, op. cit., 76.

18. James Pool and Suzanne Pool, *Who Financed Hitler* (1978), 94.

19. M. Kumar, op. cit., 295-296, citing Robert Jungk, *Brighter than a Thousand Suns: A Personal History of the Atomic Scientists* (London: Penguin, 1960), 44; Gilder (2009), 91-92.

20. Robert S. Wistrich, *Hitler and the Holocaust* (2001), 113.

21. [151] Adolf Hitler, "Table Talk," cited in Allan Bullock, *Hitler: A Study in Tyranny* (New York: Konecky and Konecky, 1962), 672-673; D. Aikman, *The Delusion of Disbelief*, 131-132; see also H.R. Trevor-Roper, ed., *Hitler's Table Talk, 1941-1944* (London, 1973), 78-79. A later edition was published in 2002 by Enigma Books.

22. Robert S. Wistrich, *Hitler and the Holocaust* (2001), 131-132, citing the following edition: H.R. Trevor-Roper, ed., *Hitler's Table Talk, 1941-1944* (London, 1973), 78-79.

23. Wistrich, op. cit., 132-133, also citing *Hitler's Table Talk.*

24. Although the Wannsee Mansion was the site for planning one of the greatest evils the world has ever known, in his book *What About Us?* Eitan Shishkoff shares how a more recent worship service of German Christian believers and Israeli Messianic leaders – held in the very same spot where the Wannsee Protocol was adopted – was filled with remorse and forgiveness (E. Shishkoff, *'What About Us? The end-time calling of Gentiles in Israel's revival*, 87).

25. Paraphrase of the Wannsee Protocol text cited by IDF General Elazar Stern in his book, *Struggling Over Israel's Soul* (Jerusalem: Gefen, 2012), p. 106. Another translation of the Wannsee Protocols merely says, "The final remnant, doubtlessly consisting of the toughest and most resilient individuals, would have to be treated accordingly, since they would have survived by natural development." (taken from Jeno Levai, Ed., *Eichmann in Hungary Documents* (Budapest: Pannonia Press, 1961, pp. 24-28, reproduced in R. Mendes-Flohr and Jehuda Reinharz, *The Jew in the Modern World: A Documentary History* (New York: Oxford University Press, 1980), p. 506.

26. Dr. David Hartman notes how indelibly the Holocaust continues to implant itself on Jewish consciousness today, and he recognizes the need for Jews to escape from being defined as victims: "No matter how powerful and compelling the experience of the Holocaust is for Jews today, we must not define ourselves as victims but must move from Auschwitz to Jerusalem." D. Hartman cited in *I Am Jewish* book of essays, 113.

27. Gilder, op. cit., 42.

28. Noah Efron, *A Chosen Calling* (2014), 68 and footnote 13, page 127.

29. N. Efron, op. cit., 76, 83.

30. D. Senor & S. Singer, *Start-Up Nation*, 212, citing America-Israel Friendship League, "Facts About Israel and the U.S.," http://www.aifl.org/html/web/resource_facts.html (CHECK for ACCESS and Date)

31. George Gilder, *The Israel Test* (2009), 3-4.

32. Gilder relates Jewish achievement and excellence to the Hebrew word for "alacrity" (*zerizus* or *zerizut*), citing Rabbi Zelig Pliskin, who defines it as "the blessed willpower and aspiration that leads to exceptional achievement." (Gilder, 12, 257)

33. G. Gilder (2009), 4-5.

34. Yuri Slezkine, *The Jewish Century* (2004), 1.

35. G. Gilder, op. cit., 62, 69. Although Gilder goes with this percentage of less than 0.1%, as noted elsewhere, other sources put the percentage at 0.2%. If we look at Israel alone, then we are closer to the figure of less than 0.1%.

36. Dan Senor and Saul Singer, *Start-Up Nation: The Story of Israel's Economic Miracle* (2011 edition), xvi.

37. "Israel's Silicon Valley, a global power in hi-tech," *The Washington Times*, July 8, 1998, p. A7.

38. Alla Borisova, Interview with Semyon Litsin. "Creator of flash technology – there is no happy Jew." ("Sozdatel' fleshki: 'Dovol'nogo evreya ne byvaet"). Jewish.ru. January 8, 2016. Russian language article. www.jewish.ru/style/science/2016/01/news994332173.php.

39. Senor & Singer, *Start-Up Nation,* 11, 19.
40. Todd L. Pittinsky, "A high-tech light unto the nations," The Times of Israel, November 3, 2016, http://blogs.timesofisrael.com/a-high-tech-light-unto-the-nations/
41. G. Gilder, op. cit., 6.

Chapter Seven

1. Steven Silbiger, *The Jewish Phenomenon,* 8.
2. Eric Weiner, *The Geography of Genius* (2016), 169. Journalist Daniel Schorr also expressed this feeling in his comments about what it means to be Jewish in the book, *I Am Jewish,* when he said: "...having grown up poor in the Bronx, I had a need to prove myself to the *goyim.* There! I've said it." (D. Schorr in *I Am Jewish,* 25).
3. A. Chua and J. Rubenfeld, *The Triple Package,* 12, 15-17, 58.
4. S. Silbiger, op. cit., 157, 159.
5. See the fascinating section on this in Amos Oz and Fania Oz-Salzberger, *Jews and Words,* 158, as these two self-identified Jewish atheists seek to define their own identity apart from Judaism.
6. Ioan James, 23.
7. Natan Sharansky, cited in Senor & Singer, *Start-Up Nation* (2009), 127.
8. Sergey Brin, cited in Senor & Singer, *Start-Up Nation* (2009), 124.
9. Kazin quote cited in Amy Chua and Jed Rubenfeld, *The Triple Package: How Three Unlikely Traits Explain the Rise and Fall of Cultural Groups in America,* 11.
10. Senor & Singer, op. cit., 158.
11. Steven Silbiger, *The Jewish Phenomenon,* 186.
12. Amy Chua and Jed Rubenfeld, *The Triple Package,* 151.
13. James Gleick, *Genius: The Life and Science of Richard Feynman,* 28, citing Melville Feynman's correspondence to his son Richard on 10 September 1944. During World War II, Richard Feynman was one of the key physicists at Los Alamos involved in the creation of the atomic bomb.
14. Steven Silbiger, 163.
15. "Hava Nagila (The Movie)," PBS television program. 2012 by Katahdin Productions. Steven Pease notes that "Alfred Adler, Erik, Erikson, Erich Fromm, Bruno Bettelheim, Frieda Fromm-Reichmann, and David Rapaport are but a few of the more prominent Jewish leaders in psychoanalysis." (Steven L. Pease, *The Golden Age of Jewish Achievement,* 54).
16. Alla Borisova, Interview with Semyon Litsin. "Creator of flash technology – there is no contented Jew." ("Sozdatel' fleshki: 'Dovol'nogo evreya ne byvaet"). Jewish.ru. January 8, 2016. Russian language article. www.jewish.ru/style/science/2016/01/news994332173.php.
17. Steven Silbiger, *The Jewish Phenomenon,* 35-36.
18. Steven L. Pease, "Julius Rosenwald," *The Golden Age of Jewish Achievement,* 369-371.
19. Morley Safer profile of David Rubenstein, "All-American," on the CBS "60 Minutes" television program, May 3, 2015. www.cbsnews.com/news/patriotic-philanthropist-david-rubenstein-morley-safer-60-minutes/
20. S. Silbiger, op. cit., 42; Pease, op. cit., 376-378.
21. Kenneth Chang, "9 Scientists Receive a New Physics Prize," *The New York Times,* July 31, 2012. http://nyti.ms/M6Tnm5
22. "Yuri Milner and Stephen Hawking announce $100 million Breakthrough Initiative to dramatically accelerate search for intelligent life in the Universe," July 20, 2015. http://www.astrobio.net; Max Taves, "Russian billionaire patiently listens for alien sounds," CNET, October 7, 2015 www.cnet.com/news/russian-billionaire-patiently-listens-for-alien-sounds/
23. Cited in "Philanthropic People" (Carl Icahn), www.philanthropicpeople.com/profiles/carl-icahn/. [Accessed Sept. 29, 2015).

Chapter Eight

1. Eric H. Yoffie, cited in the *I Am Jewish* book of essays (2004, 2015 ed.), 116.
2. Tina Levitan, "The First Jew in America, *First Facts in American Jewish History* (1996), 3-4.
3. T. Levitan, op. cit., 10.
4. Steven Silbiger, *The Jewish Phenomenon* (2009), 18. This group of 23, consisting of primarily Dutch and Italian Sephardim and made up of at least thirteen Jewish children, arrived in New Amsterdam aboard the French ship *Ste. Catherine* (Howard M. Sachar, *A History of the Jews in America,* 13-14).

5.   See Howard M. Sachar, op. cit., 14.
6.   Peter Stuyvesant, "Petition to Expel the Jews from New Amsterdam (Sep. 22, 1654), cited in Paul Mendes-Flohr and Jehuda Reinharz, Ch. IX, "The American Experience," *The Jew in the Modern World: A Documentary History,* 452, and response of the Dutch West India Company (453-454).
7.   Instead of listening to Megapolensis and Stuyvesant, the Dutch West India Company granted the Jews of New Amsterdam "the same liberty that is granted to them in this country [the Netherlands]...extended with respect to civil and political liberties," although they did not have the right "to exercise and carry on their religion in synagogues and gatherings." ("Dutch West India Company: Rights of Jews of New Amsterdam (March 13, 1656)," 453, cited in Paul Mendes-Flohr and Jehuda Reinharz, Ch. IX, "The American Experience," *The Jew in the Modern World: A Documentary History*. Mendes-Flohr and Reinharz note that pressure from the Amsterdam Jewish community on the Dutch West India Company was an important factor, but the main thing is that, in the end, the Company did the right thing by allowing the small Jewish community to remain.
8.   Sachar, 16.
9.   H. Sachar, op. cit., 16-20.
10. H. Sachar, 23.
11. Steven L. Pease, *The Golden Age of Jewish Achievement*, 60.
12. Charles E. Silberman, *A Certain People: American Jews and Their Lives Today*, 40.
13. Paul Mendes-Flohr and Jehuda Reinharz, Ch. IX, "The American Experience," *The Jew in the Modern World: A Documentary History,* 449.
14. S.J. Whitfield, Ch. 9: "Declarations of Independence: American Jewish Culture in the Twentieth Century," cited in David Biale, *Cultures of the Jews: A New History*, 1103.
15. Rob Richards, *Has God Finished with Israel?* 179.
16. Anita Libman Lebeson, *Jewish Pioneers in America, 1492-1848* (New York: Brentano's Publishers, 1931), 314.
17. One terrible example of anti-Semitism in America was the lynching of Jewish factory superintendent Leo Frank in 1915 in Georgia, who had been convicted (probably wrongfully) of murdering and raping a 13-year old female employee. Part of Frank's legal defense included the lawyer father of Daniel Boorstin. Boorstin, who came from a Jewish family, went on to become one of the most distinguished of American historians and the Librarian of Congress. The Frank case led to a rise of anti-Semitism in Georgia.
18. Of the 908 Jewish refugees on board the MS *St Louis* at the time the ship was denied entry to the U.S. in 1939, one person returned to his native Hungary, 287 persons eventually found refuge in Great Britain and the "remaining 620 passengers found refuge in France, Belgium, and the Netherlands." Of those, 254 perished in the war or the Holocaust (J. Grymes, *Violins of Hope*, 74-75).
19. J. Grymes, *Violins of Hope* (2014), 20.
20. George Washington, "Letter to the Jews of Newport", 18 August 1790, *Washington Papers*, 6: 284-85, cited in "George Washington and His Letter to the Jews of Newport," http://tourosynagogue.org/index.php/history-learning/gw-letter
21. David A. Hollinger, *Science, Jews, and Secular* Culture, 39 (footnote 45).
22. Rafael Medoff, "Document sheds new light on Jewish vote in 1944 race." October 15, 2012. JNS.org.
23. R. Medoff (2012), op. cit.
24. R. Medoff (2012), op. cit.
25. Raphael Patai, op. cit., 354.
26. Tina Levitan, Preface, *First Facts in American Jewish History* (1996), xiii.
27. "Broadway Musicals: A Jewish Legacy" television program (2012).
28. Howard M. Sachar, *A History of the Jews in America*, 764.
29. David A. Hollinger, "Why Are Jews Preeminent in Science and Scholarship? The Veblen Thesis Reconsidered," *Aleph* 2 (2002), 149. Elsewhere, Hollinger has offered one explanation as to why this success story of Jewish integration into American academia has received such little attention: "...one reason Jews have rarely been treated as a distinctive group in the discussions of academia during the multiculturalist 1980s and 1990s is that Jews long since come to be perceived as part of an empowered white, or European-American, demographic bloc." (David A. Hollinger, *Science, Jews, and Secular Culture: Studies in Mid-Twentieth-Century American Intellectual History,* 13-14).
30. Howard M. Sachar, op. cit., 753, 756.

31. Hollinger, op. cit., 29.

32. Steven Silbiger, *The Jewish Phenomenon*, 83.

33. Although in pre-war Europe, there were some amazing statistics emerging prior to the two world wars that would soon follow: "In 1885, out of a total attendance of 3,609 at the University of Berlin, 1,302, or 35 per cent, were Jews. In 1888 the figures stood at 2,500 out of 6,350 at the University of Vienna, and 1,194 out of 2,679, or 45 per cent, in the University of Budapest... Yet the Jews form only 5 per cent of the population of these countries." (A.E. Thompson, *A Century of Jewish Missions*, 1902, pp. 72-73).

34. Leonard Silk and Mark Silk, *The American Establishment* (1980), 41.

35. Josh Kun, music critic, recorded in the television show, "Broadway Musicals: A Jewish Legacy".

36. Avraham Burg, cited in *I Am Jewish* (Jewish Lights Publishing, 2015), 5.

37. James Gleick, *Genius: The Life and Science of Richard* Feynman, 23.

38. George Gilder, *The Israel Test* (2014), 41; see also Gilder, "Capitalism, Jewish Achievement, and the Israel Test," *The American*, July 27, 2009, http://www.discovery.org/a/11771

39. The first volume of this two-volume set is titled *Judaica Americana: A Bibliography of Publications to 1900, Volume I, Chronological File 1676 to 1889* (1990). Compiled by Robert Singerman.

40. William Hubbard, *The Happiness of a People in the Wisdome of their Rulers Directing And in the Obedience of their Brethren Attending Unto What Israel Ought to Do.* Boston: 1676, p. 59.

Conclusion - Part 1

1. Goethe quote cited in McMahon, *Divine Fury* (2013), 147. In Goethe, *Conversations with Eckermann*, 317-318 (March 2, 1831), 319 (March 8, 1831), 199-205 (March 11, 1828).

2. Daniel C. Juster, *The Irrevocable Calling*, 12.

3. Sander L. Gilman, critiquing Herrnstein and Murray's controversial book, *The Bell Curve,* cited Leon Wieseltier, at the time the literary editor of *The New Republic*. Wieseltier was troubled by the potential implications of this idea of innate giftedness. He wrote that he was "repelled" by this whole notion (referring to purported Jewish superior intelligence as related by Herrnstein and Murray), because, according to Gilman, Wieseltier "wishes to believe that he is responsible for his own achievements rather than that they are a reflex of a group of which he happens to be a member." (Gilman, 1996a), 65.

Chapter Nine

1. See Joel Richardson, "The Restoration of the Jewish Kingdom," *When a Jew Rules the World*, 89-92.

2. Jim R. Sibley, "The 'Lost Gospel' of Jerusalem," LCJE *Bulletin,* No. 121 (August-September 2015), 13.

3. Joel Richardson, *When a Jew Rules the World* (2015), 7.

4. See Sean Carroll, *The Particle at the End of the Universe: How the Hunt for the Higgs Boson Leads Us to the Edge of a New World* (2012), 20. See also Jim Baggott, *Higgs: The Invention and Discovery of the 'God Particle'.* (Oxford University Press, 2012).

5. Edward J. Larson and Larry Witham, "Leading scientists still reject God," *Nature* **394,** No. 6691, 313 (1998) www.nature.com/nature/journal/v394/n6691/full/394313a0_fs.html.

6. See Sean Carroll, *The Particle at the End of the Universe: How the Hunt for the Higgs Boson Leads Us to the Edge of a New World* (2012).

7. Cited in Joel Richardson, *When a Jew Rules the World* (2015), 201. See also S. Snobelen, "'The Mystery of This Restitution of All Things': Isaac Newton on the Return of the Jews," Chapter 7 in J.E. Force and R.H. Popkin (Eds.), *Millenarianism and Messianism in Early Modern European Culture: The Millenarian Turn*, 95, citing Newton's Papers, Yahuda MS 6, f. 12r. at the Jewish National and University Library (Jerusalem).

8. While there is evidence that Isaac Newton was non-Trinitarian in his views, this area is still somewhat murky. Regardless, it is absolutely clear from his writings that Newton believed in the literal prophecies of the Hebrew Scriptures that God would indeed bring about a restoration of the Jewish people both to their ancient homeland and that they would someday be saved *as a nation.*

224 Jewish Giftedness and World Redemption

9.   Barry Horner, *Future Israel,* 333, Appendix A, "Jonathan Edwards and the Future of Israel."
10.   Jonathan Edwards, *Works, A History of the Work of* Redemption, Vol. 9, John F. Wilson, Ed. (New Haven, CT: Yale University Press, 1989), 469-470. Also cited in Iain Murray, *The Puritan Hope* (1971), 61; Horner, op. cit., 335.
11.   S. Snobelen, op. cit., 101. However, Snobelen adds elsewhere that Newton's view of Romans 11 differed from the traditional restorationist interpretation. Newton reportedly believed that Romans 11 "referred to the moment at the end when all Israel – Jew and Gentile alike – would convert together to true Christianity." (op. cit., 110).
12.   Cited in Iain Murray, *The Puritan Hope* (1971), 100.
13.   Kelvin Crombie, *For the Love of Zion* (1991), 11.
14.   Increase Mather, *The Mystery of Israel's Salvation Explained and Applied* (London: 1669), 1.
15.   Joel Chernoff, "The Restoration of Israel" album and song. Produced by Galilee of the Nations. See www.galileeofthenations.com/products/the-restoration-of-israel
16.   In his 2010 book on the Soviet Jewish emigration movement, author Gal Beckerman observes that Soviet Jews under Stalin's reign "were discouraged in every way from being Jews – synagogues were shuttered, and Yiddish writers and actors were executed..." This was done "by a regime that wanted no trace of Jewish communal life, extinguishing even that which was permitted by the Bolsheviks.... It was obvious to most observers that within a generation or two, the total assimilation, or spiritual genocide, of Soviet Jewry would be complete." (Gal Beckerman, *When They Come for Us, We'll Be Gone: The Epic Struggle to Save Soviet Jewry,* 5).
17.   Some Christians also strongly deny that the founding of the State of Israel had anything to do with Biblical prophecy. These Christians range from those who simply believe in *replacement theology,* or, as one author terms it, "revocation theology" – a tongue-in-cheek phrase meaning that God has "revoked" His irrevocable promises to the Jewish people – a view that this author denounces (see also J. Richardson, *When a Jew Rules the World,* 63).
18.   James Bicheno, *The Restoration of the Jews, The Crisis of All Nations* (1807), 229.
19.   Rob Richards, *Has God Finished with Israel?* (2000 ed.), 54, 151.
20.   I. Murray, *The Puritan Hope,* 66.
21.   Daniel C. Juster, *The Irrevocable Calling: Israel's Role as a Light to the Nations* (2007 ed.), 2.
22.   J.C. Ryle, *Coming Events,* V, 88-90.
23.   Douglas W. Kittredge, *God's Plan for Peace in the Middle East* (2006), 31.

Chapter Ten

1.   Adolph Saphir, in a manuscript found among his papers and first published in *The Scattered Nation* in 1898, later re-published in *Christ and Israel,* 16.
2.   A. Saphir, op. cit., 103, 107, from a sermon given on May 18, 1868.
3.   Saphir, op. cit., 107.
4.   "Life from the Dead." Interview with Julia Fisher. 2008. The Olive Tree Reconciliation Fund. http://www.olivetreefund.org/life-from-the-dead/
5.   Adolph Saphir addressed his congregation on this theme in 1885: "...although they [the Jews] are not clearly conscious of its nature, they feel that they have a special position and mission in the history of the world." (A. Saphir, from a January 18, 1885 sermon, Chapter IV, "The Everlasting Nation," *Christ and Israel,* 74).
6.   Douglas W. Kittredge, *God's Plan for Peace in the Middle East* (2006), 29.
7.   L.H. Feldman has been the "strongest advocate for Jewish missionary activity...who has made the case repeatedly and with powerful documentation." See L.H. Feldman in M. Mor, Ed., *Jewish Assimilation, Acculturation and Accommodation* (Lanham, MD, 1992): 24-37). See footnote 206 (page 274) in Erich S. Gruen, *Diaspora: Jews Amidst Greeks and Romans* (Cambridge, MA: Harvard University Press, 2002). Gruen himself rejects that view and claims that "no unambiguous testimony exists to show that Jews went about accosting Gentiles and endeavoring to turn them into good Jews..." (Gruen, 46).
8.   Adolph Saphir, *Christ and Israel,* 56.
9.   D. Kittredge, op. cit., 29-30.
10.   D. Kittredge, op. cit., 39.
11.   G. Gilder, op. cit., 246.
12.   Avi Snyder, "Life from the Dead." Interview with Julia Fisher. 2008. The Olive Tree Reconciliation Fund. http://www.olivetreefund.org/life-from-the-dead/
13.   See David Aikman's discussion of this in his book, *One Nation Without God: The Battle for Christianity in an Age of Unbelief* (Baker Books, 2012), pp. 69-73.

14. David Aikman, op. cit., p. 73.
15. Adolph Saphir, *Christ and Israel*, 111, from a sermon dated May 18, 1868.
16. Marvin R. Wilson, *Our Father Abraham: Jewish Roots of the Christian Faith* (1989), 321.
17. H. Bonar (1855), 350.
18. Sam Harris, *The End of Faith* (2004), 153.
19. While the Apostle Paul used the word "Greek" in Romans 1:16 and again in 2:9-10 (and by it he meant the Hellenic world at large), it is also clear from the later context a few verses later in Romans 2:14 that he has expanded that meaning beyond the Greek world to include all the non-Jewish nations of the world as well. In verse 14 he uses the word *ethos*, which refers to "tribes, Gentiles, heathens, nations or peoples."
20. From a sermon by Rev. Robert Murray M'Cheyne (November 17, 1839), cited in Jerry Marcellino with Yochanan Ben Yehuda, *Should the Church Have a Heart for Israel? A Historical Perspective*, 40-41.
21. See Michael Brown's *Our Hands Are Stained with Blood*; and David A. Rausch, *A Legacy of Hatred: Why Christians Must Not Forget the Holocaust* (Chicago: Moody Press, 1984).
22. Horner, op. cit., xviii.
23. Frederic Raphael, *Anti-Semitism* (2015), 35.
24. Ephraim Sevela, *Farewell, Israel!* (1977), 295.
25. Matthew Wilson, *The Ruth-like Church* (2013), 261.
26. D. Gruber, *The Church and the Jews* (Hanover, NH: Elijah Publishing, 1997), 401-402; also cited in Barry Horner, *Future Israel*, 320-321.
27. Richard Dreyfuss, cited in *I Am Jewish*, 75-76.
28. Martin Buber, "Hebrew Humanism," in *Israel and the World: Essays in a Time of Crisis* (Syracuse, NY: Syracuse University Press, 1997), 240 & 250, cited by Amy Chua and Jed Rubenfeld, *The Triple Package: How Three Unlikely Traits Explain the Rise and Fall of Cultural Groups in America* (2015), 63 & 269.

Chapter Eleven

1. I am indebted to well-known Bible song-writer Michael Card and his "Biblical Imagination Series" for rekindling my interest in the debates between Shammai and Hillel. I had studied these long ago, but Michael's discussion of them at a seminar in September 2015 at New Life in Christ Church (Fredericksburg, Virginia) at just the time I was writing this section of the book was very helpful and relevant.
2. *The Jewish Encyclopedia* (1906), http://jewishencyclopedia.com/articles/12391-proselyte (accessed April 2015)
3. Thomas Coke Commentary on the Bible. (for Matthew 23:15)
4. But there is debate over that point. According to John J. Collins: "The idea of a Jewish mission, or of active Jewish proselytism, however, which was a virtual dogma of scholarship in the early twentieth century, has been widely discredited in recent years." (John J. Collins, Chapter 7, "Jews and Gentiles," *Between Athens and Jerusalem: Jewish Identity in the Hellenistic Diaspora*. Grand Rapids, Michigan: William B. Eerdmans and Dove Booksellers, Second Edition, 2000, 261). But do we really know? Is a view that has gone from "a virtual dogma of scholarship in the early twentieth century" to becoming "widely discredited in recent years" (to quote Collins) really a settled matter?
5. Horace, *The Satires*, Book I, Satire IV, "A Defense of Satire," verse 142 (138-143).
6. The first version appears in the Thomas Coke commentary on Matthew 23:15. The second appears in a modern English translation of Horace of Book I, Satire IV, appearing in http://www.poetryintranslation.com/PITBR/Latin/HoraceSatiresBkISatIV.htm (accessed April 2015). Erich S. Gruen takes exception to the view expressed in these other translations: "There is no good reason," he claims, "to think that Horace is here speaking of conversion. The Jews never, on any reckoning, 'compelled' persons to convert!" I am not a scholar in this area, but this sounds to me very much like an over-reaction. Gruen continues: "…it is taking the lines too seriously to interpret them as showing that the Jews constituted a known pressure group in Rome." (Erich S. Gruen, *Diaspora: Jews Amidst Greeks and Romans*, Cambridge, MA: Harvard University Press, 2002, p. 275).
7. J. J. Collins, op. cit., 264, footnote 14, citing Seneca, in Augustine, *De Civitate Dei* 6.11.
8. J.J. Collins, op. cit., 262, fn. 6, citing Cassius Dio, *Historia Romana* 57.18.5a and Tacitus, *Annals* 2.85.5.

9.   Harald Hegermann, Chapter 4, "The Diaspora in the Hellenistic Age," W.W. Davies and Louis Finkelstein, Eds., *The Cambridge History of Judaism*, Vol. II, 157.
10.   *Encyclopedia Judaica* 10:55, s.v. "Jewish Identity." 1971 edition.
11.   Michael Avi-Yonah, *The Jews of Palestine* (Oxford, 1976), 37.
12.   Donald A. Hagner, "Paul as a Jewish Believer – According to His Letters," in Oskar Skarsaune and Reidar Hvalvik, Eds., *Jewish Believers in Jesus: The Early Centuries*, Peabody, Massachusetts: Hendrickson Publishers, 2007, 125.
13.   H. Hegermann, op. cit.
14.   Amos Oz and Fania Oz-Salzberger, *Jews and Words*, 176-177.
15.   Alfred Edersheim discusses examples of this antipathy at length in *The Life and Times of Jesus the Messiah*: "To begin with, every Gentile child, as soon as born, was to be regarded as unclean…" Further, he wrote that even "milk drawn by a heathen, if a Jew had not been present to watch it," as well as "bread and oil prepared by them," were considered unlawful for Jews. And as far as wine was concerned, "the mere touch of a heathen polluted a whole cask…" (A. Edersheim, *The Life and Times of Jesus the Messiah*, 62-63).
16.   Daniel C. Juster, *The Irrevocable Calling*, 22-23; see also 12-13.
17.   *The Babylonian Talmud*, Gemara, Tractate Sukkah 55b, Vol. III, Chapter V, p. 269.
18.   Eitan Shishkoff, '*What About Us?*', 12, 42.
19.   Daniel Juster, *Jewish Roots: Understanding Your Jewish Faith* (Shippensburg, PA: Destiny Image Publishers, Inc., 1013, Fourth Revised Edition), 114.

Chapter Twelve

1.   Adolph Saphir, from a sermon given on May 18, 1868, *Christ and Israel*, 111.
2.   Iain Murray, *The Puritan Hope: Revival and the Interpretation of Prophecy* (Edinburgh, Scotland; Carlisle, Pennsylvania: The Banner of Truth Trust, 1971).
3.   Daniel C. Juster, *The Irrevocable Calling*, 32.
4.   Daniel C. Juster, *The Irrevocable Calling*, 44.
5.   Sir Henry Finch, *The World's Great Restauration [Restoration] or Calling of the Jews* (London: William Gouge, 1621), 6.
6.   Salo Wittmayer Baron, "French and English Ambiguities," *A Social and Religious History of the Jews*. Vol. 15: *Late Middle Ages and Era of European Expansion, 1200-1650, Resettlement and Exploration* (1973 edition), 145-146.
7.   Elnathan Parr, *A Plaine Exposition upon the whole eighth, ninth, tenth, eleventh, twelfth Chapters of the Epistle of Saint Paul to the Romanes* (London, 1620), 366, 409.
8.   James Bicheno, *The Restoration of the Jews; The Crisis of All Nations* (1807), 102.
9.   Horatius Bonar, "The Jew," *Quarterly Journal of Prophecy* (July 1870), 209-211, cited in Joel Richardson, *When a Jew Rules the World*, 197-198; see also Barry Horner, op. cit, 10.
10.   Daniel C. Juster, *The Irrevocable Calling*, 47.

Bibliography

Aczel, Amir D. 2009. *Uranium Wars: The Scientific Rivalry that Created the Nuclear Age.*New York: Palgrave Macmillan.

Aikman, David. 2012. One Nation Without God? The Battle for Christianity in an Age of Unbelief. Grand Rapids, Michigan: Baker Books.

_____. 2008. The Delusion of Disbelief. Carol Stream, Illinois: Saltriver, Tyndale House.

American Jewish Desk Reference. 1999. Editorial Director Ralph Carlson. New York: Random House, The Philip Lief Group, Inc.

Aronson, Josh. 2011. "Orchestra of Exiles: The Story of the Israel Philharmonic." www.seenandheard-international.com/2011/04/orchestra-of-exiles-the-story-of-the-israel-philharmonic *The Babylonian Talmud.*

Baggott, Jim. 2011. *The Quantum Story: A History in 40 Moments.* Oxford: Oxford University Press.

_____. 2012. *Higgs: The Invention and Discovery of the 'God Particle'.* Oxford: Oxford University Press.

Baron, Salo Wittmayer. 1967, 1973. *A Social and Religious History of the Jews.* Vol. 15: *Late Middle Ages and Era of European Expansion, 1200-1650, Resettlement and Exploration.*

Bauman, Mark K. 2011. *Jewish-American Chronology: Chronologies of the American Mosaic.* Santa Barbara, CA: Greenwood.

Beckerman, Gal. 2010. *When They Come for Us, We'll Be Gone: The Epic Struggle to Save Soviet Jewry.* Boston: Mariner Books.

Belkin, Douglas. 2015. "Harvard Accused of Bias Against Asian-Americans." *Wall Street Journal.* May 15, 2015.

http://www.wsj.com/articles/asian-american-organizations-seek-federal-probe-of-harvard-admission-policies-1431719348

Benhayim, Haya with Menachem Benhayim. 2004. *Bound for the Promised Land.* San Francisco, CA: Purple Pomegranate Productions.

Berdyaev, Nikolai. 1969. *Smysl' istorii: Opyt filosofi chelovecheskoi sud'by* (The Meaning of History: The Experience of the Philosophy of Human Destiny). Paris: YMCA-Press. 2nd Edition. See Chapter V. *Sud'ba evreistva* ("The Destiny of Jewry"). This edition is based on Berdyaev's 1920-21 lecture series.

_____. 2006. *The Meaning of History.* New Brunswick, NJ: Transaction Publishers. Original edition: London: G. Bles, 1936.

Bethe, Hans. 2013. "About Hans Bethe: Personal and Historical Perspectives of Hans Bethe." http://bethe.cornell.edu/about.html (Accessed October 2015)

Biale, David. Editor. 2002. *Cultures of the Jews: A New History.* New York: Schocken Books.

Bicheno, James. 1807. *The Restoration of the Jews, The Crisis of All Nations; to which is now prefixed,   A Brief History of the Jews, from Their First Dispersion...* Second edition. London.

The Biographical Dictionary of Scientists. 2000. Third Edition: Vol. I. New York: Oxford University Press.

Bjoraker, Bill. "Ten Narratives on the Place of Story and Orality in Christian and Messianic Jewish Theology and Ministry: Rediscovering the Lost Treasures of Hebraic Narrative Epistemology." *LCJE Bulletin.* May-June 2015: 20-23.

Bock, Darrell L. and Mitch Glaser, Eds. 2008. *To the Jew First: The Case for Jewish Evangelism in Scripture and History.* Grand Rapids, Michigan: Kregel Publications.

Boden, Margaret A. 1990. *The Creative Mind: Myths and Mechanisms.* New York: Basic Books.

Bonar, Horatius. 1855. "The Responsibilities of Christians as Regards the Jews." *The Quarterly Journal of Prophecy.* October 1855: 347-352.

Borisova, Alla. 2016. Interview with Semyon Litsin. "Creator of flash technology – there is no contented Jew." ("Sozdatel' fleshki: 'Dovol'nogo evreya ne byvaet"). Jewish.ru. January 8, 2016. Russian article. www.jewish.ru/style/science/2016/01/news994332173.php

Born, Max. 1975. *My Life: Recollections of a Nobel Laureate.* New York: Charles Scribner's Sons.

Braude, Benjamin. 2001. Review of Sander Gilman's book *Smart Jews* in *The Jewish Quarterly Review* **92**(1/2). July-October 2001: 180-181.

"Broadway Musicals: A Jewish Legacy." 2012 documentary. Great Performances series. Film by Michael Kantor. B'WAY Films LLC, Ghost Light Films, Albert M. Tapper. PBS premier in 2013.

Broocks, Rice. 2013. *God's Not Dead: Evidence for God in an Age of Uncertainty.* Nashville, TN: W. Publishing, Thomas Nelson.

Brook, Kevin Alan. 2013. "Are Russian Jews Descended from the Khazars?" www.khazaria.com/khazar-diaspora.html

Brooks, David. 2010. "The Tel Aviv Cluster." *The New York Times*. January 12.

Brown, Michael L. 2000. *Answering Jewish Objections to Jesus,* Volume One. Grand Rapids, MI: Baker Books.

_____. 1992. *Our Hands Are Stained with Blood: The Tragic Story of the 'Church' and the Jewish People.* Shippensburg, PA: Destiny Image.

Buhle, Paul. 2004. *From the Lower East Side to Hollywood: Jews in American Popular Culture.* London: Verso.

Cahill, Thomas. 1998. *The Gifts of the Jews: How a Tribe of Desert Nomads Changed the Way Everyone Thinks and Feels.* New York: Nan A. Talese/ Anchor Books.

Carroll, Sean. 2012. *The Particle at the End of the Universe: How the Hunt for the Higgs Boson Leads Us to the Edge of a New World.* New York: Dutton.

Ceoldo, Constantino. 2012. "Homage to Rita Levi Montalcini." Dec. 31, 2012. Pravda.ru. http://english.pravda.ru/society/anomal/31-12-2012/123358-rita_montalcini-0/

Chang, Kenneth. 2012. "9 Scientists Receive a New Physics Prize." *The New York Times*. July 31, 2012. http://nyti.ms/M6Tnm5

Chua, Amy and Jed Rubenfeld. 2014, 2015. *The Triple Package: How Three Unlikely Traits Explain the Rise and Fall of Cultural Groups in America.* New York: Penguin Books. Paperback edition.

Cochran, Gregory, Jason Hardy, and Henry Harpending. 2006. "Natural History of Ashkenazi Intelligence." *Journal of Biosocial Science* **38.**

Collins, John J. 2000. *Between Athens and Jerusalem: Jewish Identity in the Hellenistic Diaspora.* Grand Rapids, Michigan: William B. Eerdmans and Dove Booksellers, Second Edition. (see esp. Ch. 7, "Jews and Gentiles).

Costa, Marta D., Joana B. Pereira, Maria Pala, et al. "A substantial prehistoric European ancestry amongst Ashkenazi maternal lineages." *Nature Communications* **4** No. 2543. 8 October 2013. www.nature.com/ ncomms/2013/131008/ncomms3543/full/ncomms3543.html

Crombie, Kelvin. 1991. *For the Love of Zion: Christian witness and the restoration of Israel.* London: Hodder & Stoughton.

_____. 1998, 2007. *ANZACs, Empires, and Israel's Restoration, 1798-1948.* Nicolayson's: Jerusalem.

Cropper, William H. 2001. *Great Physicists: The Life and Times of Leading Physicists from Galileo to Hawking.* Chapter 26: "Telling the Tale of the Quarks: Murray Gell-Mann." New York: Oxford University Press.

Cuddihy, John Murray. 1974. *The Ordeal of Civility: Freud, Marx, Levi-Strauss and the Jewish Struggle with Modernity.* New York: Delta.

Day, Vox. 2008. *The Irrational Atheist: Dissecting the Unholy Trinity of Dawkins, Harris and Hitchens.* Dallas, Texas: BenBella Books.

DeRouchie, Jason S. 2015. "Counting Stars with Abraham and the Prophets: New Covenant Ecclesiology." *Journal of the Evangelical Theological Society.* Vol. 58. No. No. 3. September.

Deutsch, David. 2011. *The Beginning of Infinity.* New York: Viking.

Deutsch, Gotthard, Richard Gottheil, J. Friedlander. "Belgium." *Jewish Encyclopedia* (1906 edition). http://www.jeiwshencyclopedia.com/articles/2803-belgium. Accessed November 2015.

Deutscher, Isaac. 1968. *The Non-Jewish Jew and Other Essays.* New York: Hill and Wang.

Dimont, Max I. 1973. *The Indestructible Jews.* New York: New American Library. Revised edition.

Disraeli, Isaac. 1818, 1859 ed. *The Works of Isaac Disraeli: The Literary Character of Men of Genius Drawn from Their Own Feelings and Confessions.* London: Routledge, Warnes, and Routledge. Isaac was the father of the famed Jewish Prime Minister of England, Benjamin Disraeli, who edited this edition. Found in Google Books.

Dunlop, John. 1894. *Memories of Gospel Triumphs among the Jews during the Victorian Era.* London: S.W. Partridge & Co. Dunlop was the Secretary of the British Society for the Jews.

Edersheim, Alfred. 1874. *The Temple, its Ministry and Services, as They Were at the Time of Jesus Christ.* London.

_____. 1886, 1993. *The Life and Times of Jesus the Messiah.* Peabody, Massachusetts: Hendrickson Publishers.

Edsel, Robert M. 2006. *Rescuing Da Vinci: Hitler and the Nazis Stole Europe's Great Art. America and Her Allies Recovered It.* Dallas, Texas: Laurel Publishing LLC.

Efron, Noah J. 2014. *Chosen Calling: Jews in Science in the Twentieth Century.* Johns Hopkins University Press, Hebrew Union College Press.

Ehrenberg, Ilya and Vasily Grossman. 1980. *The Black Book.* New York: Holocaust Library, Yad Vashem.

Encyclopedia Judaica. 2007. Second Edition. Fred Skolnik, Editor in Chief. Keter Publishing House Ltd., Farmington Hills, MI: Thomson Gale. Volume 15 entries for "J. Robert Oppenheimer." "Nobel Prizes"; Volume 19 entry for "Tikkun" (p. 722)

Epstein, Varda. 2015. "The Debate Over Jewish Achievement: A Review." Huffpost Religion. August 25, 2015. http://www.huffingtonpost.com/varda-epstein/the-debate-over-Jewish-achievement_b_8027028.html

Ferreira, Pedro G. 2014, 2015. *The Perfect Theory: Century of Geniuses and the Battle Over General Relativity.* London: Abacus (paperback edition).

Feuer, Lewis S. 1963, 1992. "The Scientific Revolution Among the Jews." *The Scientific Intellectual: The Psychological and Sociological Origins of Modern Science.* New Brunswick, New Jersey: Transaction Publishers, 1992 edition.

Feynman, Richard. 1977. *The Feynman Lectures on Physics.* Reading, MA: Addison-Wesley Publishing Co.; California Institute of Technology: 1963, 1977 edition.

[Finch, Sir Henry]. 1621. *The World's Great Restauration [Restoration] or Calling of the Jews.* London: William Gouge.

The First Report of the American Society for Meliorating the Condition of the Jews. 1823. New York: Printed for the Society by Gray and Bunce. Presented May 9, 1823.

Frank, Adam and Marcelo Gleiser. "A Crisis at the Edge of Physics." *The New York Times.* June 5, 2015. http://nyti.ms/1lqkvhO

Fraser, Gordon. 2012. *The Quantum Exodus: Jewish Fugitives, the Atomic Bomb and the Holocaust.* Oxford University Press.

Friedländer, Saul. 1997. *Nazi Germany and the Jews. Volume I. The Years of Persecution, 1933-1939.* New York: HarperCollins.

Fritzsch, Harald. 2010. *Murray Gell-Mann Selected Papers.* Vol. 40. World Scientific Series in 20th Century Physics. Singapore: World Scientific Publishing.

Gell-Mann, Murray. 1994. *The Quark and the Jaguar: Adventures in the Simple and the Complex.* New York: A.W.H. Freeman; Holt Paperback.

"George Washington and His Letter to the Jews of Newport." 1790. This is Washington's letter to the Jews of Newport, Rhode Island dated 18 August 1790. Accessed August 2014. http://tourosynagogue.org/index.php/history-learning/gw-letter

Gilder, George. 2009. *The Israel Test. Why the World's Most Besieged State is a Beacon of Hope for the World Economy.* New York: Encounter Books.

_____. 2009. "Capitalism, Jewish Achievement, and the Israel Test." *The American.* July 27, 2009. http://www.discovery.org/a/11771 (accessed April 2016)

Gilman, Sander L. 1996a. "'The Bell Curve,' Intelligence, and Virtuous Jews." *Discourse.* Vol. 19. No. 1 'Secularism and the Future of Jewry'. Fall 1996: 58-80.

_____. 1996b. *Smart Jews: The Construction of the Image of Jewish Superior Intelligence.* Lincoln, Nebraska: University of Nebraska Press.

_____. 1986. *Jewish Self-Hatred: Anti-Semitism and the Hidden Language of the Jews.* Baltimore: Johns Hopkins University Press.

Glaser, Mitch and Alan Shore. 2006. *Remnant and Revival: The New Russian Messianic Movement.* New York: Chosen People Ministries.

Gleick, James. 1992. *Genius: The Life and Science of Richard Feynman.* New York: Pantheon Books.

Glenny, Misha. 2008. *McMafia: A Journey through the Global Criminal Underground.* New York: Alfred A. Knopf.

A Glimpse of Sions Glory or, The Churches Beautie Specified. 1641. Thomas Goodwin, William Kiffin, Hanserd Knollys, Jeremiah Burroughs. London: Printed for William Lamar.

Gould, Stephen Jay. 1981. *The Mismeasure of Man.* New York: W.W. Norton.

Gruber, D. 1997. *The Church and the Jews.* Hanover, NH: Elijah Publishing.

Gruen, Erich S. 2002. *Diaspora: Jews Amidst Greeks and Romans.* Cambridge, Massachusetts: Harvard University Press.

Grymes, James A. 2014. *Violins of Hope: Violins of the Holocaust – Instruments of Hope and Liberation in Mankind's Darkest Hour.* New York: HarperCollins.

Harding, Luke. 2007. "Can Russia's oligarchs keep their billions – and their freedom?" *The Guardian.* 1 July 2007. www.theguardian.com/world/2007/jul/02/lukeharding1

Harris, Sam. 2004. *The End of Faith: Religion, Terror, and the Future of Reason.* New York: W.W. Norton.

"Hava Nagila (The Movie)." 2012. PBS television program. Katahdin Productions.

Hefly, James and Marti. 1974. *Where in the World Are the Jews Today?* Wheaton, Illinois: Victor Books, SP Publications.

Hegermann, Harald. 1990. Chapter 4, "The Diaspora in the Hellenistic Age," W.W. Davies and Louis Finkelstein, Editors, *The Cambridge History of Judaism*, Vol. II. Cambridge University Press.

Heiber, Helmut. 1972. *Goebbels.* New York: Da Capo Press.

Heller, Anne C. 2009. *Ayn Rand and the World She Made.* New York: Nan A. Talese/Doubleday.

Herman, Arthur. 2001. *How the Scots Invented the Modern World: The true story of how western Europe's poorest nation created our world and everything in it.* New York: Three Rivers Press.

Herrnstein, Ricjard J. and Charles Murray. 1994. *The Bell Curve: Intelligence and Class Structure in American Life.* New York: Free Press.

Herzig, Steve. 2004. *More Jewish Culture and Customs: A Sampler of Jewish Life.* Bellmawr, NJ: Friends of Israel Gospel Ministry.

Heschel, Abraham Joshua. 1956. *God in Search of Man: a philosophy of Judaism.* New York: The Jewish Publication Society of America.

"History of the Huberman." *The Strad* 124 No. 1483 (November 2013): 51.

Hoberman, J. and Jeffrey Shandler. 2003. *Entertaining America: Jews, Movies and Broadcasting.* New York: The Jewish Museum and Princeton University Press.

Hollinger, David. 2002. "Why Are the Jews Pre-eminent in Science and Scholarship? The Veblen Thesis Reconsidered." *Aleph* 2: 145-163.

_____. 1996. *Science, Jews, and Secular Culture: Studies in Mid-Twentieth Century American Intellectual History.* Princeton, NJ: Princeton University Press.

Holt, Jim. 2012. *Why Does the World Exist? An Existential Detective Story.* London: Profile Books.

Hooper, Dan. 2008. *Nature's Blueprint: Supersymmetry and the Search for a Unified Theory of Matter and Force.* New York: HarpersCollins.

Horace. *The Satires.* Book I. Satire IV. "A Defense of Satire." verse 142: (138-143). A possible reference to Jewish proselytizing in the ancient Roman world.

Horner, Barry. 2007. *Future Israel: Why Christian Anti-Judaism Must Be Challenged.* Nashville, TN: B&H Academic.

Hubbard, William. 1676. *The Happiness of a People in the Wisdome of their Rulers Directing and in the Obedience of their Brethren Attending Unto What Israel Ought to Do.* Boston: Printed by John Foster. Hubbard was one of the most venerated ministers in the Massachusetts Bay Colony during his lifetime. Reviewed at Houghton Library at Harvard on October 31, 2015. Houghton Call No. *AC6 H8613 677na.

Isaiah. Rev. Dr. A. Cohen, Ed. 1976 printing. London: The Soncino Press.

Jacob, Alex. 2010. *The Case for Enlargement Theology.* UK: Glory to Glory Publications.

Jacobovici, Simcha. 2014. "Pink, the Oscars and the…rebirth of Israel?" blogs. timesofisrael.com/pink-the-oscars-and-the-rebirth-of-israel (March 4, 2014). Accessed August 1, 2015.

Jacobs, Joseph. 2009. *Jewish Contributions to Civilization: An Estimate.* Piscatany, New Jersey: Gorgias Press. Reprint of 1919 work. Original published by The Conant Press, 1920.

James, Ioan. 2009. *Driven to Innovate: A Century of Jewish Mathematicians and Physicists.* Peter Lang Oxford.

"Jewish American physicist says he'll send part of $3 million prize to J Street," JTA, *Haaretz*, August 4, 2012. http://www.haaretz.com/jewish-world/ jewish-world-news/jewish-american-physicist-says-he'll-send-part-of-3-to-j-street-1.455893

"Jewish Biographies: Business & Entrepreneurial Icons." Jewish Virtual Library. http://www.jewishvirtuallibrary.org/jsource/biography/businessicons.html

The Jewish Encyclopedia. 1906. http://jewishencyclopedia.com/articles/12391-proselyte (accessed April 2015). Definition of "proselyte".

"Jewish Recipients of the Pulitzer Prize for General Non-Fiction." www.jinfo. org/Pulitzer_Non-Fiction.html

"Jewish Recipients of the Pulitzer Prize for Fiction" www.jinfo.org/Pulitzer_ Fiction.html

"Jewish World Chess Champions," http://www.jinfo.org/Chess_Champions. html. Accessed August 2014

"Jewish Nobel Prize Winners." http://jinfo.org/Nobel_Prizes.html (between 1901-2012).

"Jewish Violinists." http://www.jinfo.org/Violinists.html (Accessed August 2014)

Johnson, George. 1999. *Strange Beauty: Murray Gell-Mann and the Revolution in Twentieth-Century Physics.* New York: Alfred A. Knopf, Inc.

Johnson, Paul. 1987. *A History of the Jews.* New York: Harper & Row.

Jones, Leslie. 2004. "Demographic Pillars of Civilization." A review of *Human Accomplishment. The Occidental Quarterly.* Vol. 4. No. 4 (Winter 2004): 71-80.

Josephson, Paul. 2003. "Science, Ideology and the State." *The Cambridge History of Science,* Volume 5. *The Modern Physical and Mathematical Sciences.* Edited by Mary Jo Nye. Cambridge University Press. Paul and I were graduate students together at Harvard's Soviet Union Program.

_____. 2000. *Red Atom: Russia's Nuclear Power Program from Stalin to Today.* Pittsburgh, PA: University of Pittsburgh Press.

Josephus. *The Antiquities of the Jews,* Book IX, Chapter IV, Part 3. Found in *Josephus Complete Works.* Grand Rapids, Michigan: Kregel Publications, 1960. 1976 printing.

Judaica Americana: A Bibliography of Publications to 1900, Volume I, Chronological File 1676 to 1889. Compiled by Robert Singerman. New York: Greenwood Press, 1990.

Juster, Daniel C. 2015. "Jewish Roots: God's Plan for Reconciliation and Redemption." YouTube.com. Presentation at Wheaton College, Wheaton, Illinois. December 9, 2015.

_____. 2014. "A Deeper Look at Atheism." *Israel's Restoration: Tikkun International Newsletter.* March 2014: Vol. 23. No. 3.

_____. 2013. *Jewish Roots: Understanding Your Jewish Faith.* Shippensburg, PA: Destiny Image Publishers, Inc. Revised Fourth Edition.

_____. 1996, 2007. *The Irrevocable Calling: Israel's Role as a Light to the Nations.* Clarksville, Maryland: Lederer Books, Messianic Jewish Publishers.

Khovanova, Tanya and Alexey Radul. 2011. "Jewish Problems," arXiv.org: arXiv:1110.1556v2. October 18, 2011 http://arxiv.org/pdf/1110.1556.pdf.

Kleiman, Yaakov. "The Cohanim – DNA Connection." Aish.com. http://www.aish.com/ci/sam/48936742.html?tab=y

Kyriazis, Nicholas. 2012. *Why Ancient Greece? The birth and development of democracy.* Greece: Psichogios Publications S.A.).

Kittredge, Douglas. 2006. *God's Plan for Peace in the Middle East.* West Conshohocken, PA: Infinity Publishing.

Koestler, Arthur. 1964. *The Act of Creation.* New York: Macmillan.

_____. 1976. *The Thirteenth Tribe: The Khazar Empire and Its Heritage.* New York: Random House.

_____. 1977. Letter to the author. London: March 21, 1977.

Krauss, Lawrence M. 2011. *Quantum Man: Richard Feynman's Life in Science.* New York: W.W. Norton & Company.

Kumar, Manjit. 2008. *Quantum: Einstein, Bohr, and the Great Debate about the Nature of Reality.* New York: W.W. Norton.

Larson, Edward J. and Larry Witham. 1998. "Leading scientists still reject God." *Nature* **394.** No. 6691. 313 (1998) www.nature.com/nature/journal/v394/n6691/full/394313a0_fs.html

Lebeson, Anita Libman. 1931. *Jewish Pioneers in America.* New York: Brentano's Publishers.

Leichman, Abigail Klein. 2014. "Meet Mr. Gaist, cyber-security wunderkind." Israel21c. February 4, 2014 http://israel21c.org/people/meet-nir-gaist-cyber-security-wunderkind/

_____. 2011. "Israel's top 45 greatest inventions of all time." Israel21c. September 26, 2011. http://www.israel21c.org/israels-top-45-greatest-inventions-of -all-time-2/

Levitan, Tina. 1996. *First Facts in American Jewish History.* Northvale, New Jersey: Jason Aronson, Inc.

Lynn, Richard. 2011. *The Chosen People: A Study of Jewish Intelligence and Achievement.* Whitefish, Montana, USA: Washington Summit Publishers. Pease describes Lynn's book as "an outspoken advocacy for genetics as the reason behind disproportionate Jewish achievements."

Malseed, Mark. 2007. "The Story of Sergey Brin." *Moment.* February-March 2007. http://www.momentmag.com/the-story-of-sergey-brin/

Marcellino, Jerry with Yochanan Ben Yehuda. 2001. *Should the Church Have a Heart for Israel? A Historical Perspective.* Hartsville, Tennessee: Heart for Israel.

"Mathematician-Apologist Leonhard Euler." www.christianity.com/church/church-history/timeline/1701-1800/mathematician-apologist-leonhard-euler-11630191.html. Updated May 2007.

Mather, Increase. 1669. *The Mystery of Israel's Salvation Explained and Applied.* London.

McClelland, David. 1961. *The Achieving Society.* Princeton, NJ: D. Van Nostrand Company.

McMahon, Darrin. 2013. *Divine Fury: A History of Genius.* New York: Basic Books.

Mead, Rebecca. 2003. "The All-time Greats." *New Yorker.* November 10, 2003. www.newyorker.com/magazine/2003/11/10/the-all-time-greats

Medawar, Jean and David Pyke. 2000. *Hitler's Gift: Scientists Who Fled Nazi Germany.* London: Richard Cohen Books in association with the European Jewish Publications Society.

Melnick, Arseny James (Jim). 2015. "The Quantum World: A Fine-Tuned Multiversal Reality?" *Journal of Interdisciplinary Studies.* XXVII: 45-60.

_____. 2014. "David Deutsch's strange reality." *Journal of Creation* 28 (1) 2014: 32-33.

_____. 2011. "The Underside of Russian Jewish Ministry in Israel and around the World Today." *Mishkan.* Issue 69 (2011). "Russian Jewish Ministry" special issue.

_____. 2005. "The Struggle within Chabad and Orthodox Judaism," *Mishkan.* Issue 43 (2005): 47-62.

Mendes-Flohr, Paul. 1991. *Divided Passions: Jewish Intellectuals and the Experience of Modernity.* Detroit: Wayne State University Press.

Mendes-Flohr, Paul R. & Jehuda Reinharz. 1995. *The Jew in the Modern World: A Documentary History.* New York: Oxford University Press, Second edition.

Murray, Charles. 2003. *Human Accomplishment: The Pursuit of Excellence in the Arts and Sciences. 800 B.C. to 1950.* New York: HarperCollins.

_____. 2007. "Jewish Genius." *Commentary.* April 1, 2007. https://www.commentarymagazine.com/articles/jewish-genius/

Murray, Iain H. 1971. *The Puritan Hope: Revival and the Interpretation of Prophecy.* Edinburgh, Scotland; Carlisle, Pennsylvania: The Banner of Truth Trust.

Nadis, Steve and Shing-Tung Yau, *A History in Sum: 150 Years of Mathematics at Harvard, 1825-1975.* Cambridge, Massachusetts: Harvard University Press.

Netanyahu, Benzion. 2001. *The Origins of the Inquisition in Fifteenth-Century Spain.* 2nd edition. New York: New York Review of Books.

"New Book Looks at Debate Over Jewish Achievement." Religion News Service. June 10, 2015. http://religionnews.com/2015/06/10/new-book-looks-at-debate-over-jewish-achievement/

Oz, Amos and Fania Oz-Salzberger. 2012. *Jews and Words.* New Haven, CT: Yale University Press.

Pais, Abraham. 1991. *Niels Bohr's Times: In Physics, Philosophy, and Polity.* Oxford: Clarendon Press.

Parr, Elnathan. 1620. *A Plaine Exposition upon the whole eighth, ninth, tenth, eleventh, twelfth Chapters of the Epistle of Saint Paul to the Roman[e]s.* London.

Patai, Raphael. 1977. *The Jewish Mind.* New York: Charles Scribner's Sons.

Pease, Steven L. 2009. *The Golden Age of Jewish Achievement: The Compendium of a Culture, a People, and Their Stunning Performance.* Sonoma, California: Deucalion.

_____. 2015. *The Debate over Jewish Achievement: Exploring the Nature and Nurture of Human Accomplishment.* Sonoma, California: Deucalion. Paperback edition.

_____. 2015. "The debate over Jewish achievement." Aish.com. *Chicago Jewish News.* June 19-25, 2015.

Pearl, Judea and Ruth, Eds. 2004, 2015. *I am Jewish: Personal Reflections Inspired by the Last Words of Daniel Pearl.* Woodstock, Vermont: Jewish Lights Publishing/Gefen. 2015 Paperback edition.

Penrose, Roger. 1994. *Shadows of the Mind: A Search for the Missing Science of Consciousness.* Oxford: Oxford University Press.

Pew Research Report (October 2013). "A Portrait of Jewish Americans." http://www.pewforum.org/2013/10/01/jewish-american-beliefs-attitudes-culture-survey/.

The full Pew survey is available at: http://www.pewforum.org/files/2013/10/jewish-american-full-report-for-web.pdf

PhilanthropicPeople.com

Pinsker, Sanford. 1997. "Smart[Academic] Jews." *The Georgia Review* **51** (1). Spring 1997: 161-166.

Pittinsky, Todd L. 2016. "A high-tech light unto the nations." The Times of Israel. November 3, 2016. http://blogs.timesofisrael.com/a-high-tech-light-unto-the-nations/

Plaut, Steven. 2007. "The Khazar Myth and the New Anti-Semitism." JewishPress.com. May 9, 2007. www.jewishpress.com/indepth/front-page/the-khazar-myth-and-the-new-anti-semitism/2007/05/09/

Pool, James and Suzanne Pool. 1978. *Who Financed Hitler: The Secret Funding of Hitler's Rise to Power, 1919-1933.* New York: The Dial Press.

Prager, Dennis and Joseph Telushkin. 1983, 2003. *Why the Jews? The Reason for Anti-semitism.* Revised edition. New York: Touchstone, Simon & Schuster.

Rabi, Isidor Isaac. 1970. *Science: The Center of Culture.* New York and Cleveland: The New American Library, Inc. and the World Publishing Company

Raphael, Frederic. 2015. *Anti-Semitism.* London: Biteback Publishing Ltd.

Rausch, David A. 1984. *A Legacy of Hatred: Why Christians Must Not Forget the Holocaust.* Chicago: Moody Press.

Richards, Rob. 1994, 2000. *Has God Finished with Israel?* Milton Keynes, England: Word Publishing.

Richardson, Joel. 2015. *When a Jew Rules the World. What the Bible Really Says about Israel in the Plan of God.* Washington, DC: WND Books.

Roth, Cecil. 1938. *The Jewish Contribution to Civilisation.* London: Macmillan and Co. Ltd.

Rubenstein, Richard L. 1966. *After Auschwitz: Radical Theology and Contemporary Judaism.* New York: The Bobbs-Merrill Company, Inc.

Runes, Dagobert D. 1951. *The Hebrew Impact on Western Civilization.* New York: Philosophical Library.

Ryle, John Charles. 1867, 1879. *Coming Events and Present Duties, being Miscellaneous Sermons on Prophetical Subjects Prophecy.* London: William Hunt and Company, 2nd Edition. Available online via Google Books. (Accessed June 2015)

Sachar, Howard M. 1992. *A History of the Jews in America.* New York: Alfred A. Knopf.

Saphir, Adolph. 1864-1868. *Christ and Israel.* Jerusalem: Yanetz Ltd. (Modern reprint). Earlier version edited by D. Baron. *Christ and Israel: Lectures and Addresses on the Jews.* London: Morgan and Scott, 1911.

Sarton, George. 1932, 1961. *Introduction to the History of Science*, Volume II, *From Rabbi Ben Ezra to Roger Bacon.* Baltimore: Carnegie Institution of Washington, The Williams and Wilkins Company, 1931. Reprinted 1962.

"Saul Perlmutter." Undated. The Jewish Virtual Library. https://www. jewishvirtuallibrary.org/jsource/biography/saulperlmutter.html

Savage, Sean. 2015. "'Lapsed Presbyterian' author carves an unlikely niche: Jewish achievement." JNS.org http://www.jns.org/latest-articles/2015/11/12/lapsed-presbyterian-author-carves-   an-unlikely-niche-jewish-achievement#.VkT4H7crK00=

Scammell, Michael. 2009. *Koestler: The Literary and Political Odyssey of a Twentieth Century Skeptic.* New York: Random House.

Schaeffer, Edith. 1975. *Christianity is Jewish.* Wheaton, IL: Tyndale House Publishers.

Schama, Simon. 2014. "The Story of the Jews" television series. Program: "A Leap of Faith." PBS. WNET. BBC, Thirteen Productions LLC. http:// www.pbs.org/wnet/story-jews/

_____. 2013. *The Story of the Jews: Finding the Words, 1000 BC-1492 AD.* New York: HarperCollins.

Schlesinger, Andrew. 2005. *Veritas: Harvard College and the American Experience.* Chicago: Ivan R. Dee.

"Scientometrics." http://link.springer.com/journal/11192

Senor, Dan and Saul Singer. 2011 edition. *Start-Up Nation: The Story of Israel's Economic Miracle.* Toronto, ON: McClelland & Stewart Ltd.

Sevela, Ephraim.1977. *Farewell, Israel!* South Bend, Indiana, USA: Gateway Editions, Ltd.

Shanks, Hershel. 2015. "Renowned Collector Shlomo Moussaieff Dies at 92." *Biblical Archaeology Review* (November/December 2015). Vol. 41 (6): 62-64.

Shishkoff, Eitan. 2013. *"What About Us?"- The End-time Calling of Gentiles in Israel's Revival.* Bedford, Texas, USA: Burkhart Books.

Sibley, Jim. 2015. "The 'Lost Gospel' of Jerusalem." *LCJE Bulletin.* Issue 121. August-September 2015: 13-19.

Silberman, Charles E. 1985. *A Certain People: American Jews and Their Lives Today.* New York: Summit.

Silbiger, Steven. 2009. *The Jewish Phenomenon: Seven Keys to the Enduring Wealth of a People* Lanham, Maryland: N. Evans. Revised edition.

Silk, Leonard and Mark Silk. 1980. *The American Establishment*: New York: Basic Books, Inc.

Simonton, Dean Keith. 1999. *Origins of Genius: Darwinian Perspectives on Creativity.* NY: Oxford University Press.

Skarsaune, Oskar and Reidar Hvalvik. 2007. *Jewish Believers in Jesus: The Early Centuries.* Peabody, Massachusetts: Hendrickson Publishers.

Slezkine, Yuri. 2004. *The Jewish Century.* Princeton, NJ: Princeton University Press.

Snobelen, S. 2001. "'The Mystery of This Restitution of All Things": Isaac Newton on the Return of the Jews." Chapter 7 In J.E. Force and R.H. Popkin, Eds. *Millenarianism and Messianism in Early Modern European Culture: The Millenarian Turn.* The Netherlands: Kluwer Academic Publishers: 95-118.

Snyder, Avi. 2015. "Ever Again." *Issues: A Messianic Jewish Perspective* **20**(9).

_____. 2014. "Created to Proclaim – Israel, An Evangelistic Light to the Nations." LCJE *Bulletin* #116 (May 2014): 20-22.

_____. 2011. "The Fervent Years." *Mishkan* 69: 7-12.

_____. 2008. "Life from the Dead." Interview with Julia Fisher. The Olive Tree Reconciliation Fund. http://www.olivetreefund.org/life-from-the-dead/

Sowell, Thomas. 2014. "Achievement under attack" column. Cited from *The Vindicator* (Youngstown, Ohio). August 13, 2014. See also Townhall.com, August 12, 2014. http://townhall.com/columnists/thomassowell/2014/08/12/attacking-achievement-n1877398

Stenger, Victor. 2014. *God and the Multiverse.* Amherst, New York: Prometheus.

Stern, Elazar. 2012. *Struggling Over Israel's Soul: An IDF General Speaks of His Controversial Moral Decisions.* Jerusalem: Gefen Publishing House Ltd.

Storfer, Miles D. 1990. *Intelligence and Giftedness: The Constitutions of Heredity and Early Environment.* San Francisco: Jossey-Bass.

Taves, Max. 2015. "Russian billionaire patiently listens for alien sounds." CNET. October 7. www.cnet.com/news/russian-billionaire-patiently-listens-for-alien-sounds/

Ten Boom, Corrie. with John and Elizabeth Sherrill. 1971. *The Hiding Place.* Washington Depot, CT: Chosen Books.

Thomas, Kelly D. 2013. "The Advent and Fallout of EPR." Institute for Advanced Study. Fall 2013. http://ww.ias.edu/about/publications/ias-letter/articles/2013-fall/epr-fallout (Accessed October 2015).

"Tikkun Olam: The Spiritual Purpose of Life." http://www.innerfrontier.org/Practices/TikkunOlam.htm Accessed October 15, 2015.

Tilles, Murray. 2011. *Devoted to Israel: Devotions for those who Love Israel, the Jewish People, and Our Jewish Roots.* Roswell, GA: Devoted to Israel.

Topping, Seymour. Undated. "Pulitzer biography." Joseph Pulitzer (1847-1911). www.pulitzer.org/biography

Turok, Neil. 2012. *The Universe Within: From Quantum to Cosmos.* Toronto, Canada: Anansi Press.

Twain, Mark. 1899. "Concerning the Jews." [Samuel L. Clemens]. *Harper's New Monthly Magazine.* Volume XCIX. June, 1899 to November, 1899. New York & London: Harper & Brothers.

VanDeMark, Brian. 2003. *Pandora's Secrets: Nine Men and the Atomic Bomb.* New York: Bay Back Books.

Van Gelder, Lawrence. 1969. "C.P. Snow Says Jews' Success Could Be Genetic Superiority." *New York Times.* April 1, 1969: 37.

Vara, Vauhini. 2007. "Just How Much Do We Want to Share on Social Networks?" *Wall Street Journal* (Online). Updated Nov. 28, 2007. http://online.wsj.com/news/articles/SB119621309736406034

Veblen, Thorstein. 1919. "The intellectual pre-eminence of the Jews in Modern Europe." *Political Science Quarterly* 34, No. 1 (March): 33-42.

Watson, Peter. 2005. *Ideas: A History of Thought and Invention, from Fire to Freud.* New York: Harper.

Weiner, Eric. 2016. *The Geography of Genius: A Search for the World's Most Creative Places, from Ancient Athens to Silicon Valley.* New York: Simon & Schuster.

"WhatsApp co-founder Jan Koum: New billionaire once lived on food stamps." NDTV.com. February 21, 2014. http://gadgets.ndtv.com/apps/features/whatsapp-co-founder-jan-koum-new-billionaire-once-lived-on-food-stamps-486290

Whitfield, Stephen J. 1984. *Jewish Voices of Jacob, Hands of Esau: Jews in American Life and Thought.* Hamden, Connecticut: Archon Books.

Wiesel, Elie. 1966. *The Jews of Silence.* New York: Holt, Rinehart and Winston.

_____. 1969. *Night.* New York: Avon Books.

Wigoder, Geoffrey. 1991. *Dictionary of Jewish Biography*. New York: Simon & Schuster. The Jerusalem Publishing House Ltd.

Wilson, Marvin R. 1989. *Our Father Abraham: Jewish Roots of the Christian Faith.* Dayton, Ohio: William B. Eerdmans Publishing Co. and Center for Judaic-Christian Studies.

Wilson, Matthew T. 2013. *The Ruth-like Church vs. The Role of Christians in Israel's Redemption as Prophesied in the Book of Ruth.* Woodland Hills, California: Yeshua's Harvest.

Wisse, Ruth R. 2007. *Jews and Power.* New York: Schoken Books.

Wistrich, Robert. 2001. *Hitler and the Holocaust.* New York: Modern Library.

Witten, Edward. "Edward Witten." Biography-Center. http://www.biography-center.com/biographies/3741-Witten_Edward.html. Accessed December 2014.

Wouk, Herman. 2010. *The Language God Talks: On Science and Religion.* New York: Little, Brown and Company.

Index

First Time in History!

General Editor: Rabbi Barry Rubin
Theological Editor: Dr. John Fischer

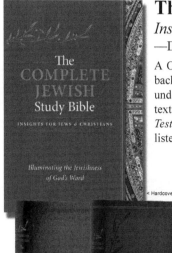

< Hardcover Edition

The Complete Jewish Study Bible

Insights for Jews and Christians

—Dr. David H. Stern

A One-of-a-Kind Study Bible that illuminates the Jewish background and context of God's word so it is more fully understandable. Uses the updated *Complete Jewish Bible* text by David H. Stern, including notes from the *Jewish New Testament Commentary* and contributions from Scholars listed below. 1990 pages.

Hardback	978-1619708679	$49.95
Flexisoft	978-1619708693	$79.95
Leather	978-1619708709	$139.95

Leather Edition w/color gift box   Flexisoft Edition w/color sleeve

CONTRIBUTORS & SCHOLARS

Rabbi Dr. Glenn Blank	Rabbi Dr. David Friedman	Rabbi Elliot Klayman	Dr. Michael Rydelnik
Dr. Michael Brown	Dr. Arnold Fruchtenbaum	Jordan Gayle Levy	Dr. Jeffrey Seif
Rabbi Steven Bernstein	Dr. John Garr	Dr. Ronald Moseley	Rabbi Tzahi Shapira
Rabbi Joshua Brumbach	Pastor David Harris	Rabbi Dr. Rich Nichol	Dr. David H. Stern
Rabbi Ron Corbett	Benjamin Juster	Rabbi Mark J. Rantz	Dr. Bruce Stokes
Pastor Ralph Finley	Rabbi Dr. Daniel Juster	Rabbi Russ Resnik	Dr. Tom Tribelhorn
Rabbi Dr. John Fischer	Dr. Walter C. Kaiser	Dr. Richard Robinson	Dr. Forrest Weiland
Dr. Patrice Fischer	Rabbi Barney Kasdan	Rabbi Dr. Jacob Rosenberg	Dr. Marvin Wilson
Rebbitzen Malkah Forbes	Dr. Craig S. Keener	Rabbi Isaac Roussel	

QUOTES BY CURRENT JEWISH SCHOLARS & ANCIENT JEWISH SAGES

Dr. Daniel Boyarin	Rabbi Gamaliel	Rabbi Akiva
Dr. Amy-Jill Levine	Rabbi Hillel	Maimonides
Rabbi Jonathan Sacks	Rabbi Shammai	and many more

Complete Jewish Bible: *An English Version*
—Dr. David H. Stern (Available March 2017)

Now, the most widely used Messianic Jewish Bible around the world, has updated text with introductions added to each book, written from a biblically Jewish perspective. The CJB is a unified Jewish book, a version for Jews and non-Jews alike; to connect Jews with the Jewishness of the Messiah, and non-Jews with their Jewish roots. Names and terms are returned to their original Hebrew and presented in easy-to-understand transliterations, enabling the reader to say them the way *Yeshua* (Jesus) did! 1728 pages.

Paperback	978-1936716845	$29.95
Hardcover	978-1936716852	$34.95
Flexisoft Cover	978-1936716869	$49.95

Jewish New Testament
—Dr. David H. Stern

The New Testament is a Jewish book, written by Jews, initially for Jews. Its central figure was a Jew. His followers were all Jews; yet no other version really communicates its original, essential Jewishness. Uses neutral terms and Hebrew names. Highlights Jewish references and corrects mistranslations. Freshly translated into English from Greek, this is a must read to learn about first-century faith. 436 pages

Hardback	978-9653590069	**JB02**	$19.99
Paperback	978-9653590038	**JB01**	$14.99
Spanish	978-1936716272	**JB17**	$24.99

Also available in French, German, Polish, Portuguese and Russian.

Jewish New Testament Commentary
—Dr. David H. Stern

This companion to the *Jewish New Testament* enhances Bible study. Passages and expressions are explained in their original cultural context. 15 years of research. 960 pages.

Hardback	978-9653590083	**JB06**	$34.99
Paperback	978-9653590113	**JB10**	$29.99

Will the Nazi Eagle Rise Again?
What the Church Needs to Know about BDS and Other Forces of Anti-Semitism
–David Friedman, Ph.D.

This is the right book at the right time. exposing the roots of Anti-Semitism being resurrected in our days, especially in our Christian Church.
—Dr. Hans-Jörg Kagi, Teacher, Theologian, Basle, Switzerland

Timely and important response to the dangerous hatred of the State of Israel that is growing in society and in the Church.
—Michael Rydelnik, Prof. of Jewish Studies, Moody Bible Inst., Chicago, Ill.

Israel is not an apartheid state and bears absolutely no resemblance to the institutionalized racial oppression that I lived under in South Africa. I am deeply offended by this comparison.
—Luba Mayekiso, Africa for Israel Christian Coalition, Republic of South Africa

Paperback (278 Pages)   978-1936716876 $19.99

Messianic Judaism *A Modern Movement With an Ancient Past*
—David H. Stern

An updated discussion of the history, ideology, theology and program for Messianic Judaism. A challenge to both Jews and non-Jews who honor Yeshua to catch the vision of Messianic Judaism. 312 pages

978-1880226339   **LB62** $17.99

Restoring the Jewishness of the Gospel
A Message for Christians
—David H. Stern

Introduces Christians to the Jewish roots of their faith, challenges some conventional ideas, and raises some neglected questions: How are both the Jews and "the Church" God's people? Is the Law of Moses in force today? Filled with insight! Endorsed by Dr. Darrell L. Bock. 110 pages

| English | 978-1880226667 | **LB70** | $9.99 |
| Spanish | 978-9653590175 | **JB14** | $9.99 |

Come and Worship *Ways to Worship from the Hebrew Scriptures*
—Compiled by Barbara D. Malda

We were created to worship. God has graciously given us many ways to express our praise to him. Each way fits a different situation or moment in life, yet all are intended to bring honor and glory to him. When we believe that he is who he says he is [see *His Names are Wonderful!*] and that his Word is true, worship flows naturally from our hearts to his. Softcover, 128 pages.

978-1936716678   **LB88** $9.99

His Names Are Wonderful
Getting to Know God Through His Hebrew Names
—Elizabeth L. Vander Meulen and Barbara D. Malda

In Hebrew thought, names did more than identify people; they revealed their nature. God's identity is expressed not in one name, but in many. This book will help readers know God better as they uncover the truths in his Hebrew names. 160 pages.

978-1880226308   **LB58** $9.99

The Return of the Kosher Pig *The Divine Messiah in Jewish Thought*
—Rabbi Tzahi Shapira

The subject of Messiah fills many pages of rabbinic writings. Hidden in those pages is a little known concept that the Messiah has the same authority given to God. Based on the Scriptures and traditional rabbinic writings, this book shows the deity of Yeshua from a new perspective. You will see that the rabbis of old expected the Messiah to be divine. Softcover, 352 pages.

"One of the most interesting and learned tomes I have ever read. Contained within its pages is much with which I agree, some with which I disagree, and much about which I never thought. Rabbi Shapria's remarkable book cannot be ignored."
—Dr. Paige Patterson, President, Southwest Baptist Theological Seminary

978-1936716456   **LB81** $ 39.99

Proverbial Wisdom & Common Sense

A Messianic Commentary

—Derek Leman

A Messianic Jewish Approach to Today's Issues from the Proverbs
A devotional style commentary, divided into chapters suitable for daily reading. An encyclopedia of practical advice on topics relevant to everyone. 248 pages

Paperback	978-1880226780 **LB98**	$19.99

Matthew Presents Yeshua, King Messiah *A Messianic Commentary*

—Rabbi Barney Kasdan

Few commentators are able to truly present Yeshua in his Jewish context. Most don't understand his background, his family, even his religion, and consequently really don't understand who he truly is. This commentator is well versed with first-century Jewish practices and thought, as well as the historical and cultural setting of the day, and the 'traditions of the Elders' that Yeshua so often spoke about. Get to know Yeshua, the King, through the writing of another rabbi, Barney Kasdan. 448 pages

978-1936716265 **LB76** $29.99

Rabbi Paul Enlightens the Ephesians on Walking with Messiah Yeshua

A Messianic Commentary

—Rabbi Barney Kasdan

The Ephesian were a diverse group of Jews and Gentiles, united together in Messiah. They definitely had an impact on the first century world in which they lived. But the Rabbi was not just writing to that local group. What is Paul saying to us? 160 pages.

Paperback	978-11936716821 **LB99**	$17.99

James the Just Presents Application of Torah

A Messianic Commentary

—Dr. David Friedman

James (Jacob) one of the Epistles written to first century Jewish followers of Yeshua. Dr. David Friedman, a former Professor of the Israel Bible Institute has shed new light for Christians from this very important letter.

978-1936716449 **LB82** $14.99

Jude On Faith and the Destructive Influence of Heresy

A Messianic Commentary

—Rabbi Joshua Brumbach

Almost no other canonical book has been as neglected and overlooked as the Epistle of Jude. This little book may be small, but it has a big message that is even more relevant today as when it was originally written.

978-1-936716-78-4 **LB97** $14.99

Psalms & Proverbs *Tehillim* תְּהִלִּים-*Mishlei* מִשְׁלֵי
—Translated by Dr. David Stern

Contemplate the power in these words anytime, anywhere: Psalms-*Tehillim* offers uplifting words of praise and gratitude, keeping us focused with the right attitude; Proverbs-*Mishlei* gives us the wisdom for daily living, renewing our minds by leading us to examine our actions, to discern good from evil, and to decide freely to do the good. Makes a wonderful and meaningful gift. Softcover, 224 pages.

978-1936716692   LB90 $9.99

At the Feet of Rabbi Gamaliel
Rabbinic Influence in Paul's Teachings
—David Friedman, Ph.D.

Paul (Shaul) was on the "fast track" to becoming a sage and Sanhedrin judge, describing himself as passionate for the Torah and the traditions of the fathers, typical for an aspiring Pharisee: "...trained at the feet of Gamaliel in every detail of the Torah of our forefathers. I was a zealot for God, as all of you are today" (Acts 22.3, CJB). Did Shaul's teachings reflect Rabbi Gamaliel's instructions? Did Paul continue to value the Torah and Pharisaic tradition? Did Paul create a 'New' Theology? The results of the research within these pages and its conclusion may surprise you. Softcover, 100 pages.

978-1936716753   **LB95** $8.99

Debranding God *Revealing His True Essence*
—Eduardo Stein

The process of 'debranding' God is to remove all the labels and fads that prompt us to understand him as a supplier and ourselves as the most demanding of customers. Changing our perception of God also changes our perception of ourselves. In knowing who we are in relationship to God, we discover his, and our, true essence. Softcover, 252 pages.

978-1936716708   **LB91** $16.99

Under the Fig Tree *Messianic Thought Through the Hebrew Calendar*
—Patrick Gabriel Lumbroso

Take a daily devotional journey into the Word of God through the Hebrew Calendar and the Biblical Feasts. Learn deeper meaning of the Scriptures through Hebraic thought. Beautifully written and a source for inspiration to draw closer to Adonai every day. Softcover, 407 pages.

978-1936716760   **LB96** $25.99

Under the Vine *Messianic Thought Through the Hebrew Calendar*
—Patrick Gabriel Lumbroso

Journey daily through the Hebrew Calendar and Biblical Feasts into the B'rit Hadashah (New Testament) Scriptures as they are put in their rightful context, bringing Judaism alive in it's full beauty. Messianic faith was the motor and what gave substance to Abraham's new beliefs, hope to Job, trust to Isaac, vision to Jacob, resilience to Joseph, courage to David, wisdom to Solomon, knowledge to Daniel, and divine Messianic authority to Yeshua. Softcover, 412 pages.

978-1936716654   **LB87** $25.99

The Revolt of Rabbi Morris Cohen

Exploring the Passion & Piety of a Modern-day Pharisee
—Anthony Cardinale

A brilliant school psychologist, Rabbi Morris Cohen went on a one-man strike to protest the systematic mislabeling of slow learning pupils as "Learning Disabled" (to extract special education money from the state). His disciplinary hearing, based on the transcript, is a hilarious read! This effusive, garrulous man with an irresistible sense of humor lost his job, but achieved a major historic victory causing the reform of the billion-dollar special education program. Enter into the mind of an eighth-generation Orthodox rabbi to see how he deals spiritually with the loss of everything, even the love of his children. This modern-day Pharisee discovered a trusted friend in the author (a born again believer in Jesus) with whom he could openly struggle over Rabbinic Judaism as well as the concept of Jesus (Yeshua) as Messiah. Softcover, 320 pages.

978-1936716722　　**LB92**　　$19.99

Stories of Yeshua

—Jim Reimann, Illustrator Julia Filipone-Erez

Children's Bible Storybook with four stories about Yeshua (Jesus).
Yeshua is Born: The Bethlehem Story based on Lk 1:26-35 & 2:1-20; *Yeshua and Nicodemus in Jerusalem* based on Jn 3:1-16; *Yeshua Loves the Little Children of the World* based on Matthew 18:1–6 & 19:13–15; *Yeshua is Alive-The Empty Tomb in Jerusalem* based on Matthew 26:17-56, Jn 19:16-20:18, Lk 24:50-53. Ages 3-7, Softcover, 48 pages.

978-1936716685　　**LB89**　　$14.99

To the Ends of the Earth – How the First Jewish Followers of Yeshua Transformed the Ancient World

— Dr. Jeffrey Seif

Everyone knows that the first followers of Yeshua were Jews, and that Christianity was very Jewish for the first 50 to 100 years. It's a known fact that there were many congregations made up mostly of Jews, although the false perception today is, that in the second century they disappeared. Dr. Seif reveals the truth of what happened to them and how these early Messianic Jews influenced and transformed the behavior of the known world at that time.

978-1936716463　　**LB83**　　$17.99

Passion for Israel: *A Short History of the Evangelical Church's Support of Israel and the Jewish People*

—Dan Juster

History reveals a special commitment of Christians to the Jews as God's still elect people, but the terrible atrocities committed against the Jews by so-called Christians have overshadowed the many good deeds that have been performed. This important history needs to be told to help heal the wounds and to inspire more Christians to stand together in support of Israel.

978-1936716401　　**LB78**　　$9.99

Jewish Roots and Foundations of the Scriptures I & II
—John Fischer, Th.D, Ph.D.

An outstanding evangelical leader once said: "There is something shallow about a Christianity that has lost its Jewish roots." A beautiful painting is a careful interweaving of a number of elements. Among other things, there are the background, the foreground and the subject. Discovering the roots of your faith is a little like appreciating the various parts of a painting. In the background is the panorama of preparation and pictures found in the Old Testament. In the foreground is the landscape and light of the first century Jewish setting. All of this is intricately connected with and highlights the subject—which becomes the flowering of all these aspects—the coming of God to earth and what that means for us. Discovering and appreciating your roots in this way broadens, deepens and enriches your faith and your understanding of Scripture. This audio is 32 hours of live class instruction - audio is clear and easy to understand.

9781936716623 **LCD03 / LCD04** $49.99 each

The Gospels in their Jewish Context
—John Fischer, Th.D, Ph.D.

An examination of the Jewish background and nature of the Gospels in their contemporary political, cultural and historical settings, emphasizing each gospel's special literary presentation of Yeshua, and highlighting the cultural and religious contexts necessary for understanding each of the gospels. 32 hours of audio/video instruction on MP3-DVD and pdf of syllabus.

978-1936716241 **LCD01** $49.99

The Epistles from a Jewish Perspective
—John Fischer, Th.D, Ph.D.

An examination of the relationship of Rabbi Shaul (the Apostle Paul) and the Apostles to their Jewish contemporaries and environment; surveys their Jewish practices, teaching, controversy with the religious leaders, and many critical passages, with emphasis on the Jewish nature, content, and background of these letters. 32 hours of audio/video instruction on MP3-DVD and pdf of syllabus.

978-1936716258 **LCD02** $49.99

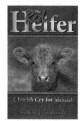

The Red Heifer *A Jewish Cry for Messiah*
—Anthony Cardinale

Award-winning journalist and playwright Anthony Cardinale has traveled extensively in Israel, and recounts here his interviews with Orthodox rabbis, secular Israelis, and Palestinian Arabs about the current search for a red heifer by Jewish radicals wishing to rebuild the Temple and bring the Messiah. These real-life interviews are interwoven within an engaging and dramatic fictional portrayal of the diverse people of Israel and how they would react should that red heifer be found. Readers will find themselves in the Land, where they can hear learned rabbis and ordinary Israelis talking about the red heifer and dealing with all the related issues and the imminent coming and identity of Messiah.

978-1936716470 LB79 $19.99

The Borough Park Papers
—Multiple Authors

As you read the New Testament, you "overhear" debates first-century Messianic Jews had about critical issues, e.g. Gentiles being "allowed" into the Messianic kingdom (Acts 15). Similarly, you're now invited to "listen in" as leading twenty-first century Messianic Jewish theologians discuss critical issues facing us today. Some ideas may not fit into your previously held pre-suppositions or pre-conceptions. Indeed, you may find some paradigm shifting in your thinking. We want to share the thoughts of these thinkers with you, our family in the Messiah.

Symposium I:
The Gospel and the Jewish People
248 pages

978-1936716593	LB84	$39.95

Symposium II:
The Deity of Messiah and the Mystery of God
211 pages

978-1936716609	LB85	$39.95

Symposium III:
How Jewish Should the Messianic Community Be?

978-1936716616	LB86	$39.95

On The Way to Emmaus: *Searching the Messianic Prophecies*
—Dr. Jacques Doukhan

An outstanding compilation of the most critical Messianic prophecies by a renowned conservative Christian Scholar, drawing on material from the Bible, Rabbinic sources, Dead Sea Scrolls, and more.

978-1936716432	LB80	$14.99

Yeshua *A Guide to the Real Jesus and the Original Church*
—Dr. Ron Moseley

Opens up the history of the Jewish roots of the Christian faith. Illuminates the Jewish background of Yeshua and the Church and never flinches from showing "Jesus was a Jew, who was born, lived, and died, within first century Judaism." Explains idioms in the New Testament. Endorsed by Dr. Brad Young and Dr. Marvin Wilson. 213 pages.

978-1880226681	**LB29**	$12.99

Gateways to Torah *Joining the Ancient Conversation on the Weekly Portion*
—Rabbi Russell Resnik

From before the days of Messiah until today, Jewish people have read from and discussed a prescribed portion of the Pentateuch each week. Now, a Messianic Jewish Rabbi, Russell Resnik, brings another perspective on the Torah, that of a Messianic Jew. 246 pages.

978-1880226889 **LB42** $15.99

Creation to Completion *A Guide to Life's Journey from the Five Books of Moses*
—Rabbi Russell Resnik

Endorsed by Coach Bill McCartney, Founder of Promise Keepers & Road to Jerusalem: "Paul urged Timothy to study the Scriptures (2 Tim. 3:16), advising him to apply its teachings to all aspects of his life. Since there was no New Testament then, this rabbi/apostle was convinced that his disciple would profit from studying the Torah, the Five Books of Moses, and the Old Testament. Now, Rabbi Resnik has written a warm devotional commentary that will help you understand and apply the Law of Moses to your life in a practical way." 256 pages

978-1880226322 **LB61** $14.99

Walk Genesis! Walk Exodus! Walk Leviticus! Walk Numbers! Walk Deuteronomy!
Messianic Jewish Devotional Commentaries
—Jeffrey Enoch Feinberg, Ph.D.

Using the weekly synagogue readings, Dr. Jeffrey Feinberg has put together some very valuable material in his "Walk" series. Each section includes a short Hebrew lesson (for the non-Hebrew speaker), key concepts, an excellent overview of the portion, and some practical applications. Can be used as a daily devotional as well as a Bible study tool.

Walk Genesis!	238 pages	978-1880226759	**LB34**	$12.99
Walk Exodus!	224 pages	978-1880226872	**LB40**	$12.99
Walk Leviticus!	208 pages	978-1880226926	**LB45**	$12.99
Walk Numbers!	211 pages	978-1880226995	**LB48**	$12.99
Walk Deuteronomy!	231 pages	978-1880226186	**LB51**	$12.99
SPECIAL! Five-book Walk!		5 Book Set **Save $10**	**LK28**	$54.99

Good News According To Matthew

—Dr. Henry Einspruch

English translation with quotations from the Tanakh (Old Testament) capitalized and printed in Hebrew. Helpful notations are included. Lovely black and white illustrations throughout the book. 86 pages.

| | 978-1880226025 | **LB03** | $4.99 |
| Also available in Yiddish. | | **LB02** | $4.99 |

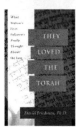

They Loved the Torah *What Yeshua's First Followers Really Thought About the Law*

—Dr. David Friedman

Although many Jews believe that Paul taught against the Law, this book disproves that notion. An excellent case for his premise that all the first followers of the Messiah were not only Torah-observant, but also desired to spread their love for God's entire Word to the gentiles to whom they preached. 144 pages. Endorsed by Dr. David Stern, Ariel Berkowitz, Rabbi Dr. Stuart Dauermann & Dr. John Fischer.

978-1880226940   **LB47** $9.99

The Distortion *2000 Years of Misrepresenting the Relationship Between Jesus the Messiah and the Jewish People*

—Dr. John Fischer & Dr. Patrice Fischer

Did the Jews kill Jesus? Did they really reject him? With the rise of global anti–Semitism, it is important to understand what the Gospels teach about the relationship between Jewish people and their Messiah. 2000 years of distortion have made this difficult. Learn how the distortion began and continues to this day and what you can do to change it. 126 pages. Endorsed by Dr. Ruth Fleischer, Rabbi Russell Resnik, Dr. Daniel C. Juster, Dr. Michael Rydelnik.

978-1880226254   **LB54** $11.99

God's Appointed Times *A Practical Guide to Understanding and Celebrating the Biblical Holidays* – **New Edition.**
—Rabbi Barney Kasdan

The Biblical Holy Days teach us about the nature of God and his plan for mankind, and can be a source of God's blessing for all believers–Jews and Gentiles–today. Includes historical background, traditional Jewish observance, New Testament relevance, and prophetic significance, plus music, crafts and holiday recipes. 145 pages.

English	978-1880226353	**LB63**	$12.99
Spanish	978-1880226391	**LB59**	$12.99

God's Appointed Customs *A Messianic Jewish Guide to the Biblical Lifecycle and Lifestyle*
— Rabbi Barney Kasdan

Explains how biblical customs are often the missing key to unlocking the depths of Scripture. Discusses circumcision, the Jewish wedding, and many more customs mentioned in the New Testament. Companion to *God's Appointed Times*. 170 pages.

English	978-1880226636	**LB26**	$12.99
Spanish	978-1880226551	**LB60**	$12.99

Celebrations of the Bible *A Messianic Children's Curriculum*

Did you know that each Old Testament feast or festival finds its fulfillment in the New? They enrich the lives of people who experience and enjoy them. Our popular curriculum for children is in a brand new, user-friendly format. The lay-flat at binding allows you to easily reproduce handouts and worksheets. Celebrations of the Bible has been used by congregations, Sunday schools, ministries, homeschoolers, and individuals to teach children about the biblical festivals. Each of these holidays are presented for Preschool (2-K), Primary (Grades 1-3), Junior (Grades 4-6), and Children's Worship/Special Services. 208 pages.

978-1880226261	**LB55**	$24.99

Passover: *The Key That Unlocks the Book of Revelation*
—Daniel C. Juster, Th.D.

Is there any more enigmatic book of the Bible than Revelation? Controversy concerning its meaning has surrounded it back to the first century. Today, the arguments continue. Yet, Dan Juster has given us the key that unlocks the entire book—the events and circumstances of the Passover/Exodus. By interpreting Revelation through the lens of Exodus, Dan Juster provides a unified overview that helps us read Revelation as it was always meant to be read, as a drama of spiritual conflict, deliverance, and above all, worship. He also shows how this final drama, fulfilled in Messiah, resonates with the Torah and all of God's Word. — Russ Resnik, Executive Director, Union of Messianic Jewish Congregations.

978-1936716210	**LB74**	$10.99

The Messianic Passover Haggadah
Revised and Updated
—Rabbi Barry Rubin and Steffi Rubin.

Guides you through the traditional Passover seder dinner, step-by-step. Not only does this observance remind us of our rescue from Egyptian bondage, but, we remember Messiah's last supper, a Passover seder. The theme of redemption is seen throughout the evening. What's so unique about our Haggadah is the focus on Yeshua (Jesus) the Messiah and his teaching, especially on his last night in the upper room. 36 pages.

English	978-1880226292	**LB57**	$4.99
Spanish	978-1880226599	**LBSP01**	$4.99

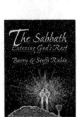

The Messianic Passover Seder Preparation Guide
Includes recipes, blessings and songs. 19 pages.

English	978-1880226247	**LB10**	$2.99
Spanish	978-1880226728	**LBSP02**	$2.99

The Sabbath *Entering God's Rest*
—Barry Rubin & Steffi Rubin

Even if you've never celebrated Shabbat before, this book will guide you into the rest God has for all who would enter in—Jews and non-Jews. Contains prayers, music, recipes; in short, everything you need to enjoy the Sabbath, even how to observe havdalah, the closing ceremony of the Sabbath. Also discusses the Saturday or Sunday controversy. 48 pages.

978-1880226742	**LB32**	$6.99

Havdalah *The Ceremony that Completes the Sabbath*
—Dr. Neal & Jamie Lash

The Sabbath ends with this short, yet equally sweet ceremony called havdalah (separation). This ceremony reminds us to be a light and a sweet fragrance in this world of darkness as we carry the peace, rest, joy and love of the Sabbath into the work week. 28 pages.

978-1880226605	**LB69**	$4.99

Dedicate and Celebrate!
A Messianic Jewish Guide to Hanukkah
—Barry Rubin & Family

Hanukkah means "dedication" — a theme of significance for Jews and Christians. Discussing its historical background, its modern-day customs, deep meaning for all of God's people, this little book covers all the how-tos! Recipes, music, and prayers for lighting the menorah, all included! 32 pages.

978-1880226834	**LB36**	$4.99

The Conversation
An Intimate Journal of the Emmaus Encounter
—Judy Salisbury

"Then beginning with Moses and with all the prophets, He explained to them the things concerning Himself in all the Scriptures." Luke 24:27
If you've ever wondered what that conversation must have been like, this captivating book takes you there.

"The Conversation brings to life that famous encounter between the two disciples and our Lord Jesus on the road to Emmaus. While it is based in part on an imaginative reconstruction, it is filled with the throbbing pulse of the excitement of the sensational impact that our Lord's resurrection should have on all of our lives." ~ Dr. Walter Kaiser President Emeritus Gordon-Conwell Theological Seminary. Hardcover 120 pages.

Hardcover	978-1936716173	**LB73**	$14.99
Paperback	978-1936716364	**LB77**	$9.99

Growing to Maturity
A Messianic Jewish Discipleship Guide
—Daniel C. Juster, Th.D.

This discipleship series presents first steps of understanding and spiritual practice, tailored for the Jewish believer. It's purpose is to aid the believer in living according to Yeshua's will as a disciple, one who has learned the example of his teacher. The course is structured according to recent advances in individualized educational instruction. Discipleship is serious business and the material is geared for serious study and reflection. Each chapter is divided into short sections followed by study questions. 256 pages.

978-1936716227	**LB75**	$19.99

Growing to Maturity Primer: *A Messianic Jewish Discipleship Workbook*
—Daniel C. Juster, Th.D.

A basic book of material in question and answer form. Usable by everyone. 60 pages.

978-0961455507	**TB16**	$7.99

Conveying Our Heritage A Messianic Jewish Guide to Home Practice
—Daniel C. Juster, Th.D. Patricia A. Juster

Throughout history the heritage of faith has been conveyed within the family and the congregation. The first institution in the Bible is the family and only the family can raise children with an adequate appreciation of our faith and heritage. This guide exists to help families learn how to pass on the heritage of spiritual Messianic Jewish life. Softcover, 86 pages

978-1936716739	**LB93**	$8.99

That They May Be One *A Brief Review of Church Restoration Movements and Their Connection to the Jewish People*
—Daniel Juster, Th.D

Something prophetic and momentous is happening. The Church is finally fully grasping its relationship to Israel and the Jewish people. Author describes the restoration movements in Church history and how they connected to Israel and the Jewish people. Each one contributed in some way—some more, some less—toward the ultimate unity between Jews and Gentiles. Predicted in the Old Testament and fulfilled in the New, Juster believes this plan of God finds its full expression in Messianic Judaism. He may be right. See what you think as you read *That They May Be One*. 100 pages.

978-1880226711   **LB71** $9.99

The Greatest Commandment
How the Sh'ma Leads to More Love in Your Life
—Irene Lipson

"What is the greatest commandment?" Yeshua was asked. His reply—"Hear, O Israel, the Lord our God, the Lord is one, and you are to love Adonai your God with all your heart, with all your soul, with all your understanding, and all your strength." A superb book explaining each word so the meaning can be fully grasped and lived. Endorsed by Elliot Klayman, Susan Perlman, & Robert Stearns. 175 pages.

978-1880226360   **LB65** $12.99

Blessing the King of the Universe
Transforming Your Life Through the Practice of Biblical Praise
—Irene Lipson

Insights into the ancient biblical practice of blessing God are offered clearly and practically. With examples from Scripture and Jewish tradition, this book teaches the biblical formula used by men and women of the Bible, including the Messiah; points to new ways and reasons to praise the Lord; and explains more about the Jewish roots of the faith. Endorsed by Rabbi Barney Kasdan, Dr. Mitch Glaser, & Rabbi Dr. Dan Cohn-Sherbok. 144 pages.

978-1880226797   **LB53** $11.99

You Bring the Bagels, I'll Bring the Gospel
Sharing the Messiah with Your Jewish Neighbor
Revised Edition—Now with Study Questions
—Rabbi Barry Rubin

This "how-to-witness-to-Jewish-people" book is an orderly presentation of everything you need to share the Messiah with a Jewish friend. Includes Messianic prophecies, Jewish objections to believing, sensitivities in your witness, words to avoid. A "must read" for all who care about the Jewish people. Good for individual or group study. Used in Bible schools. Endorsed by Harold A. Sevener, Dr. Walter C. Kaiser, Dr. Erwin J. Kolb and Dr. Arthur F. Glasser. 253 pages.

English   978-1880226650 **LB13** $12.99
Te Tengo Buenas Noticias 978-0829724103 **OBSP02** $14.99

Making Eye Contact With God
A Weekly Devotional for Women
—Terri Gillespie

What kind of eyes do you have? Are they downcast and sad? Are they full of God's joy and passion? See yourself through the eyes of God. Using real life anecdotes, combined with scripture, the author reveals God's heart for women everywhere, as she softly speaks of the ways in which women see God. Endorsed by prominent authors: Dr. Angela Hunt, Wanda Dyson and Kathryn Mackel. 247 pages, hardcover.

978-1880226513   **LB68** $19.99

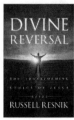

Divine Reversal
The Transforming Ethics of Jesus
—Rabbi Russell Resnik

In the Old Testament, God often reversed the plans of man. Yeshua's ethics continue this theme. Following his path transforms one's life from within, revealing the source of true happiness, forgiveness, reconciliation, fidelity and love. From the introduction, "As a Jewish teacher, Jesus doesn't separate matters of theology from practice. His teaching is consistently practical, ethical, and applicable to real life, even two thousand years after it was originally given." Endorsed by Jonathan Bernis, Dr. Daniel C. Juster, Dr. Jeffrey L. Seif, and Dr Darrell Bock. 206 pages

978-1880226803   **LB72** $12.99

Praying Like the Jew, Jesus
Recovering the Ancient Roots of New Testament Prayer
—Dr. Timothy P. Jones

This eye-opening book reveals the Jewish background of many of Yeshua's prayers. Historical vignettes "transport" you to the times of Yeshua so you can grasp the full meaning of Messiah's prayers. Unique devotional thoughts and meditations, presented in down-to-earth language, provide inspiration for a more meaningful prayer life and help you draw closer to God. Endorsed by Mark Galli, James W. Goll, Rev. Robert Stearns, James F. Strange, and Dr. John Fischer. 144 pages.

978-1880226285   **LB56** $9.99

Growing Your Olive Tree Marriage *A Guide for Couples from Two Traditions*
—David J. Rudolph

One partner is Jewish; the other is Christian. Do they celebrate Hanukkah, Christmas or both? Do they worship in a church or a synagogue? How will the children be raised? This is the first book from a biblical perspective that addresses the concerns of intermarried couples, offering a godly solution. Includes highlights of interviews with intermarried couples. Endorsed by Walter C. Kaiser, Jr., Rabbi Dan Cohn-Sherbok, Jonathan Settel, Dr. Mitchell Glaser & Natalie Sirota. 224 pages.

978-1880226179   **LB50** $12.99

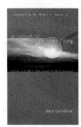

In Search of the Silver Lining *Where is God in the Midst of Life's Storms?*
—Jerry Gramckow

When faced with suffering, what are your choices? Storms have always raged. And people have either perished in their wake or risen above the tempests, shaping history by their responses...new storms are on the horizon. How will we deal with them? How will we shape history or those who follow us? The answer lies in how we view God in the midst of the storms. Endorsed by Joseph C. Aldrich, Ray Beeson, Dr. Daniel Juster. 176 pages.

978-1880226865   **LB39** $10.99

The Voice of the Lord *Messianic Jewish Daily Devotional*
—Edited by David J. Rudolph

Brings insight into the Jewish Scriptures—both Old and New Testaments. Twenty-two prominent Messianic contributors provide practical ways to apply biblical truth. Start your day with this unique resource. Explanatory notes. Perfect companion to the Complete Jewish Bible (see page 2). Endorsed by Edith Schaeffer, Dr. Arthur F. Glaser, Dr. Michael L. Brown, Mitch Glaser and Moishe Rosen. 416 pages.

9781880226704   **LB31** $19.99

Kingdom Relationships *God's Laws for the Community of Faith*
—Dr. Ron Moseley

Dr. Ron Moseley's Yeshua: A Guide to the Real Jesus and the Original Church has taught thousands of people about the Jewishness of not only Yeshua, but of the first followers of the Messiah.
In this work, Moseley focuses on the teaching of Torah -- the Five Books of Moses -- tapping into truths that greatly help modern-day members of the community of faith. 64 pages.

978-1880226841   **LB37** $8.99

Mutual Blessing *Discovering the Ultimate Destiny of Creation*
—Daniel C. Juster

To truly love as God loves is to see the wonder and richness of the distinct differences in all of creation and his natural order of interdependence. This is the way to mutual blessing and the discovery of the ultimate destiny of creation. Learn how to become enriched and blessed as you enrich and bless others and all that is around you! Softcover, 135 pages.

978-1936716746   **LB94** $9.99

Train Up A Child *Successful Parenting For The Next Generation*
—Dr. Daniel L. Switzer

The author, former principal of Ets Chaiyim Messianic Jewish Day School, and father of four, combines solid biblical teaching with Jewish sources on child raising, focusing on the biblical holy days, giving fresh insight into fulfilling the role of parent. 188 pages. Endorsed by Dr. David J. Rudolph, Paul Lieberman, and Dr. David H. Stern.

978-1880226377   **LB64** $12.99

Fire on the Mountain - *Past Renewals, Present Revivals and the Coming Return of Israel*
—Dr. Louis Goldberg

The term "revival" is often used to describe a person or congregation turning to God. Is this something that "just happens," or can it be brought about? Dr. Louis Goldberg, author and former professor of Hebrew and Jewish Studies at Moody Bible Institute, examines real revivals that took place in Bible times and applies them to today. 268 pages.

978-1880226858   **LB38** $15.99

Voices of Messianic Judaism *Confronting Critical Issues Facing a Maturing Movement*
—General Editor Rabbi Dan Cohn-Sherbok

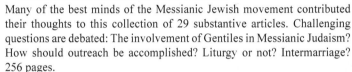

Many of the best minds of the Messianic Jewish movement contributed their thoughts to this collection of 29 substantive articles. Challenging questions are debated: The involvement of Gentiles in Messianic Judaism? How should outreach be accomplished? Liturgy or not? Intermarriage? 256 pages.

978-1880226933   **LB46** $15.99

The Enduring Paradox *Exploratory Essays in Messianic Judaism*
—General Editor Dr. John Fischer

Yeshua and his Jewish followers began a new movement—Messianic Judaism—2,000 years ago. In the 20th century, it was reborn. Now, at the beginning of the 21st century, it is maturing. Twelve essays from top contributors to the theology of this vital movement of God, including: Dr. Walter C. Kaiser, Dr. David H. Stern, and Dr. John Fischer. 196 pages.

978-1880226902   **LB43** $13.99

The World To Come *A Portal to Heaven on Earth*
—Derek Leman

An insightful book, exposing fallacies and false teachings surrounding this extremely important subject... paints a hopeful picture of the future and dispels many non-biblical notions. Intriguing chapters: Magic and Desire, The Vision of the Prophets, Hints of Heaven, Horrors of Hell, The Drama of the Coming Ages. Offers a fresh, but old, perspective on the world to come, as it interacts with the prophets of Israel and the Bible. 110 pages.

978-1880226049   **LB67**   .$9.99

Hebrews Through a Hebrew's Eyes
—Dr. Stuart Sacks

Written to first-century Messianic Jews, this epistle, understood through Jewish eyes, edifies and encourages all. 119 pages. Endorsed by Dr. R.C. Sproul and James M. Boice.

978-1880226612   **LB23** $10.99

The Irrevocable Calling *Israel's Role As A Light To The Nations*
—Daniel C. Juster, Th.D.

Referring to the chosen-ness of the Jewish people, Paul, the Apostle, wrote "For God's free gifts and his calling are irrevocable" (Rom. 11:29). This messenger to the Gentiles understood the unique calling of his people, Israel. So does Dr. Daniel Juster, President of Tikkun Ministries Int'l. In *The Irrevocable Calling*, he expands Paul's words, showing how Israel was uniquely chosen to bless the world and how these blessings can be enjoyed today. Endorsed by Dr. Jack Hayford, Mike Bickle and Don Finto. 64 pages.

978-1880226346   **LB66** $8.99

Are There Two Ways of Atonement?
—Dr. Louis Goldberg

Here Dr. Louis Goldberg, long-time professor of Jewish Studies at Moody Bible Institute, exposes the dangerous doctrine of Two-Covenant Theology. 32 pages.

978-1880226056   **LB12** $ 4.99

Awakening *Articles and Stories About Jews and Yeshua*
—Arranged by Anna Portnov

Articles, testimonies, and stories about Jewish people and their relationship with God, Israel, and the Messiah. Includes the effective tract, "The Most Famous Jew of All." One of our best anthologies for witnessing to Jewish people. Let this book witness for you! Russian version also available. 110 pages.

| English | 978-1880226094 | **LB15** | $ 6.99 |
| Russian | 978-1880226018 | **LB14** | $ 6.99 |

The Unpromised Land *The Struggle of Messianic Jews Gary and Shirley Beresford*
—Linda Alexander

They felt God calling them to live in Israel, the Promised Land. Wanting nothing more than to live quietly and grow old together in the country of refuge for all Jewish people, little did they suspect what events would follow to try their faith. The fight to make *aliyah*, to claim their rightful inheritance in the Promised Land, became a battle waged not only for themselves, but also for Messianic Jews all over the world that wish to return to the Jewish homeland. Here is the true saga of the Beresford's journey to the land of their forefathers. 216 pages.

978-1880226568   **LB19** $ 9.99

Death of Messiah *Twenty fascinating articles that address a subject of grief, hope, and ultimate triumph.*
—Edited by Kai Kjaer-Hansen

This compilation, written by well-known Jewish believers, addresses the issue of Messiah and offers proof that Yeshua—the true Messiah—not only died, but also was resurrected! 160 pages.

978-1880226582   **LB20** $ 8.99

Beloved Dissident *(A Novel)*
—Laurel West

A gripping story of human relationships, passionate love, faith, and spiritual testing. Set in the world of high finance, intrigue, and international terrorism, the lives of David, Jonathan, and Leah intermingle on many levels--especially their relationships with one another and with God. As the two men tangle with each other in a rising whirlwind of excitement and danger, each hopes to win the fight for Leah's love. One of these rivals will move Leah to a level of commitment and love she has never imagined--or dared to dream. Whom will she choose? 256 pages.

978-1880226766   **LB33** $ 9.99

Sudden Terror
—Dr. David Friedman

Exposes the hidden agenda of militant Islam. The author, a former member of the Israel Defense Forces, provides eye-opening information needed in today's dangerous world.

Dr. David Friedman recounts his experiences confronting terrorism; analyzes the biblical roots of the conflict between Israel and Islam; provides an overview of early Islam; demonstrates how the United States and Israel are bound together by a common enemy; and shows how to cope with terrorism and conquer fear. The culmination of many years of research and personal experiences. This expose will prepare you for what's to come! 160 pages.

978-1880226155   **LB49** $ 9.99

It is Good! *Growing Up in a Messianic Family*
—Steffi Rubin

Growing up in a Messianic Jewish family. Meet Tovah! Tovah (Hebrew for "Good") is growing up in a Messianic Jewish home, learning the meaning of God's special days. Ideal for young children, it teaches the biblical holidays and celebrates faith in Yeshua. 32 pages to read & color.

978-1880226063   **LB11** $ 4.99